Sexual Revolution

Laurie Penny

Sexual Revolution

Modern Fascism and the Feminist Fightback

BLOOMSBURY PUBLISHING
LONDON · OXFORD · NEW YORK · NEW DELHI · SYDNEY

BLOOMSBURY PUBLISHING
Bloomsbury Publishing Plc
50 Bedford Square, London, WC1B 3DP, UK
29 Earlsfort Terrace, Dublin 2, Ireland

BLOOMSBURY, BLOOMSBURY PUBLISHING and the Diana logo are trademarks of
Bloomsbury Publishing Plc

First published in Great Britain 2022

A catalogue record for this book is available from the British Library

Library of Congress Cataloguing-in-Publication data has been applied for

ISBN: HB: 978-1-5266-0219-0; TPB: 978-1-5266-0220-6;
eBook: 978-1-5266-0217-6; ePDF: 978-1-5266-4584-5

2 4 6 8 10 9 7 5 3 1

Typeset by Newgen KnowledgeWorks Pvt. Ltd., Chennai, India
Printed and bound in Great Britain by CPI Group (UK) Ltd, Croydon CR0 4YY

To find out more about our authors and books visit www.bloomsbury.com and
sign up for our newsletters

To David Boarder Giles

CONTENTS

INTRODUCTION

This is a story about the choice between feminism and fascism. It's a story about sex and power and trauma and resistance and persistence. It's a story about work, and who does it, and why. It's a story about how you can track the crisis of democracy against the crisis of white masculinity, and how the far right is rising in response to both. And at the centre of that story is one simple idea.

We are living, all of us, through a paradigm shift in power relations between the genders. The world is mired in a crisis of care and of reproduction that is transforming society, as millions of women and their allies struggle to build a better, fairer society – and millions of men try to stop them. The world, in other words, is in the middle of a sexual revolution.

And it matters more than most of us have been allowed to imagine. It matters because sex and gender are not political side-issues. They never have been. Sex and gender affect everything and everyone – they are, as theorist Shulamith Firestone put it, 'underpinnings'.[1] That means that any challenge to the social norms of sex and gender has to be ambitious. For example, if you want to end sexual harassment in the workplace, you must first redefine the terms of both work and sex – and how much of either can be demanded from a human being against their will. You must be prepared to imagine a world where exploitative, exhausting work and joyless, coercive sex are no longer the norm. Modern feminism is intellectually, creatively and ethically ambitious because it has to be, even though ambition in women

1

and girls is still considered morally suspect. This book is ambitious because I would rather be ambitious than waste anyone's time.

I've been a political journalist for twelve years. I've reported on activist movements around the Global North, and everywhere I've heard protesters and pundits predicting a great reckoning, a coming cultural shift that would sweep away all our socioeconomic certainties. But when that enormous change actually came, almost everyone was looking the other way. Because when it came, it came from women.

All over the world, women and queer people are rewriting the terms of a social contract that was never supposed to include us. Women of colour, Indigenous women, trans women and young women are driving this change. They are remaking the future in a shape that redefines freedom as universal and demands it for everyone, not simply for white, straight, wealthy cis men. I believe that paradigm shift will remake our civilisation – is remaking it as I write – despite the backlash from a fragile, savage minority that would rather burn the world than share it.

Sex and gender are in crisis, and that crisis is reshaping society. The pattern repeats across and beyond the Global North, as changes in the balance of power between men and women provoke a brutal political backlash – and women refuse to be intimidated into giving up their power. In the summer of 2016 a teenage girl was gang-raped in the Spanish town of Pamplona. The five men who were arrested for the attack referred to themselves as La Manada – the wolf pack. Their trial made international headlines, as a high-profile incident of sexual violence became a referendum on the nature of power in a divided nation. When the 'wolf pack' was acquitted of rape in April 2018, hundreds of thousands of women poured into plazas throughout Spain demanding changes to the law. Shortly afterwards, decrying the threat of radical feminism, the political party Vox became the first far-right party to take multiple seats in Spain since Franco. But the women of Spain would not be cowed. In the plazas, they chanted, '*Tranquila hermana, aquí está tu manada*'. Don't worry, sister. We are your wolf pack.

Almost nobody saw it coming. Nobody predicted that the greatest challenge to the social order in this century would be women, girls and queer people, particularly women, girls and queer people of colour, finally coming together to talk about sexual violence and structural abuses of power. Something has broken. Something is breaking still. Not like a glass breaks or like a heart breaks, but like the shell of an egg breaks – inexorably, and from the inside. Something wet and angry is fighting its way out of the dark, and it has claws.

This book is an attempt to describe and to challenge the material reality of sex and power in the modern age. It covers a lot of ground, but it all comes down to a few basic central themes.

Firstly – all of us are living in a political economy of patriarchy. Patriarchy is a power system based on male dominance that is designed to keep everyone, of every gender, in their assigned roles, concentrating wealth and agency in the hands of a paranoid few. Patriarchy underwrites the other key power structures that perpetuate injustice: capitalism and white supremacy. And patriarchy, crucially, does *not* mean 'a system ruled by men'. It means 'a system ruled by *fathers*'. It means a system where a handful of old, entitled white men get to tell everyone else what to do, and that's not just unfair – it's actively dangerous.

Secondly – we are living through a profound and permanent alteration in what gender means, what sex means, and whose bodies matter. This is a time of productive disobedience, where women, men and LGBTQ people everywhere are rejecting the gender binary as a mode of power, and walking quietly away from the expectations imposed on them by thousands of years of patriarchy.

These changes are calling into existence new ways of organising care, reproduction and the work of building and sustaining the human species – ways of life that are not based on competition, coercion and dominance but on consent, community and pleasure. Consent is the organising philosophy behind many of these changes. The importance of consent cannot be overstated – and consent is a concept that goes way beyond sex.

Thirdly – these changes are profoundly threatening to the social and economic certainties that form our world. They disturb existing power structures. They undermine the authority of institutions from the waged workplace to the nuclear family. This sexual revolution is, by its very nature, a threat to heterosexuality, to male supremacy, to white supremacy, to traditional ways of dividing labour, organising bodies and distributing wealth.

And those who are invested in these power structures are fighting back.

All of this is happening during a time of crisis, collapse and relentless social upheaval, as the biosphere implodes, the global economy totters, and tyrants exploit this uncertainty to seize power, promising their supporters a return to the old, violent certainties of gender, race and nation.

Lastly, and most importantly – the tyrants and bullies won't win. At least, not for long. They can't win, because they are incapable of offering any meaningful vision of the future. They want to rule, not lead. They want control, not responsibility. They have no interest in sustaining and maintaining human life, and they have no plan. Men like Putin, Bolsonaro, Trump and Johnson built political followings that baffled their critics in the political mainstream, who rushed to point out that these men were feckless wastrels who lied as easily as breathing and had spent their lives failing upwards and dodging responsibility – that these men were obviously, embarrassingly unfit to run so much as a bath, let alone a country. This, of course, was precisely their appeal. These were men who got away with it, men who laughed in the face of consequences, men who weaponised their own vacuous charisma, Gordon Gekkos of the attention economy who wanted only power and had not thought for a moment about what they might do with it.

If patriarchy is the rule of fathers, our current rulers are feckless fathers – deadbeat dads who have proven themselves dangerously inadequate to the duties of the power they caused such chaos to secure. They are weak, and they are trivial, and they know it.

Patriarchy, capitalism, heterosexism and white supremacy are not too big to fail. In fact, they do nothing but fail, and have done nothing but fail upwards for generations. The question is not whether white capitalist patriarchy will collapse. The question is how many people it will crush on the way down.

This book picks out the patterns in the contemporary wreckage of sex and power, seeking a map to a more life-sustaining world. It starts in the tender, vicious underbelly of political economy. It starts with sex.

Sexual freedom doesn't exist. Not yet. In most democracies, most of us are legally free to love who we want, live how we like and pursue pleasure however we choose – but only in the same way that most of us are free to buy a Maserati, or a mansion, or an election. In practice, most people cannot afford sexual freedom. Most women, and most LGBTQ people of all genders, cannot afford sexual liberation – because the social costs of simply naming their desires are still so high.

Sexual liberation cannot be achieved while sexual power is unequally distributed. Today, in almost every society on earth, straight men still have far more social, political and economic agency than women, girls and LGBTQ people. Patriarchy and white supremacy are political systems that give men power over women and white people power over Black, brown and Indigenous people. This isn't power that all white people and all men have. It's not power that all of them asked for. But it's power they were raised to expect, power that feels painful to lose. It is structural power, economic power, power that means that, on the whole, white people are richer, freer and more independent than people of colour, and men are wealthier and more independent than women. This means that women and queer people, particularly women and queer people of colour, still negotiate for sexual and bodily autonomy under conditions of inequality.

The best way to correct power imbalances in society is for the weaker players to organise collectively. When women come together to argue, for example, for a change in the way rape is prosecuted, that is collective bargaining. When women begin to share stories of sexual harassment at work and to demand that there be stronger consequences for abusive employers, that is collective bargaining.

When people who can become pregnant decide not to do so until the material conditions of parenthood improve, that too is collective bargaining. That's what this sexual revolution is all about.

You can't have a sexual revolution without addressing sexual violence for the same reason that you can't have an economic revolution without addressing workers' rights. A sexual 'revolution' that simply makes sex easier to access for people who have more power is in no way radical. In fact, any sort of revolution that preaches liberation while leaving the rich and powerful free to exploit, bully and abuse will inevitably begin to rot in the damp heat of its own contradictions.

This sexual revolution is different. This sexual revolution goes deeper, because it deals not just with sexual licence but with sexual liberation. It is not just about freedom *from*, but freedom *to*. It is a fundamental reimagining of gender roles and sexual rules, work and love, trauma and violence, pleasure and power. The new sexual revolution is a feminist one. And the most important thing to realise about this sexual revolution is that it is already happening.

Here's why it's happening. Not very long ago, power in most human societies was organised around a strict gender binary, based roughly on reproductive sex. There were men and women, and men were strong and powerful, and women were nurturing and powerless, and women were the property of men. On the basis of bimodal sex, humans were forced to take on the roles of soldiers or victims in a strict gendered power hierarchy. Half of humanity was coralled into the political category of 'womanhood' – which meant that their bodies and desires were men's to dispose of. Their role was to care for men and boys, to bear and raise children, and to take only a decorative role in public life unless they happened to be a hereditary monarch. The earliest political theorists explicitly excluded women and children from the 'social contract' that is the foundation of modern statehood. The economic and social structures of every modern culture were built on the bones of those assumptions. All of us were born and raised in those structures.

But over the course of the nineteenth and twentieth centuries, something changed. Advances in medical science meant that, for the first time in human history, women were able to reliably control their own fertility. Safe medical abortion and advances in contraceptive technology meant that women and girls could – in theory – decide when and if they had children, which meant that the stakes of human sexuality and society changed for ever. It meant that it was no longer so easy to keep women and girls shamed into sexual compliance and dependent on marriage. The consequences of this technological shift have been profound, and we have only begun to cope with them.

Today, despite the devastating impact of pandemics and recessions on women's employment, there are more women and queer people in the traditional male workplace than there have been for centuries; more women and queer people making art, making laws, making history. Meanwhile, the once fundamental social structures of family and faith are falling apart. More and more women and girls are boycotting marriage and motherhood. In fact, women's increasing freedom has led to a demographic time bomb, as parenthood becomes an unsustainable choice in developed nations that still refuse to pay for the work of care and childrearing.

This is work that has, until now, been done mostly by women, mostly for free. But as motherhood becomes harder and less affordable, as governments refuse to pay for the work of social care, and as women refuse to be bullied into making babies in impossible circumstances, birth rates are plummeting across and beyond the Global North. To put it another way, women and queer people, particularly women and queer people of colour, are simply refusing to be held hostage to male fragility.

They are refusing in numbers too big to ignore. As economist and journalist Paul Mason observes in his work *Clear Bright Future*, anti-feminism is now a key recruiting ground for the new right, a phenomenon Mason traces back to:

> the reversal of male biological power, through birth control and equal rights legislation, that took place during the last decades of the twentieth century...

In the fifty years following the rollout of the contraceptive pill, developed-world society has experienced what Federal Reserve chief Janet Yellen called a 'reproductive shock'. The results do not come anywhere close to women's liberation ... [but] the basic assumption behind misogyny, that women are destined to stick to their biologically determined role as child-bearers and unpaid domestic workers, has been blown to smithereens.[2]

Alongside these shifts in power relations between men and women, the 'basic assumptions' of heterosexuality and gender identity have also been exploded.

The gender binary itself is being superseded as a form of social control. Since the early 2010s there has been a seismic cultural shift in the cultural visibility of trans and non-binary people. A great many young people in particular are coming out en masse as transgender, genderqueer or non-binary, and that's a positive change. It is a great deal more normal to be openly trans than it was even a decade ago, but social conservatives are loudly resisting this change, as are many political-interest groups afraid of a world beyond the gender binary.

In this book, when I talk about 'men' and 'women' and what they do, I am not talking about biological essentialism. This book does not subscribe to any authoritarian view of gender that divides the world into immutable biological categories, pink and blue, binary and biddable, nor does it believe in imposing political destiny on diverse human bodies without their consent. Essentialism is invariably conservative. When I write about 'men' or about 'women', I am including everyone who locates themselves in those categories. I identify as genderqueer myself, meaning that the category of 'woman' does not fully describe my lived experience.

Gender roles and gender stereotypes are imposed on our bodies from birth, without our consent – and the process of learning to occupy the gender you have been assigned is often traumatic. A great many cis men I interviewed in the course of writing this book carry profound emotional scars from decades of savage social policing, of being punished for any deviance from perceived 'masculine' norms. There is no universal experience of womanhood or of manhood. Instead, this book describes many common experiences of sex, consent and power, and invites every reader of every gender to try them on for size.

The sexual scripts of our generation vindicate dominance and venerate violence while censoring queerness, community and pleasure. Well before a young woman comes of age, she is made aware that her body is a commodity, and that that commodity is not wholly hers to command. Legislation has not eradicated the cultural logic of male entitlement to women's bodies – and particularly to the bodies of Black, brown and Indigenous women, who live with the historical trauma and vestigial memory of having been, quite literally, traded as commodities. In Britain, 38 per cent of girls aged fourteen to twenty-one report verbal harassment in public places at least once a month,[3] and one BBC survey documented that more than half of British women had experienced sexual harassment in the workplace.[4] A study of 42,000 people in the European Union found that every second woman (55 per cent) has experienced sexual harassment at least once since the age of fifteen.[5]

When women speak out of turn, we can expect to be punished. We're being provocative. We should know our place. For me, I had been writing about politics for two years when I found the first hate site dedicated to fantasies about my rape and murder. I was twenty-three years old. All I had ever wanted to do was to describe my life as I experienced it and take part in a public political conversation. I didn't expect to be punished for it so savagely. I didn't expect the pile-ons, the violent fantasies, the vicious hatemongering – from dedicated attack sites to the comments sections of more respectable publications. I didn't expect the frightening emails, the badly doctored porn with my face pasted on it. I didn't expect to have to explain any of that to my family, my friends, my bosses, all of whom were wondering what I'd done to make these people so angry. It was assumed that

I must have done something. I thought so, too. I assumed I had brought it on myself, assumed that I had asked for it, somehow. And if I ever mentioned it, that's what I was told – *don't read the comments. Suck it up. Grow a thick skin. This is just what the internet is like.* I was scared and ashamed, and I was very young.

I soon realised I was far from the only one who'd been made to feel scared and ashamed. Slowly, women and queer people who were going through the same thing started to find each other. The men who were attacking us – and it was almost exclusively men – were serious, and they were organised. In 2011, I started to speak openly about the experience of online abuse, rather than being ashamed of it in private. I wrote that having an opinion is the short skirt of the internet – if you go out with one in public you're assumed to be inviting violence. You deserve everything you get. You're provocative. You asked for it.

Two generations have gone by since Germaine Greer wrote in *The Female Eunuch* that 'women have no idea how much men hate them.'[6] Well, we do now. Much of the harassment women faced online in the mid-2010s was driven and managed by sites like Breitbart that later became soapboxes for the far right. In the new mob misogyny, the emerging far right saw a key recruiting ground.

As we'll explore later in this book, the political strategies that are currently being used to mobilise angry young men to vote for populist thugs were first developed and deployed in the online culture war against women – and often by the same people. This frightening trend reached its first frenzied crisis point in 2013–14 with 'Gamergate'[7] – a concocted controversy in the video-games industry, in which one female creator's vengeful ex-boyfriend's accusation of cheating mushroomed into a global misogynist movement involving hundreds of thousands of angry young men incensed that women had dared invade their sacred space. Suddenly, harassment of women online became organised and gamified – and the game didn't stop there.

Misogyny and anti-feminism are the backlash to the sexual revolution – and nowhere is this backlash more apparent than in the election of 'strong men' in and beyond the Global North. From Britain and the United States to India and Brazil, self-serving narcissists coast to power on a swell of weaponised male resentment and racial supremacy, incoherently promising to bring back a lost age of national greatness, of law and order and 'family values', where women are forcibly returned to their traditional roles as wives and mothers, sexually submissive and socially sidelined. Most attention focuses, not without justification, on the attacks by these regimes on designated 'outsiders' – whether they be immigrants, people of colour, LGBTQ people, Muslims or Jews. But a certain strain of revanchist sexism, with its promise to restore a particular form of domineering patriarchy, is often the point of entry to these movements – the underlying philosophy that draws men and women alike to the new cause of 'nationalist oligarchy'.

It is overwhelmingly white men who vote for these neo-masculinist leaders, and part of the promise these leaders make is a return to 'traditional values' – to a fictional past where men were real men and women were grateful. The fantasy imagines a restoration of the rule of fathers, of a society strictly corralled into monogamous, heterosexual, Christian, largely Caucasian family units, with women and children subservient to a male head of the household. A vengeful entitlement to the bodies and affection of women and girls is a common chorus in the new far-right song sheet. It's an explicitly violent sexual paradigm – but it refuses to understand itself as sexually violent. Instead, sexual violence is reimagined as an outside threat – not something that white men do, but something that foreign or immigrant men do to 'our' women, who must be protected not because they are people but because they are property.

That's why it's a mistake to talk about modern misogyny without talking about race and racism. The two are not structurally the same, but they cannot be separated, either. This is, in part, what theorist Kimberlé Crenshaw meant when she coined the term 'intersectionality'. Different forms of oppression overlap and 'intersect', and cannot be properly understood on their own. White supremacy as a political system is deeply gendered – it relies on a specific ideology of white male power that entitles white men to the control of all women's bodies. That is why, since the days of the campaign for the abolition of slavery in America, the movements for the liberation of women and for the emancipation of people of colour have been connected – although that connection, as this book explores later, has never been comfortable. White women are continually called on to challenge their own prejudices and centre women of colour, who have historically been the first to take on the risk of speaking out against sexual violence and to expose the political economy of misogyny.

In an insecure and frightening economic climate, 'nothing seems to stimulate or threaten conventional stability so deeply as the shifting terrain of gender', writes science reporter Frank Browning in his book *The Fate of Gender*.[8] 'Backlash and resentment run deeply through middle- and working-class white America, evidenced not least by the surge in misogynist messages that have surfaced across social media.'[9] Much of that resentment is directed at women who appear to be seeking more power than they deserve. 'Moral outrage', according to researchers, is still the predominant response to women seeking power. During the 2016 American Presidential primaries, when voters were asked questions designed to remind them that many women now earn more than men, men became less likely to support Hillary Clinton.[10] Moral outrage that women are taking up space in public life without apology drives a great deal of the voting behaviour of conservatives and neo-conservatives around the world. The difference in voting behaviour between men and women is as significant – and in many nations, more significant – than it is between people of colour and whites. In the UK, millennial men were twenty percentage points more likely to back a right-wing or far-right candidate than millennial women.

This moral outrage takes many forms. Some are explicit, such as the regimes of Viktor Orbán in Hungary, Jair Bolsonaro in

Brazil and Vladimir Putin in Russia, all of which have legalised domestic violence against women; others are indirect, as in Britain, where the Conservative administration under successive prime ministers simply made tens of thousands of women workers redundant, slashed salaries and cut funding to domestic violence and legal-aid provisions, making it economically impossible for battered women to leave violent partners or challenge them in court.

'Conservatives,' as the American journalist Amanda Marcotte writes, 'prefer a system where men's freedom is contingent on women's servitude.'[11] Marcotte quotes the American senator Josh Hawley, who believes that 'freedom is undesirable if it is "a philosophy of liberation from family and tradition, of escape from God and community, a philosophy of self-creation and unrestricted, unfettered free choice"'.[12] By 'family and tradition', Hawley – and many others – mean 'women in their place'.

In the modern conservative imagination, the ideal of 'freedom' was never intended to include people of colour or white women. Wealthy right-wing men wax lyrical about the importance of responsibility with the desperate confidence that comes from never having had to scrub their own toilets and not caring to start. As cultural commentator Franklin Leonard has observed, 'When you're accustomed to privilege, equality feels like oppression.'

But the real measure of oppression is not how angry you are, it's how angry you are allowed to be. That's why the anger of straight white men in the Global North often feels so overwhelming, while the rage of women and of men of colour against structural violence and historical oppression is pathologised, excluded from the political conversation. Women speaking out against institutional rape 'go too far' and 'lose control'; young people of colour protesting against police violence are simply 'thugs'; white men, by contrast, have 'legitimate concerns'.

Across and beyond the Global North, patriarchy is running scared and fighting dirty.

The aggrieved entitlement of ordinary men trying to carve a philosophy out of their refusal to manage a moment's discomfort is easy to exploit. It can be marshalled. It can be channelled. The promise of restoring lost white masculine pride sells policy, delivers votes and anoints emperors. And sexual entitlement is the language in which that promise is spoken.

Around the world, the far right is on the rise – and feminism has been identified as its enemy. Steve Bannon – the Breitbart CEO, former chief advisor to Donald Trump and the man more responsible than any other individual in the world for shaping the 'alt-right' into the political force it is today – explicitly used male fear of female power to build a movement. Bannon called modern feminism 'the single most powerful potential political movement in the world'[13]... 'or what I call the "anti-patriarchy movement".'[14] And Bannon was not the only right-wing demagogue to weaponise misogyny for his own ends.

The new far right uses tools of political coercion that evolved from dating strategies designed to work around women's sexual consent. You can trace many of the tactics and cod philosophies of modern fascism back to the cultural sewer of online men's groups – to communities of miserable, frustrated young men drawn together by common resentment of womankind. As we'll see in later chapters, modern fascism targets vulnerable young white men and convinces them that feminism, anti-racism and liberalism are a threat to the very soul of white Western manhood.

In fact, modern masculinity is its own worst enemy. In the years since the financial crash of 2008, countless millions of men have grown up and grown older facing insecurity, lack of stability, lacking everything that was supposed to give their lives meaning. Among the few things they have left to give them a sense of familiarity and purpose are traditional gender roles – specifically the social scripts that reserve respect and status for 'strong' men who can attract and dominate submissive women. This convinces many men that what's really lacking in their lives is not economic justice or social security but simply a woman – any woman – to care for them and prop up the shards of an ego shredded by modern life; a woman to make them feel important, needed, seen and heard, when so little else does. It is easier, after all, to blame women, feminism and 'woke culture' for everything that feels unfair in modern life than it is to blame the economy, or the government, or yourself.[15]

When society becomes unstable and men feel fragile and insecure, women suffer. As daily life becomes more precarious and public funding for healthcare, welfare, housing, education and social care is cut by governments around the world, women are expected to step in and provide more and more of that vital work of care, either for free, within relationships, or in the low-paid, low-status, insecure domestic jobs that are filled overwhelmingly by immigrant and working-class women. During the Covid-19 lockdowns of 2020, as millions of people were forced to 'shelter in place' with abusive partners and spouses, domestic violence more than doubled.[16] Of course, women have also had to grow up and build lives in the same toxic, demeaning job market on the same burning planet; women have had to survive falling wages and rising rents, unmanageable debts and career insecurity, and on top of all of that, women have also had to survive the men who blame them for it all.

All over the world, women are under attack as a political class. The barrage is social, economic and interpersonal, and it is happening on every front. There has been an enormous rise in reports of sexual harassment in recent years, thanks in part to the #MeToo movement – and that rise is not all down to increased reporting. According to the US National Crime Victimization Survey,[17] self-reported incidence of rape or sexual assault more than doubled from 2017 to 2018. In the UK, despite a similar rise in self-reported experiences of violence,[18] prosecutions of rape cases are currently at a ten-year low.[19] While violent crime as a whole has declined around the developed world since the 1990s, gendered violence is a consistent and increasing danger to the lives of women and girls – and the response from traditional institutions of justice has been deafening disinterest. Intimate partner violence against women is still treated as a private matter, rather than an issue of public justice.

Meanwhile, abortion provision is being violently undermined across the globe. Newly emboldened by the appointment of conservative Associate Justice Brett Kavanaugh to the US Supreme Court, states across America have been passing bills virtually banning the practice. In countries like Poland and Spain, hard-won laws enshrining women's right to choose to terminate pregnancy have been rolled back. Again, it's crucial to understand where this started: that the right-wing movement against reproductive rights has been gathering momentum for decades. It began in the 1980s as a deliberate response to second-wave feminism and the new freedoms some women were beginning to enjoy – and as a way to unite Southern conservatives against Black liberation.

There is a pattern here, a single thread running from the #MeToo movement to the surge in misogynist violence, from the backlash against abortion rights across the Global North to the dramatic decline in birth rates around the world and the terrifying rise in young men committing mass murder in the name of sexual revenge, as this book explores in depth in later chapters. There's a pattern behind all of it. The common denominator is fear. Fear of change. Fear of irrelevance. Fear of women. Fear of how women are changing, becoming freer, braver, less inclined to place men's comfort above their own human rights. The common denominator is moral outrage. Outrage that oppressed people are daring to name their own oppression, that victims of abuse are no longer sticking to their prescribed social role, no longer hiding the damage done to them, beginning to demand consequences.

This sexual revolution confronts abuse of power at every level. And this book deals explicitly with abuse, exploitation and trauma, not just as individual problems but as political phenomena. The logic of abuse is central to the way in which power operates – from world governments, institutions and industries, to individual families. This book argues that many traditional models of social organisation, from the nuclear family to parliamentary politics, do not simply enable abuse – they require abuse. They require that exploitation, bullying, male supremacy and white supremacy be normal and normalised.

Our culture is shaped and reshaped by abuse, and by the scars it leaves on the individual and collective psyche. But abuse has rarely been deemed worthy of political attention. Instead, where it is spoken of at all, it is usually something that has to be borne in private, healed in isolation – and that's useful, because it places all the responsibility for change on the individual who suffers, and not on the systems that cause suffering. Just in case anyone fails to get the message, those who do speak out about abuse can expect punishment and public humiliation, especially if they are women.

But speaking about abuse, exploitation and trauma are crucial if we want to understand how oppression operates. People who learn from a young age that adults are allowed to hurt children, that men are allowed to hurt women, that police officers are allowed to hurt people from marginalised communities, that the strong are allowed to prey upon the weak and the weak cannot rely on help arriving, will reshape their imaginations around that narrative. They will be more, not less, likely to accept bullying and exploitation as a normal part of their working lives. And this logic of exploitation has been upheld, time and time again, in recent years of political upheaval. Even as women and children have begun to speak out in ever-more confident chorus about their experience of abuse, known abusers have been elevated to the highest positions of public office and political responsibility. Watching violent bullies be rewarded hurts in a way that is hard to look away from if you have been a victim of abuse yourself, as a very great many of us have, even if we don't like to think of ourselves that way. Victims, in fact, routinely seem to burden themselves with the shame that should properly belong to those who victimise others. In fact, the amount of shame still attached to being a person who has experienced violence or persecution today has everything to do with the desire to silence victims and normalise abuse.

Again, on every level, from the institutional to the individual, the attempt to come to terms with the injustice and scale of abuse has created chaos. People and communities have torn themselves apart trying to square their desire for justice with their desire not to think about wrongdoing. Victims and survivors have struggled to hold the centre of themselves in the storm of cognitive dissonance that buffets anyone who knows that something terrible and unfair has happened to them, but who still thinks on some level that it was their fault, that they're wrong to complain, that they don't deserve to be believed, that they cannot allow themselves to believe the evidence of their own experience.

Revolution does not begin in the streets. Revolution begins in the head, and in the heart. Sexual revolution happens whenever a person decides, in the face of years of carefully nurtured self-loathing, in a culture that tells her every day that her body does not belong to her, that her sexuality is a commodity for men's consumption, that her pleasure does not matter, that her ambition makes her unlikeable and her desires make her disgusting and her exhaustion make her weak – sexual revolution happens when a person who has learned all these things decides to like herself anyway and to treat herself as if she were a person worthy of respect, as if she were a person who does not owe her body or her energy or the work of her life as the rent for existing in a man's world. When a woman behaves as if her life matters and her happiness counts, a tiny revolution takes place. And when many millions of them do, all at once, the world changes for ever. As Shulamith Firestone wrote in *The Dialectic of Sex*:

> Just as to ensure elimination of economic classes requires the revolt of the underclass (the proletariat) and, in a temporary dictatorship, their seizure of the means of production, so to assure the elimination of sexual classes requires the revolt of the underclass (women) and the seizure of control of reproduction: not only the full restoration to women of ownership of their own bodies, but also their (temporary) seizure of control of human fertility.[20]

18

In the early autumn of 2017, something snapped. Women and a few brave men finally began to come forward to speak, in numbers too big to dismiss, about the sexual harassment and abuse they had endured. It had been coming for years, but when the dam finally broke, it began in Hollywood.

In 2017, the exposé of the mega-producer and serial rapist Harvey Weinstein started a flood of women's stories, and a seismic shift in the way that most of us think and speak about sexual violence. Weinstein had been a public figure for decades, the personification of patriarchy gone to rot in a standing pool of self-satisfaction, groping and raping his way through decades of moneyed entitlement, strategising to silence every one of his sixty-plus victims, fully aware that what he was doing was vile. His victims were the first to stand up together, many of them after years of being shamed into silence, threatened with lawsuits, and iced out of the industry. At the clogged heart of mass culture, rich and beautiful women who had spent their lives being paid to speak lines men had written for them started to use their own voices to tell a different story. When one woman names her abuser, that is an act of rebellion. When many do, that is a resistance movement.

Connected by the #MeToo hashtag, first coined ten years ago by US activist Tarana Burke, the movement raced across industries, across oceans, to the very heart of politics. Powerful men began to retreat with their reputations between their legs. Frantic conversations started at the highest levels: what did these women want? How might they be stopped? The story was veering wildly off-script, but the cameras were still rolling, and men who for a long time had believed themselves the protagonists of their own cosy narratives started panicking. Weinstein's lawyer defended him as a clueless fool, an unreconstructed 'old dinosaur'; other men in his position scrambled to control the narrative with the wide-eyed panic of Jurassic predators trying to negotiate with an asteroid.

As women all over the world came forward to talk about their experiences of sexual violence, old certainties about what constituted normal, acceptable behaviour between men and women, between those with power and those without it, began to peel away like dead skin.

Half a decade later, it's still happening. It's not just Hollywood, and it's not just Silicon Valley. It's not just in the White House or behind the scenes at Fox News. It's happening in the art world and in mainstream political parties. It's happening in the London radical left, in the US Democratic Party, in the Australian parliament and in the world of international aid. It's happening in academia and in the media and in legal and therapeutic professions. It's been happening for decades. It's still happening. Wandering hands and daily dehumanisation remain a weary assault course not just for women trying to make their mark in entertainment or finance or media or politics, but for the many millions fighting to survive in lower-paid, lower-status jobs. Shortly after the #MeToo movement broke, tens of thousands of domestic workers started speaking out about their experience of abuse. McDonald's workers declared that their bodies were not on the menu.

The movement against male domination and sexual coercion appeared, for a brief moment, to bridge divides of race and class. Migrant agricultural labourers spoke out against domestic violence at the same time as Hollywood actors, journalists, politicians and technologists were organising to bring down serial predators in their industries. Defiance, for these women, began the only way workplace defiance ever does: at the point where people decide that the risk of staying silent is greater than the risk of speaking out. When people realise that their struggles aren't unique, that their pain is real and it matters, the sensation is terrifying and liberating at once. There is an exhilaration to realising that you are allowed to trust yourself, that it's not crazy to want another world, or that even if you are crazy, it doesn't mean you're wrong.

A great many alleged abusers and their allies responded to these revelations with pleas for more understanding, with insistence that accusers consider the context of these crimes. Well, of course. Context is vital. It is crucial to consider the context in which this all-out uprising against toxic white male entitlement is taking place. The context is a historical moment where it has become obvious that white male entitlement is the greatest collective threat to the survival of the species.

That isn't a metaphor. Political consent and sexual consent are not analogous. They are *correlative*. They feed one another. The search for a more human understanding of power and consent is not simply stage dressing for a bigger fight. It *is* the big fight. It's all about the grabby old men, and the young men groping for power in their wake, and it always has been. 'What will happen when women everywhere flick on every light in the house ... and men no longer have any darkness left to hide in?' asks writer Caitlin Johnstone at Medium. 'It is unimaginable. Power structures will be disrupted from the basic family unit all the way up to the highest echelons of influence.'[21] This book deals directly with the implications of this seismic shift – and the threat it poses to traditional systems of power.

Modern states are sexist and racist by their very nature, because their power structures are built on the exploitation of people of colour and of white women. Sexual violence and racist oppression are fundamental to how work, money and resources are organised in most modern societies. This is not a new idea. Theorists like Catharine A. MacKinnon have observed how fundamental gendered power is to the formation of the modern state. MacKinnon, however, believed that sexual violence is the source code of that power differential – that the state was constructed to facilitate male sexual violence against women. This book argues otherwise. Sexual violence is not the end goal of white supremacist patriarchy – it's an enforcing mechanism.

The real point of maintaining hierarchies of gender and race, the hierarchies that scaffold most modern political systems, is not controlling sex, but controlling *work*. Our architectures of racist and sexist violence are designed to coerce people of colour and most white women into doing the hard, repetitive, essential labour of sustaining life so that a minority of white, wealthy men don't have to – an arrangement that is, ultimately, to everyone's detriment.

Sex is part of this story. My generation inherited a world where sex was cheap but not free. We inherited a culture of boring, violent, coercive heterosexuality. We grew up being warned that sex was something dangerous, something violent that boys did to girls, something that men needed and women controlled, something that strong men wanted and nice girls didn't let them have too easily. We grew up marinated in a flood of mainstream pornography that rephrased sex as a factory line of bodies battering each other into submission, of ritual violence being done to women and girls, of hammering, nailing, smashing, wrecking, choking, slapping, destroying, a language of sex that was as strait-laced, joyless and competitive as everything else in our lives.

Modern society conflates sex and power, creating an environment where the idea of freedom is fetishised in theory and flattened in practice. Where every desire must become the desire to dominate. Where power, violence and authority are eroticised, sex itself becomes authoritarian.

Authoritarian tendencies are baked into mainstream political culture. A more specific term for this tendencies are what some people call neoliberalism. Neoliberalism is, quite simply, a way of organising society – from politics to culture and commerce – so that the needs of the market and of private gain take precedence over everything else. It describes a specific form of global capitalism where nothing is more important than what can be sold, and to whom, and for how much. Where human life itself has no inherent value, where every human urge is channelled towards greater productivity and most of us spend most of our time working ourselves to the raw nerves for someone else's profit. More than anything else, neoliberalism is allergic to the idea of human beings living, organising and caring for one another collectively – instead, it imagines a world order where individuals and their families struggle alone in a world of ruthless competition where only the strongest and luckiest survive. This is why neoliberalism eventually becomes authoritarianism. And neoliberalism, like every form of authoritarianism, is not just about controlling what people do; it is about controlling how they think and feel. But eventually, something is bound to snap.

Something usually does. Wilhelm Reich was one of the first philosophers to pay attention to the way in which sexual frustration was being whipped up and manipulated by the despots of the 1930s and channelled towards violent imperialist and racist ends. He observed in *The Mass Psychology of Fascism* that 'the suppression of natural sexual gratification leads to various kinds of substitute gratifications ... Natural aggression, for example, becomes brutal sadism which then is an essential mass-psychological factor in imperialistic wars.'[22]

The same is true today, from Islamic State to the American far right: the strategic use of sexual frustration and weaponised misogyny in the radicalisation of young men is consistent across ideologies. Sadly, the entitlement that underlies it is not exclusive to fascist movements. The opposite of consent culture is not rape culture – it is authoritarianism.

Sexual authoritarianism occurs when straight men can no longer count on women's sexual compliance. Again, this is more than a metaphor. Sexual repression is more than simply an analogy for political oppression. Sexual repression is real, and political oppression is real, and the two are related. Both tend to involve powerful men grabbing whatever they feel entitled to, whatever the cost, and getting away with it – because the laws that ought to hold them accountable were written by and for people just like them. This is the very essence of privilege, a word which literally means 'private law'.

To challenge sexual exploitation is ultimately to challenge male privilege on every level, from the political to the personal. It is to insist on the right of all bodies not just to equality before the law, not just to dignity and agency, but to self-mastery and pleasure and adventure. This book argues that the sexual revolution, and its urgent demands for a reorganisation of care and labour, is a threat to the modern economic order. And it is a challenge to sexual repression.

This sexual revolution is a revolution in redefining terms – an exercise in taxonomy. It is about naming and nailing down the contours of a world of violent incoherence. Words matter in sexual politics. In 2018 the actress Alyssa Milano suggested a 'sex strike' as a way for women to escalate the #MeToo movement – denying men sex so long as they deny the rest of us basic bodily autonomy. This was the right instinct, but the wrong strategy. A general sex strike is a stupid idea as well as a socially conservative one, given that female sexual desire is a real and active thing that requires extensive social and economic strategy to repress. Priests and politicians have been trying to squash women's sexuality for centuries. However, one specific sex strike – the one that chauvinists are afraid of – is already well underway. A widespread adoption of consent practices *is* the 'sex strike' that the chauvinists are afraid of.

What has been happening, quietly and for quite some time, is women and girls opting out of the old patriarchal bargain whereby we traded our sexuality and the work of our lives for security and protection. Today, fewer women are obliged by economic necessity, social pressure, isolation or fear to enter or stay in relationships they don't want. It's all well and good to say that feminism is about women having choices, but what happens when we start making choices – en masse – that men don't approve of?

What happens is a fundamental disturbance in the 'sexual contract', which, according to theorist Carole Pateman, is the very basis of what we think of as democratic freedom. Interrogating the idea of the Hobbesian 'social contract', Pateman explains[23] that the fundamental assumptions of Enlightenment liberation rely on an enforced power differential between men and women – an unspoken sexual contract whereby women owe men a duty of care, attention, sexual access and unpaid domestic labour. If women break the terms of that contract by refusing subservience, they deserve to be punished for it – and in the course of writing this book I spoke to countless women who have been punished for it, who carry wounds that ache in relentless reminder of the cost of non-compliance.

In order to heal injustice in the future, it is necessary to name and claim the hurts of the past. This is one of the greatest challenges when it comes to constructing cultures that value human life and building human lives that resist oppression. Most of us would prefer the version of the story where we were in control the whole time, where all the hurt and disappointment we have suffered was our fault, because that way it's easier to own the horrible things that have happened to us and make sense of the way they make us feel. It is terribly human to want to avoid reliving the pain of the past. It can often feel as if denying past atrocities is the only way to fully survive them. But acknowledging harm that has already happened is often what it takes to stop it happening again.

We cannot have sexual liberation without freedom from abuse, and we cannot be free from abuse without naming it. A great deal of the work of social change is about giving people permission to tell the truth about their own experiences, to articulate the hurt they have suffered so that others might not have to suffer the same. That's what happened in the 1960s and 1970s when feminists first began to speak about the sexual abuse and domestic violence that were and remain the ugly secrets gnawing at the core of our communities, families and political institutions. It was a brave and dangerous thing to do then, just as it is now. The shame of abuse was supposed to be borne by the survivors, largely women and children, who were expected to stay silent about what had happened to them, shielding their abusers from the consequences of their actions and – more importantly – protecting everyone else from the discomfort of other people's pain.

Today, we're moving from a culture that tacitly permits the rape and abuse of women and children but criminalises homosexuality, abortion and birth control, and considers female sexual pleasure to be fundamentally suspect, to one where the important thing isn't who you have sex with, or how often, or with how many, but whether or not everyone wants it. More broadly, sexual revolution imagines a world where people are free to have sex and form relationships and build families in whatever way they choose, so long as they are not hurting or violating anyone else. It imagines a world where the moral schematic is not how much sex is being had, or what kind, but whether it's wanted, whether it's fun for everyone involved. And that schematic of consent doesn't just apply to sex.

These ideas are an affront to current orthodoxies of work and love and sex. They are an affront to the assumption that men are owed something by women. To the assumption that women owe men sex, affection, emotional labour and domestic service. These assumptions are disturbed when women, girls and children come together to insist that, in fact, powerful men are not automatically entitled to have access to the bodies of others. And when a woman finally finds herself able to question whether she really owes men anything at all, whether she might be the one that's owed something by the world, that is an act of resistance.

I've learned the hard way what happens when I make men uncomfortable. When I refused to make myself small and powerless so that men could feel large and in charge, there were consequences. But there are also consequences for staying clenched and closed, for forgetting your own selfhood. There are consequences for hollowing out your heart. Consequences for putting up with violence and disrespect. The most immediate is that the violence and the disrespect keep happening. To you, and to others.

Karah Frank, who finally left a violent and abusive relationship, said in a letter that was presented during the court case against her abuser: 'In Judith [Lewis] Herman's now-foundational text "*Trauma and Recovery*", she outlines the process of psychological domination. The final stage in this process is known as total surrender, where the victim becomes utterly complicit in their own abuse.' Herman explains the necessity of this 'in the mind of the abuser' using a quote by George Orwell, from *1984*:

> We are not content with negative obedience, nor even with the most abject submission. When finally you surrender to us, it must be of your own free will. We do not destroy the heretic because he resists us; so long as he resists us we never destroy him. We convert him, we capture his inner mind, we reshape him. We burn all evil and all illusion out of him; we bring him

over to our side, not in appearance, but genuinely, heart and soul.[24]

This, in Judith Lewis Herman's estimation, is also how abusers work, the creation of a cowed and complicit loyalty being 'necessary for the justification and continuation of the abuse cycle. The perpetrator insists on total loyalty; mind, body and soul.'[25]

Complicity can curdle anyone's courage. It is extremely uncomfortable to acknowledge historical violence that has been done in your name. That's one reason why women and girls, gay and trans people, Black and brown and Indigenous people remain bit-part players in the notion of history as it is simply and collectively understood. That matters. It matters because if we don't know our history, we can't learn from it, and those who can't learn from history are doomed to speak in ignorant clichés and to live them, too.

But something is changing. Suddenly a great many unspoken things are being uttered, softly at first, and then building to an uncomfortable crescendo. Young people are no longer prepared to accept the popular consensus about whose stories get to matter. The notions of race and gender as we have come to understand them, however they may mark themselves on our bodies, have been refined over generations to justify and excuse exploitation, colonial conquest and inequality. This does not mean that race and gender are not things we know and experience in our bodies. These things are stories we tell each other about who gets to be human on what terms in this world, and ignorance of history leaves those who steer culture free to write and rewrite the story of what it means to be a decent man, a strong woman, a good girl. Inevitably, those definitions seem to settle around the outlines of what it means to be an obedient citizen, a docile worker or a compliant subject.

In order for power to be able to face itself in the mirror, certain things must be shunted down the collective memory hole. This is a normal response to trauma – especially other people's trauma. For a long time, one of the special privileges of being part of the group that got to write history has been not having to read the footnotes. This applies whether you're a man, a white person, a straight person, a wealthy person, American, European or any other class of human being usually guaranteed a speaking role in the long, weird hero's drama of recent history. Everyone else is obliged to protect you from the knowledge of what it took to keep you there – for their own good as much as yours.

It is easier to believe that you are unworthy than it is to believe that the world is unjust, because you cannot change the world by yourself. It is easier to lie to yourself and to allow yourself to be lied to. It's easier, when you have to watch petty despots bully and cheat their way to power, when you are forced to confront the real extent of rape and abuse being revealed all around you, to try to believe that somehow you chose this. That somehow you wanted it. That somehow you asked for it.

'Asking for it' – as if we really lived in an age of consent. As if coercion were not a formative part of how we find work, form families and fight to survive. What happens when enough people stop believing that they ever wanted a world like this? What might happen to us as a society, as a species, if enough of us began to take consent seriously? What might happen if enough of us stood up together and refused to spend another second watching rich old white men do whatever they want to our bodies and call it freedom? It will be exhilarating, of course, but it will also be frightening.

'We have been raised to fear the yes within ourselves, our deepest cravings,' writes Audre Lorde in *Uses of the Erotic*. 'The fear of our deepest cravings keeps them suspect, keeps us docile and loyal and obedient, and leads us to settle for or accept many facets of our oppression as women.'[26]

So many people have learned to mistrust their own desire. That's because so many desires are still stigmatised and punished by a culture that exploits and wants to control bodies that are female and femme and trans and queer and poor and Black and brown and disabled. From the first time she catches herself craving something she has been told will put her in danger and make her deserving of violence, a young girl learns to squash and stifle her own desires. When she wants to touch a forbidden body with her own. When she wants to create something bold and daring. When she wants to compete with the boys. When she wants to talk back to authority. When she feels outrage at the unfairness of the world pressing against her clenched teeth; when she wants more than she has been told to want. It is dangerous for a woman to want things, when she is supposed to spend her life servicing the wants of others. And the very worst thing a person who is any combination of female or queer or of colour can do is ask for it.

Because once people start asking, it's hard to get them to stop. And more and more women are asking if things could be different. If work could be more meaningful. If sex could be better. If love could hurt less. More women are asking if they might do something bigger with their lives than wear themselves out saving the world one man at a time. More and more women and girls are choosing independence over servitude, knowing that either one will be exhausting, refusing to accept less than the respect they are due. Refusing to work to be good enough to be owned, and beginning to own themselves. Beginning to tear up the unspoken sexual contracts that have always formed the basis of our democratic and social norms.

Consent is the opposite of authoritarianism. Transforming a culture of coercion into a culture of consent can reshape what it means to be human. And that's what this revolution is about. If men and women and everyone else of every gender can move through this trauma together, can build something like justice together, then we might actually have a shot at a bright future – for all of us, this time. Coming to terms with the intimate and structural violence of the past is the only way we will survive one another long enough to make it to that future. In the century to come, only one of two things will survive: the fragile self-conception and comfort of white masculinity, or human society as we would like to know it. There is everything to fight for. All we need to do is ask for it.

29

1

Without Our Consent

The first thing to understand about consent is that it isn't a thing. Consent is not an item, or a possession. It is not an object you can hold in your hand, or a gift that can be given and then rudely requisitioned. Consent is a *state of being*. Giving someone your consent – sexually, politically, socially – is a little like giving them your attention. It's a continuous process. It's an interaction between human creatures. I believe that a great many men and boys don't understand this. I believe that that lack of understanding is causing unspeakable trauma for women, men and everyone else who is sick of how much human sexuality still hurts.

We need to talk about what consent really means, and why it matters more, not less, at a time when women's fundamental rights to bodily autonomy are under attack across the world. We still get consent all wrong, and we have to try to get it a bit less wrong, for all our sakes. So how are we supposed to summon into being a culture where consent is the baseline of sexual interaction? Let's start with the bad news.

The bad news is that there's no simple set of rules to pass around to make sure nobody violates another human being, accidentally or on purpose, ever again. Believe me, if a set of rules was all it took, a recipe for who moves first and what goes where, I'd write it down and have done. Sadly, if a simple set of rules were all it took, we wouldn't be in this mess.

The physicist Carl Sagan once wrote that if you want to make an apple pie from scratch, 'you must first invent the universe'.

It's not just a question of the right recipe, of sugar, flour, butter and fruit in the right ratios. Before that, you need to start with a complex system of food supply and farming, hundreds of years of sordid trade in cane and grain and human labour, thousands of years of agriculture, millions of years of evolution and billions more for all of that to come together out of dust exploding from the heart of a distant star. That's what it takes to make an apple pie from scratch. The same rule applies when you want to create cultural change.

You can't make human sexuality hurt less without going back to first principles, to the very basis of the unjust social contracts and sexual scripts that steer our lives. If you want to create a culture of consent, it's not just a matter of finding the right rules and following them. *You need a sexual revolution.* You need a total rethink of how sex and love and work and gender and pleasure are defined. If we want sexual freedom, we must first rework the way relationships are organised, the way violence is understood, the way bodies are controlled, the nature of femininity and the meaning of masculinity. The good news is that we should probably be doing all of that anyway. In fact, the process has already started. It started with naming the problem.

There's an extraordinary, everyday magic in naming the problem. 'Rape culture' refers to the language and customs that normalise rape and make it a policing force in women's lives. Rape culture says *don't walk down that street.* Rape culture warns women, girls and queer people to control themselves. The control is the point. The message is that the street is not for you. That the world is not for you.

The naming and shaming of rape culture is one of the most important feminist interventions of recent years – and also one of the most misunderstood. 'Rape culture' does not simply imply a society in which rape is routine. It is routine, of course – every day in the United States 600 women are raped and three are murdered by their partner or ex-partner.[1] One in five women and one in seventy-one men will be raped at some point in their lives.[2]

But rape culture isn't just a culture where this happens – it's a culture where this happens and *it's normal.*

Another term for this is 'sexual authoritarianism' – a sexuality based on dominance, where sex is a thing that one set of people imposes on or extracts from another. 'Rape culture' refers to the narratives in our everyday lives that weaponise rape and sexual assault as a way of controlling women's lives – so that male sexual violence is excused as socially inevitable, but women and girls are still raised to be afraid of rape and to guard against it.

Women's experiences of rape and the legal *definition* of rape are vastly different. While the definition of rape as a criminal offence varies from country to country, those definitions are rarely based upon what survivors actually experience. Instead they are based on the stories culture tells about what a rapist is supposed to like – stories that have largely been written by men. In one study of seventy-seven American female college students who had been 'non-consensually vaginally penetrated', researchers found that many did not classify their experience as rape – not because it was not traumatic, but because they had absorbed narratives of what 'rape' was supposed to mean.[3]

For some, their attacker 'didn't match their expectations of a rapist' – he didn't beat them, he had no weapon, he was a dear friend. For others, their own behaviour didn't seem to match a 'normal' victim's – they were drunk, they blamed themselves. In another study from 2016, of all the rapes reported to a central UK police force, not one of the 400 incidents exactly fitted the 'real rape' story, which involves 'a stranger using a weapon attacking a woman violently at night in an isolated, outdoor area', and says that 'women sustain serious injuries from these attacks'.[4]

You do not have to be a victim of rape to be affected by rape culture – you just have to grow up in a culture that warns you that if you don't control yourself, if you talk too loud or act too crazy or go out somewhere you're not supposed to be in a too-short skirt, rape will be the result and you'll only have yourself to blame. All of us grew up in a culture like that – including men.

Rape culture affects men, too. Rape culture trains men to feel entitled to women's sexual and emotional services, to measure their own self-worth by how much 'pussy they can grab', to view women both as the enemy and as the prize in life's battle, rather than as fellow human beings. Rape culture eviscerates intimacy and destroys solidarity between men and women just when that solidarity is needed most.

An individual act of rape may be 'about' many things, but rape culture is about control. Control through violence and the threat of violence. The question is: what is being controlled, and why? Who does rape culture actually work for?

It's really very simple. Rape culture is instrumental to the functioning of economies which are run on the exploitation of women's bodies. And every economy on earth is founded on the invisible labour done mostly by women, mostly for free – on the reproductive, domestic and emotional work without which every modern economy would collapse overnight. Women's reproductive and sexual freedom is an economic issue, and if you want to build a culture of consent, that's where you need to start. You need to start by asking exactly why the bodies of women and girls are treated as a resource to be exploited, why women's agency and dignity is still treated as culturally irrelevant, and how that could change for the better.

Building a culture of consent isn't about just changing the rules around rape, harassment and violence. It's about changing the underlying ethics to include the idea that the lives of women and LGBTQ people actually matter, that what we want and don't want actually matters, and that's a bigger task. Much bigger – and more uncomfortable.

A repeating motif of my twenties has been watching communities and institutions, friendship groups and political organisations implode because of their inability to confront rapists and sexual predators. Everywhere it was the same story: popular and powerful men were being called out for behaving terribly to women and girls around them. The call-outs had ghastly consequences for the victims as well as the abusers.

I saw it happen as a reporter and an activist. I saw it happen in the anarchist scene, on the Marxist left, in schools and colleges, in the Occupy movement, in geek and gamer groups, in unions, in the tech world, in the security scene, in the literary world, in the hotel trade and in the adult film industry. And every time, I saw communities struggle to cope with the shame of being forced to acknowledge what everyone, really, already knew.

When you ask a community to deal with its abusers, you ask it to deal with its own hypocrisy and complicity. That's a deeply uncomfortable thing to ask. Most people, given the option, choose convenience and comfort over self-examination; the power of inertia cannot be underestimated. That stasis has produced months and years of trauma, with women sidelined time and again because everyone else had decided they'd rather spend their empathy on abusers.

It's easier to believe that women and girls are somehow to blame for sexual assault than it is to do the dangerous work of making change – dangerous because it tends to make powerful men uncomfortable. I have regular, passionate disagreements with one of my older female relatives about this. She believes that people who are sexually assaulted should have simply taken more precautions, and I suspect that the reason she believes this is because it gives her comfort and a sense of control to think that there is choice involved. Because the alternative is worse. The alternative is that there's nothing she can do to stop it, and by extension, nothing she can do to protect her daughters, her granddaughters, her friends, herself. Feeling complicit in our own harassment allows us to survive trauma, but it also prevents us from confronting it. This is how we get a world where women, for their own safety, are counselled by the people who love them against walking alone at night. It's our choice, a choice we make for our own good, as independent women, to minimise our risk. But that's not sexual freedom. That's something else.

There can be no sexual freedom while girls remain expendable. And girls are made expendable over and over again, on college campuses and in small towns where high-school footballers are boy-kings, in hotel rooms in every county on every continent. In their own homes and online, girls are there to be used and discarded when they become inconvenient. Girls are there as spittoons for the self-disgust you won't swallow. Girls to clean your house. Girls to clear away the evidence of your shame. And the worst thing a girl can do is refuse to be that sort of mute vessel.

Girls who speak out about what has happened to them after that party, after that interview, after that soccer game, can expect to be the ones punished for the crimes committed against them. Shamed and ostracised at school, shut out of friendship groups and, later, professional circles. He made a mistake, and she will be erased for it. He was drunk, so he couldn't have known what he was doing; she was drunk, so she should have known better. She made trouble, she was difficult, she did not make it easy for him, she is a liar or a slut or both. It didn't happen and, if it did, it didn't matter, because he's got his whole future ahead of him, and she's just a girl.

Sexual assault is the language in which girlhood is spoken. Male sexual violence is a near-universal experience for girls growing up, but that does not make it fine, or normal. Sexual violence is not normal – it is *normalised*, and deliberately, savagely so.

This is the trauma that shapes our collective understanding of gender and power, and it doesn't 'get better' as we grow beyond girlhood. This ritual of violence and silence plays out right through every industry and institution of power.

There is far more at stake here than simply ending sexual violence, though that would be a start. The rabbit hole of rape culture and misogyny goes deeper than most of us have dared to contemplate. Human beings create outsized monsters so that they don't have to face up to the everyday monstrosity in their homes, their schools, their communities. In the conspiracy theories that cosset conservative culture, there is enormous anxiety about shadowy groups of elites abusing women and children. The women and children targeted by these fictional conspiracies do not exist, and, as such, don't demand anything of their rescuers. The sheer strangeness of these conspiracy theories could only have come from a culture desperate not to face the fact that sexual violence is ordinary, and everyday, and everywhere.

In the same way, most women who are raped are raped by someone who is known to them, often a close friend, a partner or a spouse – and yet our cultural and legal understanding of what a rapist looks like still seems to involve a dark alley and a stranger with suspicious facial hair. This frankly freakish othering of rapists and abusers is a crucial pressure-release valve. It allows the rest of us to live more comfortably within economic and social structures that are entirely predicated upon abuse. If rape is a unique crime perpetrated by a few 'bad apples', there's no need to dig up the whole orchard.

Sometimes people say the quiet part out loud when protecting predators. Newspapers reacted with surprise and disgust at a ruling passed down by Monmouth County Judge James Troiano on whether to charge a sixteen-year-old boy as an adult in a rape case where a sixteen-year-old girl accused the boy of raping her at a party while she was unconscious. According to media reports, the boy filmed the encounter and shared the video with his friends along with a text message that read, 'When your first time having sex was rape.'

Troiano pointed out that the boy was destined for 'a good college', was from a 'good family', and was an Eagle Scout. The defendant had no problem understanding his own actions as rape – just not the sort of rape that men like Troiano consider criminal. What had happened to the girl was not a 'traditional case of rape', Troiano said, which typically involved 'two or more generally males involved, either at gunpoint or weapon'.[5]

Like all monsters, the imagined rapist is invoked as a warning – not to men, but to women. Don't wear that dress, don't talk too loud, don't want too much. You know what happens to girls who don't follow the rules.

There's a reason why this story is so hard to shake. If rapists are monsters, rather than human beings like the rest of us, then knowing someone to be a human being with hopes and dreams and habits and feelings means we can cease to believe that he might also be a rapist. 'He's a good guy' is usually code for 'she must be lying'. This is a comforting fantasy for the frightened, angry child inside every entitled man, desperate to be loved unconditionally; it reassures him that the monsters disappear when you close the book, and that women are unreliable narrators of their own experience.

It's not that the dedicated predator, the pathological serial rapist, does not exist. But when he does, he is accommodated quite as often as he is hunted down and stopped. Hundreds of people knew something about what Harvey Weinstein was doing in Hollywood. Weinstein was protected, just as Bill Cosby was protected, just as the paedophile Jimmy Savile was protected by television companies and charities in Britain, because the reputations of powerful men and the networks they build to armour their abuses are usually valued more highly than the safety of women and children. Acknowledging the rapist in the room makes everyone uncomfortable, so collective social comfort is purchased at the cost of women's lives.

As society continues to grapple with the stigma attached to sexual assault survivors, those in power have continued to exploit that stigma. In November 2018 , a defence lawyer in a Cork rape case passed around the seventeen-year-old complainant's underwear to the jury. The article of clothing proved that the girl was 'open to meeting someone', the lawyer said. 'You have to look at the way she was dressed. She was wearing a thong with a lace front.'[6] Only months earlier in Belfast, a nineteen-year-old woman who accused several rugby players of rape was cross-examined for eight days and her underwear was also passed around to the jury.[7] If prosecutors continue to use this line of defence, it's only because it continues to work on juries and judges. Canadian Judge Robin Camp was called out in the press after asking an alleged sexual assault victim why she could not 'just keep her knees together' or put her 'bottom down into the basin so he couldn't penetrate you?'[8]

Again and again, from courts of law to intimate relationships, those with a stake in the status quo repeat the story that it is not men's responsibility to refrain from rape, but women's responsibility to guard against it, not just physically but by controlling how they behave, how they dress and where they go. The omnipresence of rape is the enforcing mechanism for heteronormative patriarchy as a political system, just as police violence and the carceral justice system is the enforcing mechanism for the political system of white supremacy – and, in many cases, police officers themselves are the disciplinary agents for both. In 2020, Louisville police broke into twenty-six-year-old emergency medical technician Breonna Taylor's home and shot her in her bedroom during a botched raid. At least one of the officers responsible for her death had been accused of sexual assault by multiple women and had twice been investigated for sexual harassment on the job but, like most American law-enforcement officers, faced no substantive consequences. This expectation of impunity is what allowed Daniel Holtzclaw, a police officer in Oklahoma, to systematically target vulnerable African American women and coerce them into sex. When Holtzclaw was finally arrested, it was on thirty-six charges, including multiple counts of rape and sexual battery.

In the United States and elsewhere, the idea that cops protect women from rape and sexual assault is often used as an argument against defunding and demilitarising the police. This argument is nonsensical, as the police have never prioritised punishing sexual violence, to the extent that the majority of rapes and sexual assaults still go unreported.

The only circumstance in which law enforcement has historically concerned itself with rape is when the accused is a Black man and the alleged victim a white woman – whether or not the allegations are true. In fact, as this book explores in more depth later, the spectre of the 'outsider' rapist – the imagined Black or brown man as a threat to fragile white women, who require protection from white men – has been weaponised for centuries to justify racist violence. This poisonous myth has been central to the narrative of white supremacy, and to the stories white people tell themselves to justify racial inequality.

White men, by contrast, can usually count on protection from law enforcement when accused of rape. During the British occupation of India, the rape of Indian women by British army officers was a routine occurrence – and it is now known that those officers 'could and did use the term "outrage" rather than "rape" when unruly soldiers raped Indian women,' according to historian Nancy L. Paxton, who notes that 'conversely, British judges could, and occasionally did, redefine an incident involving an Indian man who touched an Englishwoman, as "sexual assault".'[9] Despite this, the popular understanding of rape in British India was of a relentless sexual threat posed to colonising white women by Indian men – and these racist 'rape scripts' were used to justify the violent suppression of political unrest for generations.

In the United States and elsewhere, Black men are still imagined as sexual aggressors, and Black women and girls as promiscuous, wanton and therefore undeserving of respect or protection. These dehumanising stereotypes still serve to justify white violence and minimise white guilt – because throughout American history, it has, in fact, been white men who have sexually terrorised Black and Indigenous women, and not the other way around.

Sexual violence is a means of enforcing political and military dominance – and it always has been. During the Second World War, both the Axis and Allied powers used rape as a means of terrorising and subduing enemy civilians.[10] Gang rape and complicity with rape by conquering armies are deliberately employed to create a feeling of bonding and cohesion among soldiers, according to researchers like Dara Kay Cohen and Gayatri Spivak.

It is not only in the context of wars of invasion that rape is used to oppress civilian groups. In the United States, for many generations after the end of chattel slavery, the rape and assault of Black, brown and Indigenous women by white men was so common and so rarely prosecuted that it was functionally legal.

In 1944, in Alabama, twenty-four-year-old Recy Taylor was walking home from church when she was brutally gang-raped by six white men. The campaign to prosecute and punish Taylor's rapists was taken up by the National Association for the Advancement of Colored People – a civil rights organisation – and championed by activist Rosa Parks. Taylor and her family received death threats and had to go into hiding when their home was firebombed by racists furious that a Black woman was daring to challenge white male violence, but Parks and Taylor did not back down. The case helped galvanise the civil rights movement of the 1960s. The mere fact that women of colour were refusing to accept sexual subjugation was a profound political statement – and a challenge to a white supremacist culture that believed only white women were worth protecting from violence.

It is clear that when we speak of 'rape culture', we are speaking of a form of biopower that is intimately involved with racism and colonial logic. It is just as clear that resistance to rape culture is inseparable from resistance to white supremacy.

Challenging rape culture is not just about preventing rape. It is a direct reckoning with power. To refuse to tolerate the assault of women and children within institutions of power is to defy the articles of faith that hold these institutions together: that powerful men make the rules; that the more powerful they are, the more they are allowed to trample gleefully over other people's boundaries; that the reputation of men is worth more than the safety of women and girls; that men are worth more than women and girls, full stop. Her pain is necessary, whoever she is; his discomfort is unbearable, whatever he did. She must make allowances, because she is a girl, and that's what girls are for. He has his whole life ahead of him, or if he is older, he has a brilliant career, or if he is older still, an important legacy, one that cannot and ought not to be analysed in the context of all the lives and legacies damaged along the way. Think about his future.

But feminists and queers and radicals aren't the ones who are afraid of the future. When people who are working for a world where more of us can live meaningful lives demand better from men, from sex, from love, from government and from one another, they are thinking about how the future will work for everyone, including for men and boys. The call for a new culture of consent, a new way of treating one another, is the simple, thrilling conviction that there might be lives ahead of all of us, maybe even better ones. Consent is the queer and throbbing core of the new sexual revolution – and consent is not just about sex. It is about power. It is about agency. It is about work, and love, and desire. It is about how much we are prepared to sacrifice to protect the fragile fantasy of masculinity that flattens all human mutuality into featureless transaction or outright violence. An ethos of exploitation is the twisted thread stitching together our relationships to power, to security, to pleasure, and to each other. To talk about building a culture of consent is to speak sincerely about all the ways in which abuse and exploitation are normalised in everyday life – at work, in politics, in our homes and families, and institutions.

The opposite of consent is not only rape, but coercion and abuse of all kinds. And coercion is the logic that sustains both patriarchy and state power in oppressive societies.

Men as a political class have long been permitted to define women's experiences for them, legally and otherwise. For a very long time, male-dominated society has gone through exhausting contortions to persuade women that the violence they were experiencing was not, in fact, happening. To recast their memories as delusions and disorient their sense of self. The appropriate word for this comes from the lexicon of trauma recovery. The word is 'gaslighting'.

'Gaslighting' is a specific method of social control. It is taken from the much-adapted 1938 play *Gas Light* – a story of manipulation and emotional abuse, featuring a husband who persuades his wife that she is mad and cannot trust her own senses. He does this by moving things around in the house at night and denying that he's done it. The only evidence she has is the flicker of the gas lights downstairs. Gaslighting. It's more than simply persuading someone that they are losing their mind. It's about convincing them that what they see, hear and remember is false; that others know what really happened better than they do.

Long before it was given a name, gaslighting was a psychological tool used by abusive people and abusive societies to ensure that their subordinates stayed in line. Gaslighting about sexual, gendered and racist violence does not just take place on an individual level. It takes place on a structural level, wherever evidence of institutional abuse can even semi-plausibly be denied.

If the evidence can't be denied, the next strategy is to discredit the victims. In the past decade, as more and more women have had both the technology and the temerity to compare notes in public, a terrible truth has dawned like the morning after a war. For survivors of intimate abuse, there's something chillingly familiar about the way modern politics acts on the psyche. As *Teen Vogue* columnist Lauren Duca wrote, weeks after the US election of 2016:

> To gaslight is to psychologically manipulate a person to the point where they question their own sanity, and that's precisely what Trump is doing to this country. He gained traction in the election by swearing off the lies of politicians while constantly contradicting himself, often without bothering to conceal the conflicts within his own sound bites. He lied to us over and over again, then took all accusations of his falsehoods and spun them into evidence of bias.[11]

In the hands of morally unencumbered leaders like Bolsonaro, Putin and Trump, facts become interchangeable with opinions, and consensus reality itself becomes subject to the whims of tyrants, marooning citizens in a world where, in the words of journalist Peter Pomerantsev, 'nothing is true and everything is possible.'[12]

The same maiming of consensus reality takes place in individual abusive relationships. We've all heard stories about drunken loutish partners who persuade their battered wives every week that they are being hysterical, that they are overreacting. Those stories are so common they stray into cliché, and yet somehow the notion that these stories are common for a reason, that there might be a pattern worth actually addressing in policy, usually meets with silence. More often, these days, when stories of abuse and systemic sexism are raised in public, campaigners are told against all evidence that it's men who are the real victims, even as women's shelters are shut down for lack of funds all over the developed world.

Silence. Guilty silence. Silence you can't break without feeling a little bit crazy. Gaslighting redefines the terms of abuse to suit the abuser. If we take seriously the proposition that rape – coercing or forcing another person into sexual activity – is far more common than was previously acknowledged, we must also reckon with the fact that rape is far more normalised than we have even begun to reckon with. If there are many more rapists walking free than there are rapists convicted and in jail, we must come to terms with the fact that it has, until extremely recently, been considered far more heinous to accuse someone of rape than it is to commit it. A false accusation can never be forgiven. And unless and until he is found guilty by a court system that rarely, for a great many reasons, puts rapists behind bars, every accusation is assumed to be false.

The problem is that assuming that he is innocent is not simply a legal standard; it is also a social convention, and the assumption that *he* is innocent contains within it the assumption that *she* is guilty. That she is lying. Women's duplicity, women's inability to reliably relate or even understand what happens to their own bodies, is a cultural assumption that underpins the political logic of patriarchy.

According to a report published by the UK Crown Prosecution Service (CPS) in 2013, over a seventeen-month period there were only thirty-five prosecutions for making false allegations of rape. To put that into context, in the same period there were 5,651 prosecutions for rape.[13] However, as barrister Helena Kennedy reminds us:

Despite the evidence, the spectre of a woman willing to falsely accuse looms disproportionately large in the collective male psyche and receives similarly disproportionately prominent coverage in the media ... it is not uncommon for rape to summon up long-learned fears whispered into the ears of boys about the fickleness and deceit of women ... fears that the line which separates rape from seduction is easily crossed, and any decent fellow is at the mercy of an unscrupulous female.[14]

Repairing all this is not just about changing laws. It's just as much about enforcing laws that are already on the books. In practice, across much of the Global North, laws around sexual violence are so rarely enforced that rape and sexual assault have been tacitly sanctioned in all but the most extreme circumstances. Despite persistent myths about mushrooming false rape accusations, the evidence tells a very different story. It has never been conclusively proven that rates of false reporting of rape are higher than for any other crime.[15] More importantly, they are dwarfed by the number of real rapes that go unprosecuted. The non-profit advocacy group, RAINN (Rape, Abuse, and Incest National Network), has found that, in America, only 23 per cent of sexual assaults are reported to the police, only 4.6 per cent of sexual assaults result in arrest and only 0.5 per cent result in a felony conviction.[16]

Like police violence against men and women of colour in the United States, gendered violence against women and girls is illegal only in theory, not in practice. This means that men have successfully claimed a monopoly on the legitimate use of sexual and gendered violence. 'Legitimate', here, means violence that is tacitly or explicitly state sanctioned. 'Legitimate' violence, for political philosophers, is violence that those in power grant themselves permission to enact on the bodies of others. It's the difference between being arrested and being kidnapped. It's violence that is legal, in the way that it is legal for a police officer to wrestle you into a cage, or in the way that, in Britain and North America, it was legal until the early 1990s to rape a woman who had made the mistake of marrying you.

But 'legitimate violence' also tacitly includes crimes that are so difficult to prosecute that they become functionally legal, in the same way that most American police officers who gun down young Black men in the street escape jail, and in the same way that the majority of what are called 'date rapes' are never prosecuted. The consequences are borne instead by victims and survivors, who must decide if they want to suffer the public humiliation that invariably follows a report of rape or assault, or whether the rape itself was enough to teach them the cost of non-compliance. Gendered violence and white supremacist violence are publicly condemned by most world governments, but few world governments actually take any steps to make sure that women are protected from rape and abuse, or that men and women of colour are protected from racist murder.

The common refrain that 'rape is not about sex but about power' is not quite true. Rape is clearly and consistently about both at once. The more terrible truth is that we live in a world that conflates sex and power, where every desire must become the desire to dominate or be dominated.

The message is clear: the pain of women and girls does not matter. It is right and natural that public conversation about rape and the law is still largely about protecting men from lying women, rather than protecting everyone from violent men. It is right and natural that women bury the pain of the past so that men might enjoy that promise of a brighter future.

The connection between sexual oppression and social repression has been explored by philosophers for centuries. Oscar Wilde reportedly wrote that 'everything is about sex, except sex. Sex is about power.' The conversation being had right now is about the place where sex and power meet. It's not enough to just reframe the rules, to ask how precisely flirting and fucking should work now that women are asking to be treated at every stage like people, rather than status objects or receptacles for men's pleasure and pain. To change the culture of consent, we need to move on from talking about rules and start talking, instead, about ethics – about what sort of society we want to live in, and what it will take to get there.

Consent culture, first named by activist and sex-critical feminist Kitty Stryker, is the alternative to all this. Resisting a culture of rape and abuse must involve more than insisting on the individual right to say no, although that's both a decent starting place and a difficult concept for some people to wrap their forebrains around. There's a reason for that. The reason that the notion of real, continuous, enthusiastic sexual consent is so outrageous is that the concept of female sexual agency – let alone active desire – is still a fearful one. Our culture still has very little room for the idea that women and queer people, given the chance, want and enjoy sex just as much as men do.

We must get to grips with the idea of consent as ongoing and negotiable, rather than consent as an object, a one-time contract that can be fudged or debated in court. If people of all genders are going to stand a chance of living in this weird new world together without destroying one another, consent is going to have to mean more than that. Consent is more than the absence of no. It is the possibility of a real yes. It is the presence of mutual human agency. It is lust and lusciousness and shamelessness. It is the horizon of desire.

We are teetering, as a society, on the edge of a powerful transformation – but we could just as easily collapse back into the petty, violent certainties of the past. We could stop talking about ending ritual sexual violence in colleges, in schools, in religious and political institutions. We could stop insisting on the importance of consent as a baseline for pleasure and desire. We could stop calling out rapists and abusers. We could keep bullying and pressuring and isolating survivors until it's just too much pressure to speak out, until once again the impact of a rape accusation on a man's life is considered more important than the impact of rape itself on a woman's. We could stop all of it and pretend – if we can – that none of it ever happened.

Or we could try something new. We could try being better than we've been before. We could decide to do better than just trying not to get into trouble, trying not to actively commit rape and assault. We could start to talk about desire and consent as if they matter.

2

The Horizon of Desire

I've got a friend with a shady past. He's a clever and conscientious person who grew up in patriarchy, and he knows that he's done things that may not have been criminal but may well have hurt people, and by people he means women. My friend has hurt women, and he doesn't know what to do about that now. From time to time, we talk about it.

That's how it happened that, halfway through the first year of our friendship, halfway through an effervescent confession in a coffee shop, the following words came unselfconsciously out of his mouth: 'Technically, I don't think I've raped anyone.'

Technically. Technically, my friend didn't think he was a rapist.

That 'technically' haunted me for days. Not because I don't believe it, but because I do.

It's not the first time I've heard it, or something like it, from otherwise well-meaning male friends frantically reassessing their own sexual history in the light of the fact that shame is no longer enough to stop women from naming their abusers. 'Technically, I haven't raped anyone.' What did he mean, 'technically'? My friend went on to describe how, over years of drinking and shagging around before he got sober, he considers it a matter of luck rather than pride that he has never, to his knowledge, committed serious sexual assault. The fact is that, like any number of men growing up in the last decade, his concept of consent could have been written in crayon. Sex was something you persuaded women to let you do to them, and if she wasn't passed out, saying no, or actively trying to throw you off, you were probably OK.

What about her, though? Was she OK?

All the way home from the coffee shop I thought about consent, and why the concept is so frightening to anyone invested in not looking under the carpet of modern morality. I thought about the number of situations I've encountered where, technically, nobody committed a crime, and yes, technically, what happened was consensual. Maybe someone pushed a boundary to its breaking point. Maybe someone simply lay there and let something be done to them because they didn't feel able, for whatever reason, to say no.

That 'technically' is not just something one hears from men. You hear that same 'technically' in a different key, from girls and grown women who don't want to think of the things that happened to them that way, even though the fact that those things happened to them, with or without their say-so, is the whole problem. We learn, just as men do, that our instincts about what we feel and experience are not to be trusted. We learn that our desire is dangerous and so we tamp it down until we no longer recognise the difference between wanting and being wanted. We learn that our sexuality is contemptible and so we crush it; we become alienated from our own bodies. I've told myself before that, technically, this or that person committed no crime, so technically, I've got no reason to feel used like a human spittoon, and technically I did invite him back to my house, so technically, I should have expected nothing less, and technically, there's no reason to be angry and upset, because really, what is female sexuality but a set of technicalities to be overcome?

The problem is that technically isn't good enough. 'At least I didn't actively assault anyone' is not a gold standard for sexual morality, and it never was. Of course, we have to start somewhere, and 'try not to rape anyone' is as good a place as any, but it can't end there. Our standards for decent sexual and social behaviour should not be defined purely by what is likely to get us publicly shamed or put in prison, because we are not toddlers, and we can do better.

This is what consent culture means. It means expecting more – demanding more. It means treating one another as complex human beings with agency and desire, not just once, but continually. It means adjusting our ideas of dating and sexuality beyond the process of prying a grudging 'yes' out of another human being. Ideally you want them to say it again, and again, and mean it every time. Consent doesn't have to be sexy to be important – but there is dreadfully little joy in a model of sexuality that devolves into arguing over what you can get away with and still call consensual.

When you put it that way, consent sounds simple. Sadly, there are a great many simple ideas that otherwise sensible people choose not to understand when their self-image as decent human beings is at stake.

Right now, a lot of men and boys I know are bewildered. They are uncomfortable. They are wrestling with the spectre of their own wrongdoing. They are frightened, most of all, about how the ground rules for being a worthwhile person are changing so fast.

If you accept the idea that a woman has the absolute right to sexual choice, that she has a right to say no even if she's said yes before, even if she's naked in your bed, even if you've been married for twenty years, you must also wrestle with the prospect that she might not make the choice you want. That's the hill that far too many men mistake for the moral high ground as they prepare to die on it.

We are surrounded by so many images of sexuality that it's easy to think of ourselves as liberated. But liberation, by definition, involves everyone. Instead, the messages that bombard us, from marketing and pop culture to mainstream pornography, insist that acceptable desire goes only in one direction: from men to women. It's a homogenous, dehumanising vision of straight sex, a simple story where only men have agency, and women are passive datapoints on a spectrum of fuckability. It is sexual licence, not liberation.

The modern concept of sexual freedom, in fact, is very much like the modern concept of market freedom. Yes, the word 'freedom' is involved – but what it boils down to is freedom for people with power to dictate terms and freedom for everyone else to shut up and smile. In sexuality as in economics, a vision of freedom whereby the illusion of choice has become a modesty slip for unspeakable everyday violence.

Here's how that happens. Well before they are old enough to start thinking about having it, girls are still trained to imagine sex as something that will be done to us, rather than something we might like to do for its own sake. We grow up with warnings that sexuality in general, and heterosexuality in particular, is a fearful, violent thing; sex is something we must avoid, rather than something we might have. If we're able to recognise that we want it of our own accord, we learn that we are deviant, dirty and wicked. The legion of one-handed-typers in misogynist chat-threads wondering why on earth it's so hard for them to get laid, wondering why women don't make approaches, why they often use sexuality as a social bargaining strategy, would do well to remember that straight women didn't come up with those rules.

Most straight women, let alone queer women, learned from a very young age how to gently suffocate their own desires. Withholding sexuality is the only social power they are permitted – even if that permission is given grudgingly by a culture that calls them sluts and bitches and whores when they say yes, and refuses to hear them when they say no.

Little boys who are straight, by contrast, grow up learning three things about sex. Firstly, that sex is something you do to women, that you're entitled to do it to them, and if you don't figure out a way to do it to at least one of them, you're not a man at all. Secondly, that sex is something absolutely vital to your identity and status, not just physically – it is not really about pleasure – but emotionally, socially and as the one form of true intimacy you're actually allowed. And thirdly, that sex is violent.

Boys learn from example and indoctrination that male sexuality is inherently animalistic and savage and damaging, and that women simply do not want sex in the same way – unless there's something wrong with them. Boys are taught that sexuality

52

involves doing something disgusting and violent to another person, something that is degrading – even if she lets you. Even if she likes it. Perhaps especially if she likes it.

This means that straight boys learn to be frightened and repelled by their own sexuality, and suspicious of any woman who seems too eager to accommodate it. They learn that sex is just another violent urge to be managed. Part of this fear is often about the inevitability of someday hurting someone, of 'getting it wrong'.

I have spoken to so many men who find the notion of real, active, enthusiastic consent hard to get their heads around. Why? Because they cannot believe that any woman could really want to fuck them that much.

One of the big fears that a lot of men seem to have about the dismantling of everyday sexist dating myths and the destruction of rape culture, is rooted in the conviction that if women are not to some extent coerced into sleeping with them and dating them … it won't happen. That without the rituals and petty violences of toxic masculinity, men will not get laid at all, will not have any of their needs met, or any of their desires satisfied. While the current system leaves so many of them frustrated, it has to be better than nothing, right?

Wrong. In fact, rape culture is an attack on desire. It is about controlling female sexuality. It is anti-sex and anti-pleasure. It teaches us to deny our own desires, as an adaptive strategy for surviving a sexist world.

There are all sorts of things nice girls aren't supposed to do. Nice girls are sexy but not sexual. Nice girls are fuckable, but they don't actually fuck. Nice girls talk about victimhood, if they must, but not desire. Nice girls know that their sexual consent is a commodity, and that they must not be too free with their favours lest they devalue the collective currency by which their social worth is measured. If we give the impression that we might like a fuck, or even that we'd prefer to decide for ourselves who and how and when we fuck, we deserve violence. We are nothing.

That, at least, is what certain men on the internet tell me every day, and if it's all the same to you, I'd rather not have this conversation on their terms. I do not wish to waste any more of my one precious life than is strictly necessary debunking the crypto-Darwinian pseudoscience that all women really want is to be held down and humped thoroughly until they stop lying about the pay gap and start making Christian babies. It's the sort of disingenuous discursive slime mould that only grows the more oxygen you feed it, and that's why the terms of engagement have to shift. That's why we need to talk – more than ever – about agency, about consent, and yes, about desire.

Some time ago, I had a lover who could not get over his astonishment about how much I seemed to enjoy sex. 'You really like this, for its own sake,' he said, routinely, every time we slept together. 'You actually enjoy it.' He was surprised. I was surprised that he was surprised – though I've encountered that surprise before. My own experience is that the men who were most surprised about my sexual enthusiasm were all for it at first – and then they were the first to find it off-putting, to use it as an excuse for disrespect, to ghost when I revealed myself as a woman who has managed to hang on to my own sexuality enough to express it.

This sort of surprise is often seasoned with disgust – after all, culture still teaches us that straight and bisexual women who actually pursue pleasure are somehow dirty, worthless, less valuable, *less*. In a world where heterosexuality is flattened into a logic of dominance and ownership, there's nothing attractive about a woman who owns her own desire. Most of the men who expressed surprise at my enthusiasm quickly found their own interest waning. If they didn't have to chase me, if I didn't play a little coy, if I got bored with the game of keeping them waiting until the third date because I was horny and busy and dating is weird and I'd always rather just go to bed and see if our bodies like each other – well. That's when I got my ticket to the friendzone, usually with a short speech about how different I was from other girls. I have never understood what makes that a compliment.

I'm not knocking the friendzone; it's an exciting place to visit, nobody expects you to wear special underwear, and all the rides are free. Nobody has to continue any relationship they don't want to; 'I don't want to' is reason enough. It just happens that my particular experience is studded with men who could only understand straight sexuality as a game of predator and prey. Stating clearly what you want, whether or not you get it, complicates the standard narrative of straight sex where men are supposed to set the terms, to control both partners' pleasure, to dictate who feels what, and when, and why.

But consent is not a kink. A sexual culture predicated on violence insists that openness and honesty are unthinkable boner-killers, that 'things are better with a bit of mystery', and it leaves a lot of us unable to name abuse for what it is – much less be honest about our own desires. So what do we do about consent when active female desire is a turn-off? What do we do when women are supposed to say 'no' when we mean 'yes', and 'I've got a boyfriend' when we mean 'no'?

Men who mouth the language of erotic liberation are often secretly terrified of women's sexual agency. The sexually free woman remains a figure of popular and moral horror. She – we – are the gaping hole that can never be filled. Historically, any hint of promiscuity in women was linked to prostitution, insanity or both, and both could lose you the freedom you clearly had too much of. Upfront desire for sex was blamed on hysteria, on womb-sickness, on an imbalance of the humours. These days it's often put down to sexual abuse in childhood – oddly, this is practically the only occasion when the endemic nature of such abuse is acknowledged. As if the problem were not that little girls were being hurt, but that grown women were not adequately controlling themselves.

Women grow up learning that our own desire is dirty and dangerous. We learn it early, and hard. We learn it in our bones. We learn that the best we can expect from sexuality is to survive it. 'What I've learned from women's experience with sexuality,' writes Catharine A. MacKinnon, 'is that exploitation and degradation produce grateful complicity in exchange for survival.

They produce self-loathing to the point of extinction of self, and it is respect for self that makes resistance conceivable.'[1]

Desire is dangerous for women. Desire makes us ugly and unworthy of humane treatment. So we squash it down. We stamp it out, even in the moment. We learn that to be respected, even on an intimate, one-to-one level, we sometimes have to feign reluctance, let ourselves be chased and coerced, and this, of course, further complicates an already complicated situation. If you're a man and you've been told that attractive women often act like they don't want to fuck you, how are you meant to respect the wishes of those who really, actively don't want to fuck you? If you have eroticised female sexual hesitancy, how are you meant to suddenly switch to a culture of real consent, where the appropriate thing to do when someone is pulling away is to let them go?

Women actively wanting to fuck men is not at all heteronormative. That's why any active display of straight or queer female desire still has the power to shock on a political level and startle on a personal one. Given what's going on in the world beyond our bedrooms, it might seem like the wrong time to be talking about desire. Beset as we already are by swivel-eyed patriarchs and obtuse old men who see it as their right by birth and breeding to grab the whole world by the nethers, it's tempting to take pleasure off the table for now, to keep our mouths and legs and hearts shut.

But unless we talk about desire, about agency, about consent, then we'll only ever be fighting this culture war in retreat. And this is a culture war where either everyone wins, or nobody does. If we want to turn this battle around, we must rethink our understanding of consent. It will be difficult, and it will be uncomfortable, but for the sake of all of us – and for our bodies and our livelihoods and our relationships – we have to do better, we must do better, than 'technically'.

3

WE'RE ALL MAD HERE

'It's like finding out aliens exist.'

I was having drinks with a man I've known for years. He was two beers down and trying to process why he never spoke up, over a twenty-year period, about his best friend, who turned out to be a multiple rapist. The allegations had just become public.

'Back in the day we'd all heard stories about it, but – well, the girls telling them were all a bit crazy,' he said. 'You know, they were messed up. So nobody believed them.'

I took a sip of my drink to calm down. Perhaps, I suggested, the reason these women were 'messed up' was because they had been sexually assaulted. I reminded him that some of us had always known for sure. That I, personally, knew for sure. I didn't raise my voice. I didn't lose my temper. I did my best not to lose my temper or show my hurt. I wanted him to listen to me – and who's going to listen to a woman who's angry and in pain?

What is happening in our culture, as we collectively process the notion that women have a right to agency and dignity, is something akin to first contact. Abusers, like little green men in flying saucers, have a habit of revealing their true selves to people nobody's going to find credible – to women who are vulnerable, or women who are marginalised, or who are just, you know, women. But abusers don't come from any planet but this. We grew up with them. We've worked with them. Admired them. Loved them. Trusted them. And now we have to deal with the fact that our reality is not what it seemed. So who's crazy now?

Sanity is socially and politically determined. When we speak about gender, power and violence, the question of whose mental health matters is always on the agenda. Whose suffering is significant? Whose testimony can be trusted? And – most importantly – what does it mean, really, when we call a woman crazy for speaking her truth and demanding change?

Over and over again, in private social groups and public, professional settings, women and queer people who come forward about mistreatment they or others have suffered are dismissed as 'crazy'. That's not an accident. It's no accident that the idea of being 'crazy' encompasses two distinct qualities: that of being delusional, and that of being in pain. Where men's pain and suffering is taken as an explanation or excuse for harm they have caused, women's pain is taken as proof that they are delusional and are not worth listening to. This is very useful for those invested in ignoring how much women still suffer in a culture of male supremacy. According to the Rape, Abuse & Incest National Network (RAINN) in America, 94 per cent of women who are raped experience symptoms of post-traumatic stress disorder (PTSD) during the two weeks following the rape, and 13 per cent of women who are raped attempt suicide.[1]

It is terribly convenient that suffering is synonymous with delusion, depending on precisely who is suffering. The word 'mad' commonly means both 'angry' and 'delusional'. That matters.

To be the victim of sexual assault is to fall down a rabbit hole into a reality shaped by collective delusion: specifically, the delusion that powerful or popular or ordinary-seeming men who do good work in the world cannot also be abusers or predators. To suggest otherwise is to appear insane. You question yourself. Even before anyone calls you a liar – which they will – you start wondering if you've overreacted. Surely he couldn't be like that. Not him. Anyway, it would be madness to go against someone with so much clout. The girls who do that are sick in the head. Overdramatic. Hysterical.

In recent years, something important has changed. Suddenly women are speaking up and speaking out in numbers too big to shove aside. The public narrative around abuse and sexual entitlement and the common consensus around who is to be believed are changing so fast you can see the seams between one paradigm and the next, the hasty stitching where one version of reality becomes another. Now, instead of victims and survivors of rape and assault being written off as mentally ill, it is the abusers who are claiming to be disturbed – who need help.

'I'm hanging on in there,' said Harvey Weinstein, in the wake of revelations about a pattern of abuse that upended the entertainment industry, tipping out all of its ugliest secrets. 'I'm not doing OK, but I'm trying. I gotta get help. You know what – we all make mistakes.'[2]

Days earlier, Weinstein had emailed other Hollywood higher-ups, frantic not to be fired, asking for their assistance convincing The Weinstein Company board to keep him – and begging to be sent to therapy as an alternative. The same pleas for mercy on the grounds of mental illness have been issued on behalf of powerful predators in the tech industry. Here's the statement put out by the tech firm 500 Startups on the actions of its founder, Dave McClure, also accused of assault and harassment: 'He recognizes he has made mistakes and has been going through counseling to work on addressing changes in his previous unacceptable behaviour.'[3]

In other words, when women speak up about abuse, they are mad and therefore not to be believed; when men are accused of abuse, they are mad and therefore not to blame. Women's suffering makes them objects of suspicion; men's suffering exonerates them.

It's all about whose suffering matters. It is only when the abuse becomes impossible to deny, when patterns emerge, when photographs and videos are available and are enough to lead to conviction, that we start hearing the pleas for mercy. It was just twenty minutes of action. He's got such a bright future. Think of his mother. Think of his wife. He couldn't help himself.

These excuses are never just about the abuser and his reputation. They are desperate attempts to bargain with a rapidly changing reality. They are justifications for continuing, collectively, to deny systemic abuse. Suddenly it is Weinstein, not the dozens of women he victimised, who gets to be the one with 'demons'. He needs to see a therapist, not a judge. He's a very unhappy and very sick man. And so is Bill Cosby. And so is that guy in your industry everyone respects so much, the one with the charming smile and all those crazy ex-girlfriends.

One of the social definitions of sanity is the capacity to make peace with the way injustice operates. It stands to reason, then, that the language of mental illness functions as a shorthand for the articulation of truths that are outside the accepted political consensus. Feminists, anti-racist activists, LGBTQ people and socialists have all been on the receiving end of this kind of pathologising, sometimes formally so, in a way that has nothing to do with our day-to-day experience. The people who call women crazy every time they dare to speak in public about sexual violence or social justice are not at all concerned for their health. Anyone who challenges social convention is deemed mad by default, including women who dare to suggest that predators in positions of power might have to be held accountable for their actions. When you talk about something nobody else wants to see, you can expect to be called delusional.

There's a long, grim history behind the idea that women lie about sexual abuse because they're mentally unwell. In decades gone by, women who made a scene, who made the mistake of confronting abusers or even just closing the door on them, were routinely relegated to a very different sort of asylum – not for their own good, but for everyone else's.

Diagnoses like hysteria were always political, and they still are. Before modern psychiatry, women who displayed any sort of aberrant behaviour – from having sex outside marriage, to lesbianism, to talking back to her husband, or perhaps simply not being young and pretty any more, could be confined to a mental institution or placed under effective house arrest without her consent. Fifty years later, with similar motivation, psychiatrists in the Soviet Union collaborated with the secret police to deal with dissidents by diagnosing them as mentally ill and dispatching them to prisons that fronted as hospitals. Sanity is defined politically, and by opposing the state, the dissidents were by definition insane; so were the Victorian women who opposed the restrictions patriarchy placed on their lives.

Charlotte Perkins Gilman's haunting 1892 novella *The Yellow Wallpaper* famously describes a woman who is confined to an upstairs bedroom and forbidden to work or exercise by her husband, who is convinced that her desire to write is driving her insane. When her solitary confinement begins, she has control of her faculties, but the trauma of being shut up against her will, the weeks spent staring at the walls, drive her slowly to a genuine emotional breakdown. Gilman was a revolutionary thinker whose other writings included the feminist utopia *Herland*, which has not had such a popular afterlife as *The Yellow Wallpaper* in a culture that still prefers stories about women being tortured to the point of madness than women making a world where they don't have to answer to men.

Over a century later, the same rhetoric applies. Women are overemotional. They cannot be trusted because they are crazy, which is a word patriarchy uses to describe a woman who doesn't know when to shut her pretty mouth. They are unreliable narrators of their own lives, because they are unwell, which is a word patriarchy uses to describe women who are angry.

Well, of course they're angry. Of course they are hurt. They're angry and hurt *because they have been traumatised*, first by the abuse and then by their community's response. And they're not able to express that righteous rage without consequence, because they are not men. If you had been assaulted, forcibly penetrated, treated like so much human meat; if you had sought justice or even just comfort and found instead rank upon rank of friends and colleagues closing together to call you a liar and a hysteric, telling you you'd better shut up – how would you feel? You might well feel hurt, or angry – but you'd better not show it. Not if you want to be believed. Not if you want to be protected. Angry women are not to be trusted, which suits abusers and their enablers just fine. And when everyone around you gets together to dismiss the inconvenient truth of your experience, it is tempting to believe them, especially if you are very young.

Twelve years ago I was raped by a much older man in a hotel room. When I spoke out about it, I was told I was toxic, difficult and a compulsive liar. I was told that so consistently that eventually I came to accept it, and I moved away to heal in private while the man who had hurt me went on to hurt other people. In the intervening decade, every time women I know have spoken out about sexual abuse, they have been dismissed as mentally ill. And yes, some of them *were* mentally ill – at least one in four human beings will experience mental health problems in their lifetime, after all, and violence and trauma are contributing factors. More to the point, predators seek out victims who seem vulnerable. Sexual predators routinely target people who nobody will believe because they're already 'crazy'.

The #MeToo movement was exactly what the sanity and safety of thousands of unnamed women was once sacrificed to avoid: a giant flaming fuss. It is unbelievable what otherwise sensible people will do to avoid a fuss. They will ostracise victims, gaslight survivors and provide cover for predators; they will hire lawyers, hand out hundreds of thousands of dollars under the table and, if pressed, rearrange entire social paradigms to make it seem like anyone asking for basic justice is a screeching hysteric.

Now, however, it is the abusers who are suddenly seeking asylum. Asking to be treated as sufferers of illness, rather than as criminals. The language of lunacy is the last resort when society at large cannot deny the evidence of structural violence. We hear the same thing in the wake of a mass shooting or a white supremacist terror attack. He was always such a nice boy. Something broke. We couldn't have seen it coming. He was depressed and frustrated. We can't pretend it didn't happen, so instead we pretend that there's no pattern here, just individual maladaptation. A chemical imbalance in the brain, not a systemic injustice soaked into our culture. Harvey Weinstein can't be a rapist, because he's a 'very sick guy' – at least according to Woody Allen, who may not be able to claim strict objectivity. Now we're supposed to feel sorry for abusers, because they are damaged, because they are in pain.

Well, join the queue. All of us are in pain. All of us are damaged. That's because all of us are human. Having low self-esteem and a dark obsession with sexually intimidating the women around you aren't excuses for abuse. At best, they are explanations; at worst, they are attempts to redirect attention from the real harm women and queer people have suffered.

In fact, according to researchers like Lundy Bancroft, who has spent decades working with abusive men, abusers are no more or less likely to be mentally ill than anyone else. 'Abusiveness has little to do with psychological problems and everything to do with values and beliefs,' writes Bancroft in his foundational text *Why Does He Do That?*: 'Abusers have a distorted sense of right and wrong. Their value system is unhealthy, not their psychology.'[4]

We've all got broken hearts and complicated childhoods, and survivors have spent too long being quietly directed to seek therapy as an alternative to justice. For centuries women and children who spoke out about violence and abuse they experienced have been told that they were delusional and disturbed. That no matter how much they believed that injustice had been done, they should not trust their own memories, and nor should anyone else.

Sometimes the way this works is simply by creating a culture in which acknowledging violence and harassment is too uncomfortable. Survivors of rape and assault routinely report having their memories and sexual history questioned by police and in court when they are brave enough to report their attackers – but gaslighting happens in social circles, in families, in relationships, wherever women, children and queer people suffer things the world would rather not have to hear about.

In the early years of his pioneering talk therapy, Sigmund Freud was startled by the number of miserable women and girls who came to his rooms and confided that they had been molested and assaulted by their family members, including in early childhood. Jeffrey M. Masson, who first discovered this part of Freud's history in his archives, wrote that:

> Freud was the first psychiatrist who believed that his patients were telling the truth.
>
> Freud announced his discovery in a paper entitled 'The Etiology of Hysteria', which he gave in April of 1896 ... The address presented a revolutionary view of mental illness ... namely, the belief that such early experiences were real, not fantasies, and had a damaging and lasting effect on the later lives of the children who suffered them.[5]

The reaction in polite Viennese society was frosty – but Freud was adamant that 'the behavior of patients while they are reproducing these infantile experiences is in every respect incompatible with the assumption that the scenes are anything else than a reality which is being felt with distress and remembered with the greatest reluctance'.[6]

The professional consequences of this position, however, were severe. In anguished letters to a friend shortly after giving his lecture, Freud wrote that 'I am as isolated as you could wish me to be: the word has been given out to abandon me, and a void is forming around me.'[7]

In 1905, Freud publicly retracted what came to be called the Seduction Theory – and changed his story. He had been taken in at first, but these women had not actually been assaulted – instead, they were unconsciously obsessed with the erotic idea of the father figure, as opposed to an actual father figure who might have committed actual abuse. Freud's female patients, he now insisted, were not victims of abuse. They were delusional.

This is important, because Freud's work on the unconscious is the foundation for so many of our modern theories about how human desire works – including in politics. Freudian psychoanalysis introduced concepts like the 'subconscious' and the 'ego', which would radically change how ordinary people were allowed to understand themselves as sentient creatures. And yet some truths were too radical for Freud, or for the generations of male psychoanalysts who followed, built on and expanded his ideas. Freud was bold enough to challenge religious orthodoxy on the nature of the human soul, but not brave enough, in the end, to believe his patients. Not when they told him truths that were too inconvenient to treat as anything other than the symbolic spasming of feeble female minds.

And that's how it happened. That's how part of the way modern culture understands sexual desire was based on a lie. It was based on chosen ignorance of the extent of abuse of women and children, on an attempt to explain away trauma as delusion – and all to avoid ruffling whiskers in the gentlemen's club by giving too much credence to unhappy young girls.

Yes, young women are often traumatised by every violent indignity that comes along with being a young woman in the modern age. In England nearly one in four young women has a mental illness, with emotional problems such as depression and anxiety the most common. A recent NHS report found young women aged seventeen to nineteen were twice as likely as young men to have problems, with 22.4 per cent reporting a disorder.[8] Black, brown and immigrant girls are particularly vulnerable, and NHS data shows a 68 per cent rise in hospital admissions because of self-harm among girls under seventeen in the past decade.[9]

Despite these figures, it is not women's mental health that is treated as a public concern. One of the few concrete statistics about gender and violence that has penetrated public consciousness is the harrowing fact that men are taking their own lives in increasing numbers,[10] and dying in awful droves from suicide, substance abuse or other 'deaths of despair'. The fact that this is happening at all is horrific enough. The fact that the deaths of these men are so often weaponised as a reason to dismiss women's pain – as if mental illness were a competition between the genders – adds insult to an irreparable injury.

Over and over again, women and girls are told that they are to blame when men hurt themselves. In 2019, when women in the games industry spoke out about abuse and harassment they had experienced at work – about men in positions of power who had manipulated and extorted sex from them and then cast them aside – one of the named abusers was a developer named Alec Holowka. Holowka's employers found the claims credible, although no case was ever brought to court – and several days after the allegations became public, Holowka, who had struggled with mental health difficulties for many years, committed suicide. Social media exploded. Not with sympathy for Holowka's family, but with fury at the women who had called out his behaviour – who were directly blamed for his decision to end his life. The threat of extreme self-harm is a classic last-resort tactic for abusers who suspect that they're losing control, that their partner is about to leave them or tell someone, or both. It's effective emotional blackmail because it is almost always plausible. Who wants to be the person who put their own freedom and safety ahead of another person's life?

At the height of the #MeToo movement, as the list of names of perpetrators grew longer, so did the pleas for mercy on the grounds of mental illness. Violent men, we were reminded, suffer too, just as much as those they hurt – possibly more! Isn't it enough that they feel guilty, that they know they've got a problem, that they hate themselves for it? Didn't we care about them? Do we want them to fall apart – or worse, to do themselves damage?

The threat that men will fall apart or harm themselves if women refuse to put up with their behaviour is an age-old, tried-and-true tactic of control, and it plays on issues of identity that run hot and deep. Women are raised to put men's interests before their own. Women are supposed to protect men from the consequences of their own actions. Even if it means staying in an abusive relationship, or accepting social ostracism and shame, women are expected to suffer so that men can grow. Most women and queer people have been raised to treat men's emotions with respect and deference, even at the cost of their own happiness, because most of us have been raised with the understanding that when men get upset, bad things happen. Men, too, even decent

and non-sexist men, have grown up with this understanding –
that male suffering simply matters more, or why else would we
treat it as a public concern?

I've been there. I've been that person struggling not to prioritise
a man's pain, and I know how hard it is to break out of that
mindset. One of my ex-partners and former close friends is a
multiple rapist who sexually, physically and emotionally abused
countless women, including me. When some of his victims began
to put the pieces together, he assured us that he would end his life
if it became public. We believed him. We knew that he was fragile,
had accepted his narrative that he abused women for the same
reason he abused drugs and alcohol – because he was in pain and
could not help himself. He used the same combination of threats
and performative weakness that crops up in every narcissist's
playbook, convincing us that he was both too powerful to be
crossed and too weak to survive being held accountable. When
the stories came out anyway, despite his best efforts, he did not
choose to end his life. But yes, he did suffer. People who are held
accountable for years of abuse frequently do – and their victims
are not responsible for that suffering.

Here's a thought: what if people started thinking about the
effect on other people's mental health *before* they made the
decision to abuse, bully and rape? For so long, women and queer
people have learned not to speak about their exhaustion, their
pain and trauma. They have learned to come across as carefully
neutral, as endlessly reasonable, to hide the depression, the fear,
the anxiety. For every man whose behaviour has been excused
because of his mental health problems, there are countless women
and queer people whose mental health problems have been
weaponised against them, to dismiss what they say. The risk that
male violence poses to women's mental health is not considered
worthy of comment.

This is what happens within industries and institutions where
men have most of the power and seniority – and, crucially, it
is also how male power perpetuates within those institutions.
Women quietly drop out of professions and workplaces where

they are routinely hurt, demeaned and isolated. The damage is borne in private by the victims themselves, and by networks of women doing the emotional deep cleaning so that men don't have to be confronted with the damage they've done.

Right now, all around me, I see women working to support men, as well as each other, through this process. It's not just because we're nice, and it's not just because we're suckers, although it is probably a little bit of both. It is because we know how much this is going to hurt.

We know because we've carried it all for so long in private. We know how deep the damage goes, how much there is still unsaid. Even as we come together to demand an end to sexual violence, we worry that men are too weak to cope with the consequences of what they've done and have been allowed to do to us.

It's work, and it wears you down. I'm a person with two jobs, and I spent at least eight hours I didn't have to spare this past weekend holding space for friends who have been put in situations just like this – situations where they are powerless. If you've not been privy to that liminal sphere, if you don't know the daily work that goes into maintaining those delicate tendrils of care, then it could well seem like this is coming out of nowhere. If you don't know what it's like to watch a friend fold quietly in on herself as she tells you about a man you both know, about what he did, and why she can't ever say anything, because he can and will crush her dreams with a gesture, and he's already hurt her enough – if you've not had to learn, at your cost, that the fragility of powerful, volatile men is far more of a hazard than their strength – then you might well ask, why are women only speaking up now?

My fingers are fairly itching with all of the stories I'm not telling here because they aren't mine to share, and the consequences wouldn't only be mine to bear. Secrets that eat you up from the inside. I don't want to think about how much time I've spent over the past five years dealing with the fallout of male violence, giving advice, trying to mitigate damage, trying to protect survivors. I don't want to think about it because most of the men in my life and in my fields of work don't have to spend their energy on such things.

The abusers who are now being excused as mentally ill are not monsters, and they are not aberrations. They were acting entirely within the unhealthy value system of a society that esteems the reputation and status of men above the safety of women. Many abusers, on some level, do not know that what they are doing is wrong. They believe that they are basically decent. Most men who prey on women have had that belief confirmed over the course of years or decades of abuse. They believe they're basically decent, and a whole lot of other people believe they're basically decent too. They're nice guys who just have a problem with women, or booze, or their mothers, or all three.

Reframing serial abuse as a mental health issue stashes it conveniently on the high shelf marked 'somebody else's problem'. The trouble is that sickness does not obviate social responsibility. It never has. Sickness might give a person the overwhelming urge to act in repulsive ways, but sickness does not cover for them during business meetings or pay off their lawyers or make sure they get women dropped from films. It takes a village to protect a rapist.

I am perfectly willing to accept that toxic masculinity leaves a lot of broken men in its wake. That culture conspires to prevent men and boys from being able to handle their sexuality, their aggression, and their fear of rejection and loss of status in any adult way. That the modern world makes it unbearable, at times, to exist inside a male body without constant validation. But very few men – very few people, period – grow up with wholly healthy attitudes towards their own gender. Not everyone with fucked-up ideas about women goes on to do fucked-up things *to* women. Toxic masculinity, as Bancroft observes, is a social illness before it is a psychological one.

It is easier to cope with the idea of sick men than it is to face the reality of a sick society; we've waited far too long to deal with our symptoms because we didn't want to hear the diagnosis. The prognosis is good, but the treatment is brutal. The people finally facing the consequences of having treated women and girls like faceless pieces of property may well be extremely unhappy about it. That's understandable. I'm sure it's not a lot of fun to be Harvey Weinstein right now, but sadly for the disgraced super-producer and those like him, the world is changing, and for once, no longer cosseting the feelings of powerful men.

Some days it feels like the whole world is being held hostage by male fragility. Sometimes it seems that there's no limit to what women, girls and queer people are expected to tolerate in order to protect men from a moment's uncomfortable self-reflection. Sometimes I don't know who to trust any more. There are so many men out there who appear to be allies but do not consider their own intimate behaviour towards women to be at all relevant to the discussion. I don't know who is going to turn out to have covered up for his violent friend, or taken his low self-esteem out on his girlfriend, or iced younger women out of his industry when they refused to go on dates with him. I just want to know this:

What if we all decided to care as much about the well-being of women who have been abused as we do about the well-being of abusers? What would it be like to live and work in a world where the consequences of hurting a woman weighed heavier than the consequences of being one?

4

BAD SEX

Pain is political, and so is pleasure. The greatest delusion of modern sexuality is that one has to come at the cost of the other – that the price of straight men's pleasure, in particular, is women's pain. Time and again, when women and young people speak out against sexual violence, society reacts as if sex, rather than violence, were the problem to be solved. Here's an example of where that can lead:

In recent years the notion of 'rough sex' has become a popular defence strategy in assault and murder cases. Men who strangle or brutalise their partners routinely attempt to recast their behaviour as simply 'rough sex gone wrong' – as if murder and maiming were everyday risks that any woman getting into bed with a man in the early twenty-first century should have weighed beforehand.

Today, violence is assumed to be foundational to straight sex in a way that has little to do with kink and nothing to do with consent. Cruelty and coercion are an increasingly normal part of straight sexuality. 'More than a third of UK women under the age of 40 have experienced unwanted slapping, choking, gagging or spitting during consensual sex,' according to a BBC research unit.[1] What does it do to your sexuality when you can't know if getting into bed with a perfectly nice-seeming stranger will involve being humiliated or hurt without asking? It gets worse: one study published in *JAMA Internal Medicine*, which surveyed women aged eighteen to forty-four in the US, revealed that 'More than 3 million women experienced rape as their first sexual encounter'.[2]

Despite all this, the simple idea that women's sexual agency matters, and that the world should contain less rape, is still considered equivalent to 'hating sex'. Campaigners against sexual violence are routinely treated as if they were attacking sexuality itself. This only makes sense if you accept a definition of straight sex where men's pleasure is all that matters, where women are not allowed to set boundaries, and where humiliation, violence and ritual misogyny are part of the lexicon of intimacy.

It seems that for straight women, 'good sex' still means 'sex where you weren't seriously injured or killed'. For straight men, by contrast, 'good sex' is usually expected to involve orgasm. This discrepancy does not lead to erotic liberation. Sex can't seriously be considered free when it involves more than one person and only one of them enjoys it. What all of this means is that a lot of sex that is technically consensual is nonetheless dire and disappointing. Particularly straight sex. Particularly for women.

So many of us are starving for pleasure. Much has been made of the fact that millennials, and particularly millennial men, are having less sex than previous generations. Research by the *Washington Post* suggested that 28 per cent of young men between the ages of eighteen and thirty reported having no sex in 2018 – compared to 18 per cent of young women.[3] This was almost universally reported as a negative trend, as if quantity itself were the only worthwhile metric to measure human intercourse. The US edition of *The Economist* weighed in, suggesting that this decline in straight sex 'is likely a response to increased female empowerment, the major change in sexual politics, and ... further exacerbated by men's dread of a #MeToo-style harassment charge.'[4]

Here, female empowerment is framed as an unacceptable obstacle to male sexual freedom. If women really have agency and autonomy over who, how and whether they have sex, they might choose not to have sex with you, even if you really want them to – and that's a bridge too far in a culture where male entitlement to women's bodies still trumps women's right to basic safety. Heterosexual access is presented as a commodity essential to the health of men, and anything that disturbs that access is recast as a common threat to human flourishing.

But what if we approached this differently? What if, instead of asking how much sex is being had, we started asking how much *fun* is being had – by everyone, not just straight men? Why does the joyless, coercive sex that the rest of us so often have to settle for under patriarchy have to be the norm?

The new sexual revolution, as we have seen, is not just a fight against sexual violence – it is a fight for sexual freedom in the face of sexism, transphobia and homophobia. It shatters the dominance model of straight sex and disrupts the gender binary. Misogynists, transphobes and homophobes must not be allowed to own the language of sexual liberty. Sadly, that was exactly how the first backlash against the #MeToo movement took shape, mere days after the initial accusations about Harvey Weinstein hit the press. The charges against women's rights activists were reframed as hysteria, moral panic, hatred of sex and hatred of men. In fact, during interviews during the first months of the #MeToo movement, I was asked again and again where the line should be drawn between rape and 'bad sex' – as if women could not be trusted to tell the difference.

In the weeks after the first #MeToo exposés, much was made of an open letter in the French paper of record, *Le Monde*, decrying the movement as a 'puritanical ... wave of purification'. The actress Catherine Deneuve, along with a hundred other co-signatories of an open letter in *Le Monde*, condemned the women speaking out about assault as enemies of 'sexual freedom'.[5] The problem is that sexual freedom is not something that can be enjoyed in isolation when more than half the human race still fights for the basic agency to choose when and how and whom we fuck.

Days earlier, the critic Andrew Sullivan complained in *New York* magazine that 'the righteous exposure of hideous abuse of power had morphed into a more generalized revolution against the patriarchy'.[6] That, of course, was the point. As we have seen, exposing abuses of power is inevitably a revolution against the nature of power itself.

Sullivan was far from the only one to accuse the #MeToo movement of being in a moral panic about sex itself. Charges like 'sex panic' are too serious simply to dismiss, and I don't mean to do so, not least because I am a queer person. But why are so many people so anxious to recast this sexual revolution as a prudish purity drive?

There is at least one simple answer. It is easier, and more socially acceptable, to protest an attack on sexuality than it is to protest an attack on patriarchy. Time and again, in my years as an activist and a journalist, I have watched reactionaries fight against social change while genuinely believing themselves to be bold defenders of liberty – casting themselves as Mel Gibson in *Braveheart*, fighting for freedom against the invading forces of wokeness, when in fact they're just regular old Mel Gibson, shouting slurs at strangers.

Sex is not the problem. Sexism is the problem, along with the upsetting multitudes of men and women who seem unable or unwilling to make the distinction. A few weeks after the first Weinstein 'revelations', a radio host asked me if flirting was now banned. It wasn't, and it isn't. To the mainly female people who are on the receiving end, the difference between flirting and harassment – between sex and rape – is extremely clear. To some of the mainly male people who do these things, the distinction seems difficult to understand, and when it is explained they run, in short succession, out of excuses and out of the room.

It was not women, however, who decided that heterosexuality was always and only violent. It was male-supremacist culture that spent generations imagining sex and conquest as one and the same, conflating them in the collective imagination until there was little distinction left between acts of passion and assault. It is hardly surprising that so many women have been on the wrong end of that trajectory for so very long that they have given up trying to find a way to be intimate with men that doesn't have to hurt. It is equally unsurprising that some of those women have come to think of the male sex itself as inherently treacherous, unsalvageable and irredeemably violent.

Today, contrary to conservative opinion, we do not have to choose between fighting against sexual violence and being sexually liberal. For many years, women have been unable to demand the right to have our bodily autonomy respected while also feeling free to be sexual, to dress like that, to walk like that, to suggest that we might want something good girls don't. For many generations, women were allowed to ask men not to attack them, as long as they asked nicely and didn't make too much of a fuss, but actually showing any evidence of independent sexual desire was still dangerous. But until everyone of every gender is free to express and explore their sexuality, there can by definition be no sexual freedom.

In fact, the fight against sexual violence and the fight against sexual repression are two sides of the same struggle: to divide one from the other is to collapse the whole enterprise. So-called sexual liberationists of our parents' and grandparents' generation failed, and failed badly, by thinking they could have sexual freedom without tackling male supremacy and sexist violence, by clinging blindly to the cosy delusion that women aren't actually sensual beings in the way that men are, that women's sexual freedom can remain an afterthought, and any woman who acts as if it isn't can and should be punished. Without sexual equality, sex can never be free. It can only be cheap.

Yet again, sexism is the issue – and for some people, sexism itself has become eroticised. That *is* a problem. 'It's not flirtation that any of us take issue with,' said a friend of mine, late one night after another round of exhausting emotional work trying to shore up the shuddering self-image of the men we know so they don't collapse on top of us. 'It's entitlement. Projection. Objectification. We know when we're being dehumanised. Good flirting is the kind where they see us. They won't know how to flirt the right way until they start unlearning how to look at us.'

So whenever a man tells me that all of this new pressure to treat women, even women you'd like to have sex with, as people who matter, makes him feel that his sexuality is being policed, I don't know what to tell him. Whenever a man confesses that he's worried about what will happen if he tries to come on to someone, that he is afraid of being punished endlessly for one tiny or not-so-tiny error of judgement, I wonder if he understands that for women, that sort of frustrated, terrified longing, that yearning paralysis, is nothing new. It's normal.

If we want to have a conversation about the policing of sexuality, the sexuality of white straight men is not the place to start. I know how it feels to have my sexuality policed. Most women do. Most of us know how it feels to be judged because of who you are, not what you do. Most of the interesting women and queer people I've ever met know exactly how that goes, the difference being that what they are shamed and attacked for is not being sexually violent, but rather, being sexual at all. It's a little galling, having to watch men panic and beg for mercy now that they're being ever so slightly punished for hurting women, accidentally or otherwise, when some of us have spent our lives being relentlessly punished just for being women.

All else being equal (and when is all else ever equal?), men and women have comparable sex drives. This is still a controversial truth. The famous 1989 'Would you go to bed with me?' study[7] was once taken as hard evidence of what one researcher on the study told the BBC her male colleagues had assumed from the start: 'that men were crazy for sex at all times and women really hated it'.[8] When this study was repeated in Denmark in 2011, again, men were far more likely than women to accept an offer of casual sex from a total stranger. But no research was done on why that might be beyond the conclusion that men simply want sex more than women do.[9]

There are, of course, many other reasons for not leaping into bed with a stranger. When it comes to casual hook-ups, women report much lower levels of satisfaction than men – and much more perceived risk. Perhaps one of the reasons women are less likely to accept an offer of sex from a strange man is not that they're frightened of sex, but that they're frightened of strange men, and perhaps they have reason to believe that casual sex won't be any good. By contrast, studies that have measured both levels of arousal and theoretical willingness to have a one-night stand in conditions of complete safety have found very little difference between the sex drives of male and female human beings.

This is a truth with a circle of light at its centre, the kind you gather around on dark nights to share stories that don't make sense in the daylight. When it comes to the simple pleasure principle, to fucking for its own sake, sex and gender do not dictate appetite. Some people are just hornier than others, regardless of the sex they were assigned at birth. But the sex you were assigned at birth does influence how likely you are to own your appetites – and how free you are to act on them.

For women, sex comes loaded with all sorts of risks and reasons to avoid it, weighed down by warnings about social punishment, shame and violence, as well as pregnancy. Previous generations, including generations of women, policed sexual morality not because they did not have desires, but because they were made to pay such a heavy price for men's desires before they even thought about having their own. Before the advent of modern medical technology, between 1 and 2 per cent of pregnancies ended in the woman's death.[10] In the Renaissance, it was standard practice for women who fell pregnant to write their wills, just in case. Until very recently, in the scope of human history, sex was a hazardous prospect if you were a straight woman. It could kill you, or ruin you, and the fact that you probably wanted it made it that much worse – when your body wants something that could mean disaster, that doesn't make the wanting go away, it just makes you that much more afraid of your own desires. Sex was dangerous – and for many straight women, it still is.

Without medical intervention, pregnancy is still a far riskier undertaking for humans than it is for most species. 'The figures are just horrifying,' Jonathan Wells, a researcher at University College, London, told the BBC.[11] 'It's extremely rare for mammalian mothers to pay such a high price for offspring production.'

The World Health Organization estimates that 810 women died every day in 2017 due to preventable causes related to pregnancy and childbirth – a figure that disproportionately includes women from low and lower middle-income countries and girls aged ten to fourteen.[12] The United States has the highest rate of maternal mortality in the developed world[13] – and Black women are twice as likely to die in childbirth as white women, thanks to a medical system that systematically denies Black women's pain and undermines their experience of their own bodies, and a racist economic system that does the same.[14]

Even aside from the risks of pregnancy and childbirth, sexual relationships with men remain statistically treacherous for women and girls. When the *Washington Post* analysed all killings of women in forty-seven major US cities over the last decade – 4,484 in total – it found that nearly half had been killed by an intimate partner.[15] After four decades of declining, homicides by intimate partners have gone up, driven primarily by gun violence. A study conducted by Northwestern University criminologist James Alan Fox calculated that the number of victims killed by intimate partners rose by 19 per cent between 2014 and 2017, from 1,875 to 2,237.[16]

When sexuality is phrased as dangerous and social structures are in place to ensure that the danger is real, it is no surprise that so many women and girls remain alienated from their own sexual identity. For men, by contrast, sex is cast as a social imperative, something to shore up your status, self-confidence and intimate connection. Real men, we are told, must fuck – and fuck hard, and often, and overcome every obstacle in their way.

Straight sex, in its current form, is far more about power than it is about pleasure; straight sex is still understood as something that men want and that women control. Sex is something that men need and have a right to, and something that women give away in exchange for security, or protection, or love. This understanding of sex as a meat market excuses a great deal of violence, as scientist Emily Nagoski explains, 'When sex is conceptualised as a need, it creates an environment that fosters men's sense of sexual entitlement ... if you think that men in particular ... need to relieve their pent-up sexual energy, then you can invent justifications for any strategy a man might use to relieve himself. Because if sex is a drive, like hunger, then potential partners are like food. Or like animals to be hunted for food.'[17]

This predatory, acquisitive vision of sexuality is the paradigm that social conservatives are anxious to protect – one in which consent itself is a commodity.

Women's consent, and more specifically women's consent to provide men with sex and emotional care, has been covertly understood for a very long time indeed as a tradeable service, something that can be bought and sold. That's not just true in the sex industry. It's true everywhere. The sex industry isn't unique because it puts a price on women's sexual consent, but because it tells you what the price is.

It starts very young. It starts to happen somewhere between losing your first tooth and finding out what aspects of your face and figure don't match the models in the magazines. At some point, a young girl starts to realise that her body is a piece of property that does not belong to her, or at least not fully. Her body is both a bargaining chip – her greatest asset in the mad transactional game of adult life – and an invitation to violence. *Your body is the most important thing about you*, and if it isn't good enough then people won't like you. If your body is unacceptable, or too much on display, you might be attacked. You must control yourself. It changes you, this process of understanding that you must apologise for everything wrong with your body – chiefly the fact that it is female. It changes the way you take up space, the way you inhabit the contours of your own life.

This vision of women as trophies to be bought, sold and traded existed before modern capitalism. However, the logic of neoliberalism, whereby markets must be freed and people are free to do as they are told, is the special sauce that has smothered sexuality in delusions of its own liberation. Freedom to jostle other men for sexual access to women as objects is not the straightforward sexual repression of despots and religious demagogues – but it is sexual repression, nonetheless. You are free to fuck, or to be fucked, but only to a set script, and always under surveillance. If you are female or queer, you will not be permitted to live in your body like you own it. You will find your sexuality confiscated and sold back to you at a cost.

It is hard for women, too, to remember that they are not commodities, not simply animate meat to be traded for men's money and approval and affection. When you've spent your entire life being reminded that whatever else you are, you are a body first, and if your body is not acceptable, you have no value to men and therefore to the world; when you've always been encouraged to measure your worth by your value on the shifting market of male attention; when you've learned this in the white heat of adolescence, when you've grown up having to think, every day, about how men's desire or lack of it trumps your own dignity, it can be difficult to remember that you were always meant to be more than something owned.

Rating sexuality by the amount of sex being had is like judging an orchestra on its volume. Sex, like love, is not a discrete or measurable phenomenon. Sex is not a scarce commodity that one category of people distributes to another. Nor is sex an asset that you can acquire and collect more of. Sex isn't something you have, it's something you do – like dancing. You can dance alone, or with someone else, you can do it for fun or for money or simply out of boredom, but if nobody wants to dance with you, it makes no sense to get angry because you've decided someone's stolen all the dancing and is keeping it for themselves. Redistribution is good. Sharing resources is good. But sexuality itself is not a scarce resource.

Sex is not something that women cruelly hoard like dragons squatting on sexy piles of gold. Women's consent is not a commodity to be traded or jealously guarded to keep prices high. Sex is something that, all else being equal, women want just as much as men. But usually not with people who threaten, demean and resent them. Consider the fact that straight women are far less likely than straight men to orgasm during casual sex, with 80 per cent, in one study, 'admitting' to faking orgasms.[18] Common reasons listed were that the sex was hurting, that they wanted to 'protect their partner's feelings', or that it was 'taking too long'. Sex that is taking too long is sex you're anxious to get over, but too nervous to ask someone to stop. A culture that can only understand women's pleasure through the lens of male pride is one that has thoroughly alienated women and girls from their own desire.

Nor is the guilty omnipresence of pornography – the underbelly of modern sexuality – a sign of a great deal of fulfilling sex being had. Lonely people watch porn in the same way that hungry people watch cooking shows. In fact, the pornography that is produced en masse and available for free online often caters to a specific vision of straight sex – one in which sex is by its nature competitive, violent, racist and misogynist, more about performing gendered power than it is about actually getting off, a production line of oiled bodies pummelling each other into submission. Straight pornography hallucinates sexuality into an alternate universe entirely separate from the everyday, where men are never rejected, and nobody ever says no. This means that women in mainstream straight pornography do not have sex so much as they have sex done to them, sex that is never difficult, or emotional, or spontaneous, sex that is vengeful and degrading, sex as a form of ritual misogyny, broken down into a bleak taxonomy of body types and acts.

'Not all porn is about hatred of women, but at the moment what is being watched is about that,' said Virginie Despentes, the French feminist author and filmmaker, in an interview with the *Guardian*. 'What is going on in men's heads, in their sexuality, when women's pleasure has become a problem?'[19]

The idea that women's pleasure, women's desires and women's human agency are not just unimportant but obstacles to be overcome has penetrated every part of our culture. Much of the rhetoric of the modern far-right is inherited from the pickup artist community – a movement that began over ten years ago with books like Neil Strauss's *The Game*, all about training men to badger and hoodwink women into bed without having to risk any sort of vulnerability of their own.[20]

Pickup artistry has long been the last word in entrepreneurial, self-facilitating male sexual entitlement. According to its logic, heterosexuality is always a game and often a blood sport. There are rules, stakes and win conditions. Young men are taught a mode of bullish, entitled sexual interaction that is meant to lead to measurable success in the form of notches on the bedpost. Here's how that dynamic is described on the Return of Kings site, a 'blog for heterosexual, masculine men', which contains one of the most gruesomely clinical descriptions of human mating I've ever encountered:

> when it comes to sex, women are in far greater demand ... The question of how to divide up this relatively limited amount of desire among women is one every human society has struggled with. Basically, if you fail to regulate the market, the logical result is a small minority of men garnering the attention of the vast majority of all women ... to prevent this, societies have almost always regulated women's sexuality to some degree.[21]

The site and its readers, like many of the more misogynist corners of the internet, have two major interests: hating women, and strategising to sleep with as many of them as possible. This is not considered a contradiction in terms, because women and girls are explicitly coded as commodities, something you have to fight for more access to, chiefly by boosting your own value in the sexual 'marketplace'. The techniques for this involve a lot of complicated and bizarre rituals around cheap romantic trickery and protein shakes – anything that stands the slimmest chance of working, apart from treating women and girls like people who matter.

The whole thing is about as erotic as an insurance policy – and like an insurance policy, the detail is in the small print. The problem with this formulaic, ritual approach to the dating 'game' is that even if they play it perfectly, most men lose. Of course they do. They lose because modern masculinity is a Ponzi scheme. However you gamify it, it is impossible to 'win' at sex, unless your concept of the erotic is so asphyxiated that you cannot conceive of any intimacy, any pleasure, that does not resolve itself into a logic of profit and loss at another's expense.

The fascist erotics of today's frustrated men-children imagine sexuality as a battle fought over women's bodies, as an act of dominance and conquest in which they will one day emerge as kings. In my capacity as a woman who exists on the internet, I occasionally act as a receptacle for men's feelings about women, and what they pour in over and over again is the conviction that a fuck will somehow cure them – that women who deny them sex are also depriving them not just of pleasure but of the only possible escape from their terrible loneliness. There is vicious entitlement here, unhappily married to a strain of self-loathing acceptance that they may never get the sex they feel is their due. Sex is the screen upon which so many young men project all their anxieties, their insecurities, their expectations of care and connection, their yearning for intimacy. And that's too much to ask of sex. It leaves men fetishising the fuck as the one thing that can save them, the one way to be truly close to another person – and yet, tragically unable to have even that without shame, unable to see the person they're fucking through the fog of their own hurt and need.

'Men come to sex hoping that it will provide them with all of the emotional satisfaction that would have come from love,' writes bell hooks in *The Will to Change: Men, Masculinity and Love*. 'Most men think that sex will provide them with a sense of being alive, connected, that sex will offer closeness, intimacy, pleasure. And more often than not sex simply does not deliver the goods. This fact does not, however, lead men to cease obsessing about sex; it intensifies their lust and their longing.'[22]

Treating sex as transactional is one way of controlling its terms. It is safer to reframe the whole frightening, sticky arena of wanting and waiting and shame and lust and adventure and spasm and rejection and recovery as a clean, simple trading floor. A ledger to make the mess and confusion of desire manageable, containable. It is simpler to imagine sex as a commodity, something women have and men can acquire – something that men everywhere have a right to acquire as much of as they can.

Treating sexuality as a transaction where pleasure is traded for protection ensures a scarcity of both. It leaves men, women and everyone else caught in a quicksand of paralytic mutual longing: the women wanting to be wanted, the men wanting women to want to be wanted by them, everyone circling the drain of possible joy. Nobody gets out, and nobody gets off.

The assumption that the key to love and security and self-esteem is between a woman's legs makes the routine dehumanisation of women feel reasonable to many otherwise rational men. This is how entitlement becomes resentment, which becomes hatred, which becomes violence – because all that routine dehumanisation does not work the way it's supposed to. It doesn't provide the love, respect and self-esteem that men are lacking. Because love and respect and self-esteem cannot be taken from another person by force.

The delusion that they can means that straight sex is, in fact, far more emotionally loaded for men than it is for women. Women and queer people are permitted other ways of forming emotional connections besides sex. We are allowed to touch each other, to be vulnerable, to be silly together. Straight men romanticise straight sex as the one source of human connection and social status they are allowed to pursue without fear of social punishment. Sadly, sexism often prevents straight men from being able to respect the people they want intimacy from, and intimacy without respect is impossible.

Despite all of this, I believe that good sex is still possible. The staid, dutiful sex that straight women so often have to settle for under patriarchy does not have to be the norm. For at least three generations humans have had the technology and medical infrastructure to make sexual experience an equal-opportunity affair. We've got condoms and contraception, medical abortion and antibiotics. Heterosexuality in particular is, in theory, a far less risky prospect for women now than it once was. The fact that women aren't socially permitted to explore those new prospects without judgement is something I always felt was unfair. And so pretty early on in my own life I set out to enact my own personal liberation.

I was never a good-looking kid, or a popular one. I was socially awkward and at sea in an adolescent world where being a teenage girl seemed to mean looking sexy but never actually having sex. Growing up hungry and horny, what I most wanted was to seek pleasure where it was offered, and not be shamed for it unless I had hurt another person.

I wanted adventure, experimentation, fun; I wanted to roll out of a stranger's bed without worrying about being judged on anything but my manners and manual dexterity. More than anything, I wanted to be able to fuck like a boy. Not in the physical sense, but in the social sense. I wanted to be able to have as much fun as possible without being judged. I wanted my looks to matter less than my lust for life, my ambitions, my personality, my talents. I didn't want to stand around waiting to be seduced. I wanted to do the seducing. I wanted to be active, to flirt, to be the seeker as well as the prize. I never wanted to wait around for a man to catch me.

Along the way, I encountered violent men, frightened men, angry men, brilliant men, men who weren't much more than children with high hairlines and low self-confidence. I met men who put me down, let me down, and treated me like trash as soon as I turned up in their beds. And I met kind men, too, men who were gentle and funny and respectful. Sometimes I met all of those men in the same person. And somehow, it's still hard to speak honestly about the fact that sex can be fun.

For people who walk through the world as women, talking about the adventure and thrill and silliness of sexuality, speaking about joyful, unapologetic pleasure-seeking, is something akin to coming out. If we are going to use the word 'slut shaming' to describe the misogynist practice of pouring public scorn on women who dare to fuck without apology, pregnancy or both, then we must accustom ourselves to the idea that a 'slut' is not a shameful thing to be. Even for women who fuck men, there is something about that sort of sexual self-ownership that is only tangentially straight. Female desire expressed without shame is a threat to the way straight sex is supposed to work – it disrupts the dominance model of heterosexuality. It is, in other words, inherently queer. It may be heterosexual, but it is not straight.

My experience is not a map or a model of anything. What I wanted was sex, pleasure and intimacy on their own terms. I wanted sex unbuckled by the straitjackets of gender and double standards, and time and again I was disappointed. The best sex of our lives might not exist yet, but I never gave up looking.

Part of the reason I was able to experiment with sexual self-liberation was that I was protected by my status as white, middle-class and thin-bodied. Before I was old enough to understand why, I already knew that I could take the risk of being seen as a 'bad girl'. White, posh, slim girls have always been allowed to get away with a certain amount of sluttiness before the consequences kick in. While I might have faced sexism and dehumanisation on an individual level, I have not found myself shut out of education, denied promotion or unable to access healthcare or social services because a wealthy, white authority figure decided I was 'promiscuous' and therefore not worth helping. Black and brown women, Indigenous women and poor women have to contend with racist and classist stereotypes that deny them even the contested social capital of 'innocence' afforded to wealthy white women. As researcher Akeia A. F. Benard observes,

> We live in a culture where to an extent, White women – especially white middle-class women – are able to define, 'play with,' and explore their sexuality in ways women of color are not (e.g., the 'Slutwalk' movement) and Black women are defined by their sexuality and as their sexuality.[23]

According to the logic of white supremacist patriarchy, Black, brown, Indigenous and working-class girls are sexually incontinent and therefore undeserving of protection. Even as prepubescents, the sexuality of girls of colour is suspect. White supremacist patriarchy demonises the sexuality of women of colour and poor white women, scapegoating them as drains on the system. This means that girls who do not grow up white and wealthy often face additional pressure to stifle their own sexuality, to avoid being seen as 'fast' or 'loose'. Lashing yourself to strict standards of 'respectability' is a way to survive in a culture of racial and economic injustice that looks for any excuse to deny a Black girl her humanity. Young Black, brown and Indigenous women are often held to stricter standards of self-denial within communities and families who simply want to protect their daughters from the trauma of racism and sexual violence.

Even with the protection of whiteness, I learned shame and sexual terror as a child, and tried my hardest to unlearn it as a young woman, but by my late twenties I had had it hammered back into me by everyday sexual humiliation, by violence and harassment and rape. This is not an uncommon experience. The fact that this sort of experience is so common is precisely why it deserves attention and should not simply be filed away in a drawer marked 'Women who make too much of a fuss'.

In fact, most women don't make enough fuss. We could and should make far more of a fuss about how dull and dreadful straight sex can be for us even when it is, technically, consensual, even when no crime has been committed. We're socialised out of making a fuss, just as men are socialised into thinking about sex as something they have to bully and pester out of women. Shitty, dehumanising sex is not normal, and it is not acceptable – it's just very, very common. And because it is so common, because it is a chapter in so many of our stories, it is easier to write this sort of thing off as simply *bad sex*.

But here's the secret: good sex is still possible, once you stop looking to white supremacy and to patriarchy to define its terms. Nobody will ever convince me that all of these dull keyboard-bashers with their weary fantasies of gamified fucking will ever experience the thrill of the single spring weekend I spent in Berlin in 2018. All those Proud Boys and pearl-clutching Promise Keepers, every chatroom-addled crypto-fascist and right-wing attention grifter who's ever screamed abuse at a stranger on Twitter to stave off the howling void behind his eyes, they all wish they had the sort of fun that, so far, a lucky few of us have known. There is something in that space of daring and mutual desire that is too dangerous for straight sexuality to contemplate. Something inherently anti-authoritarian. Something *queer*.

Those who worship dominance can never really know mutual pleasure. Those who lionise bullies and are terrified of their own vulnerability are constitutionally incapable of getting even semi-decently laid. They just can't conceive of it. Disappointing sex is inevitable when even pleasure becomes a production, something that is performed and pursued for the benefit of an audience. The best sex of our lives does not exist yet.

But it can exist, if we imagine it. To defy the shame that burrows into the heart of sexuality is not an attack on sex. To protest the rigid obligations of factory-issued female beauty is not to deny beauty in the world. To cry out when love is made conditional on accepting one's own subordination is not a betrayal of love. To disturb the sterile logic that flattens all possible pleasure and adventure into stale, violent transaction is to speak sex to power. To say: I want it all, and I want it now, and the only thing that matters is whether you want it too.

One of the finest acts of rebellion comes about when a person who has long learned that she must eventually be owned in some aspect by a man, that she owes her body and her desires to him, that she must be pretty and pleasant and good enough to be owned, suddenly refuses to be told what she should want and who she should please, and chooses instead to please herself.

5

BEAUTIFUL TROUBLE

New York. Midwinter. Howling wind outside a friend's apartment; inside, a dark party vibrating with bass, full of lithe and gorgeous strangers in their underwear. I was twenty-five, new to the city, treading water in a circle of impossibly glamorous models and strippers and writers all hustling for money and a foothold, and a worrying amount of the socialising seemed to involve states of semi-undress. It was my artist friend's birthday. She'd decided to throw a 'lingerie' party. I didn't have any fancy lingerie, and at the time I dealt with my body image issues by trying to forget, whenever possible, that I had a body at all. But I didn't want to be a killjoy, so I took a deep breath and stripped down to my sensible bra and granny panties. It was bearable – fun, even – until someone started taking pictures.

The birthday girl called me over to be in a photo. She had one arm around a fashion model, and the other around Stoya – a porn actress and activist and one of the few humans I've met with a face and figure so arresting that rooms really do go quiet when she walks in. My friend was sweetly inviting me to pose with these willowy, perfect creatures – and I panicked. I couldn't bear to be in a picture like that, as a lumpy little hobbit among elves. I froze. I made my excuses. I went off to hyperventilate in the bathroom.

A few days later, I contacted Stoya to see if she'd like to get a cup of coffee and chat to me for an article I was working on. I will always be grateful for the email she sent in response. She'd love to meet me, she said, but she had some concerns. She'd noticed that, at that party, I hadn't wanted to be in a picture with her. She told me she understood. She said she knew why someone like me – a feminist, a writer, someone with a reputation to protect – might not want to be associated with someone like her – a porn actress – in public. But all the same, she had found it hurtful.

There have been very few genuine light-bulb moments in the parts of my life where the political fuses with the personal, but this was one of them. I emailed back right away to explain that, no, I hadn't been ashamed to be seen with her – I had been reading off an entirely different script of internalised sham. We sent 'virtual hugs'. We followed them up with real ones. I trailed her when she went to work at a porn convention, spending hours meeting fans, working harder than I thought possible to maintain an approachable, desirable front, while making sure nobody got too handsy. I realised, for the first time, how much I had misunderstood about the work of beauty, how it imposes duties on women against our will – and how it divides us from each other.

When I was in my teens, I thought that girls like that – the gorgeous girls who got all the attention – were the lucky ones. In the brutal game of gendered power that all of us had been entered into when we were too young to consent, those girls had won. I never wondered if they actually wanted the boys to follow them about, pestering and pressuring them. I simply resented them, and I was scared of them, so to make myself feel less horrific, I persuaded myself that I was somehow better than them. That I was less superficial and more liberated. That was an ugly thing to do. I wish I could go back and apologise to all those girls I looked down on when I was younger purely because I believed that they were 'beautiful' and I was not. It was only as I got older and began to move through many different social circles that I realised that beautiful women have not 'won' anything. That the power that beauty grants you is only ever on loan, and it comes with conditions and caveats, and it does not help you walk through a world of men with your head held high.

While actual beauty comes in many forms, there is a conventional definition of acceptable female attractiveness, a scale that shifts in relation to how white supremacist patriarchy requires women to be. These rules are not actually about controlling the way women look, but the way they behave; they are steeped not just in sexism but in racism, too.

The rules of beauty are determined, largely, by white men, and the standards are increasingly specific. When researchers at one North Carolina university asked thousands of interviewees to select images of 'attractive' men and women, the heterosexual women had a far broader definition of what it meant for a man to be 'good looking'.[1] The straight male consensus was almost universal: an attractive woman is thin, in her twenties, with subtle curves, long, straight hair and small, symmetrical Caucasian features. There are, apparently, many ways for a man to be physically attractive, but only one standard for women, a standard that idealises not just youth and compliance but a particular vision of whiteness. Women and girls of colour are held to standards of beauty that define white womanhood as the aspirational aesthetic. Curves, curls and hairstyles like box braids and cornrows designed to protect Black hair are tolerated, even celebrated, on white women – but young women of colour are discouraged from associating the Black or brown body with beauty in a culture that insists that every woman be beautiful if she wants to be treated with respect.

These things are not frivolous. They matter. Five years after that party, during a panel event in Frankfurt, Germany, a teenage girl approached me to ask a 'small, stupid' question. She wanted to know how I dealt, in my work, in my life, with 'the pressure to be pretty'. She asked me how I 'dealt with beauty culture'. I was stunned. This girl was clear-skinned and straight-toothed and tall enough that I had to peer up her perfect nose to notice that she was on the edge of tears. When I was her age, I didn't understand that girls who looked like that don't get to feel good about it any more than the rest of us ordinary-looking girls did. Something inside me stiffened at the reminder that there's still no way to win. That girls still don't get to decide what counts as beautiful, or how much it matters. This girl had waited to ask her question because she was shy, because she thought that worrying about her looks made her 'stupid'.

But it's not stupid, and it's not silly. Nobody just 'deals' with beauty culture. The question of beauty and what it means and who gets to embody it is far from frivolous when it's phrased as a duty you owe to the world, a set of commandments stamped on your body without your consent. Beauty, at least in the stereotypical sense, is still a weapon wielded against female solidarity. The relentless pressure on women and girls to achieve a certain standard of 'beauty' is one of the most intimately painful issues in feminist politics. So often, though, talking about it, let alone acknowledging that you care about it, makes women and girls feel ashamed. Or vain. Or stupid.

That's one reason why the young women who have asked me these questions rarely do so in front of other people. They wait until the quietest, most private moment to admit that while of course they care about economic justice, about reproductive rights, about violence and power and privilege, they also worry, deep down, that they're not pretty enough, and they want that worry to stop. They wonder if working harder at being pretty might take the worry away. They wonder if the worry is frivolous. It isn't. It is *foundational*.

The cultural insistence that women and queer people are worth less if they are not 'beautiful' is a way of alienating them from their own bodies. In his 1844 *Economic and Philosophic Manuscripts*, Karl Marx described his theory of estranged labour: workers under capitalism encounter their product as something 'hostile and alien'.[2] *Hostile and alien* is exactly how our understanding of female beauty makes a great many women feel about their own bodies: that their actual flesh is a product that doesn't fully belong to them, that their bodies are abject and disposable rather than precious and indispensable, especially if those bodies are elderly, ill or disabled, Indigenous, brown or Black.

'Beauty' is phrased as both an obligation and a provocation. It is every woman's job to make herself as beautiful as she can physically and financially manage, but when she does – if she does – she has issued an invitation to disrespect and disdain. She is either 'too beautiful' or 'too ugly' to be worthy of basic respect and human dignity, and either way her looks are all that matter, and it's all her fault. It's almost as if women are reduced to their bodies as a way of dismissing their human agency. It's almost as if there's no way a girl can look that will translate into being treated like a human being rather than a set of appendages and enticing angles. Almost as if there's no way to win.

No wonder more women than ever, of every age, are reporting that preoccupation with the way they look is making them miserable. The latest research suggests that women in their teens and early twenties are now considered a 'high-risk group' for anxiety, depression and other mental illnesses – and 'body image' is listed as a key contributing factor to all of this silent suffering.[3]

That phrase – 'body image' – implies that appearance-related anxiety is something that occurs spontaneously in the feeble female brain. 'Body image', in the public imagination, is a synonym for silly girls worrying about how skinny they are. It has something to do with Instagram or advertising and nothing at all to do with centuries of inequality predicated on the idea that women are bodies first and people second, and all our hopes and dreams and ideas and achievements collapse into irrelevance if we are not 'beautiful'.

'Body-image issues' don't emerge out of a vacuum. Little girls aren't born believing that their bodies are unacceptable. Someone is making them feel that way. I consider it an insult to my overpriced education to be informed every single time I open a magazine, turn on the television or try to buy a goddamn yogurt that my body does not meet the required trading standards – and then to be concern-trolled about my 'problem with body image'.

The qualities deemed beautiful in women vary dramatically from decade to decade. Female desirability is not, as some crankish armchair evolutionary psychologists insist, an artefact of nature, of men's helpless drive to pursue women who look 'fertile' – if that were so, the most alluring accessory imaginable would surely be a baby. Beauty is a force of culture, not nature, and men are recruited to enforce it – willingly or no.

For young men in particular, the pressure to acquire a 'hot' woman has little to do with the woman herself – and everything to do with other men. Having a hot woman on your arm and in your bed signifies status. Being with a hot woman means that other men will respect you – and that you are allowed to respect yourself. That's especially important in a culture which offers young men so few ways to prove their worth. It's not about the sex. It's about the status.

'Hotness' has become a duty women owe to male self-respect. I have almost never met a woman or girl who is not somewhat aware of where she ranks on the 'hotness' scale. However complicated their relationship with the image in the mirror, most women and girls, apart from those suffering from extreme body dysmorphia, have a reasonable idea of what the rest of the world sees when it looks at their bodies through men's eyes. That knowledge is part of the defensive arsenal a girl builds up as she prepares to run the psychological gamut of womanhood. But she must never admit that she knows. Women are supposed to seek beauty, to aspire to beauty – but if they actually achieve it, they can't enjoy it. Women are not supposed to know that they are beautiful. Men are supposed to tell them.

I wish I could go back and tell every girl who's ever asked me about beauty culture that the whole thing is a con, that it's designed to waste your time, drain your energy and make you suspicious of other women and other women suspicious of you. I would tell that shy girl in Frankfurt that she does not have to be physically lovely to make amends for the 'sin' of being female. That whether or not you feel pretty, whether or not anyone ever tells you you're beautiful, basic respect and human dignity are your birthright.

Women's self-esteem is a political and an economic issue. If you feel worthless because of the way you look, you are easier to exploit. If you feel that your body makes you less worthy, you are less likely to insist on being treated according to your true worth socially, sexually and economically – at work, in communities and in relationships. The woman who makes her life into an apology for her body will find it harder to stand up for herself when she is assaulted, exploited or abused. The girl who believes that she is worthless because she doesn't look like the sort of girl men are supposed to want will find it hard to ask for what *she* wants, to set her own boundaries, to say no when she means it.

The power to determine which women's bodies have worth is still a power all men are granted, whether they want it or not, but some wield that power more responsibly than others. I had a partner, not long ago, who would continually undermine me by pointing out women who were feminine, curvier, blonder than me, younger than me (I was twenty-six). When I got upset about this, I was told I was a killjoy and a prude, trying to control his freedom to express his desires by making me aware of all the ways I didn't meet his standards. It made me contort my body into a thousand painful excuses, drove me to be even more passive and accommodating in bed, even quicker to put up with his horrible behaviour outside it. I had to compete for his attention, for his respect – and if my body was not good enough, I would have to make it up to him in other ways.

Beauty orthodoxy enrols women and girls in a competition they didn't sign up for. Images of beauty undermine solidarity between women and girls of all ages by pitting us against one another, one generation against another, larger versus smaller, those deemed beautiful against everyone else.

Reclaiming beauty can be radical. Living in our bodies without apology, celebrating what we find gorgeous and sexy and appealing about ourselves and each other is still radical. It is radical when a woman or a girl claims her own beauty and does not wait for patriarchy to define it for her or deny it to her, but it's not enough. We will never escape beauty culture if beauty, however we define it, is still the social rent women have to pay for existing in the world. We will never advance as long as women are bullied into pouring money, time and energy into our appearance when we could be working on things that will last, things that give us real power over our own lives.

It is no accident that the things that the world currently deems 'beautiful' in women are the appearance of fragility, vulnerability and youth. Older women, for example, are not supposed to be considered 'beautiful'. That's partly because women often become more independent, capable and powerful as they get older, and power in women is rarely phrased as attractive. If 'beauty' as it is currently understood was something that increased with experience and confidence, it would not be valued so much in women.

In fact, from a ridiculously young age, girls learn that 'ageing' is something to worry about. By the time I was in my mid-twenties, many of my female peers were already anxious about running out of time, about looking older, because they'd internalised the ugly old adage that women age like milk, and men like wine – that men become mature, and women just rot. Beauty orthodoxy tells women and girls that their bodies are not just commodities, but *perishable* commodities. Beauty orthodoxy, along with the special misogyny directed at older women, teaches us that our futures are not worth planning for. Rather than looking forward to getting the raging, insecure horror show of young adulthood over and done with, like our male friends, the prospect of finally growing old enough to work out what the hell we're doing with our lives is no match for the fear of having to live inside bodies that might be deemed unbeautiful.

Nor is it an accident that just as feminism broke into the mainstream again in the mid-2010s, there was an enormous uptick in body-policing, a quiet epidemic of eating disorders and fat-shaming, and a real increase in the work that was required from girls and women to maintain an acceptable standard of hotness in order not to shatter men's already fragile sense of status.

'The qualities that a given period calls beautiful in women,' writes Naomi Wolf in *The Beauty Myth*, 'are merely symbols of the female behaviour that that period considers desirable: The beauty myth is always actually prescribing behaviour and not appearance.'[4] The time and attention a person spends on ensuring she is adequately beautiful signifies her commitment to a certain model of good behaviour. Down the rabbit hole of dating apps, I have encountered countless potato-faced men specifying that what they're really looking for is a woman who 'takes care of herself'. They don't mean that they're looking for someone in regular therapy who owns cosy slippers and has a retirement plan. They're looking for evidence of discipline. Someone who puts in work to maintain a standard of hotness.

We've seen that women's bodies are sites of work, of production and reproduction. When women are alienated from their own bodies, they are denied ownership of that body of work. When a woman works to become 'beautiful', she may gain temporary privileges, but they come with a catch. The catch is this: she will be assumed by some to be signalling that she is available to anyone who sees her body, desires her as a body and feels entitled to grab that body, grope it or yell at it in the street if the inconsiderate creature inhabiting that body fails to turn around and smile. If she didn't want those things, why did she dress like that? Why leave the house at all?

Beauty is a discipline that requires constant attention. Women and girls are expected to discipline their bodies and to display that discipline. The work that goes into self-denial, into thinking about how to dress, into learning how to apply make-up and look after the obligatory long, glossy, Caucasian-style hair, is not supposed to be optional, and nor is the enormous amount of money it takes to support that work, the endless lotions and potions and creams and treatments and injections and dresses and shoes and paints and powders and tiny bottles of chemicals that cost more than your heating bills. All of this is supposed to be part of the rent paid for being allowed to exist as female or queer in a world where straight men write the rules. When a woman ceases to pay attention to her face and figure, she is castigated for 'letting herself go'. She has ceased to be her own jailer. Once she 'lets herself go', who knows how far she might get?

It is still radical when women and queer people start to redefine for themselves what beauty might mean – particularly women who have always been denied their femininity by white supremacy and heteropatriarchy. Black women, brown women, trans women, disabled women and older women have all been defined, in umpteen crass and painful ways, as less beautiful and therefore less important, less deserving of respect and protection, than the minority of women who happen to be young, white, able-bodied and cisgendered.

But, again, reclaiming beauty can only go so far if the basic notion that beauty is the core of a woman's worth in the world remains unchallenged. Lasting change will come not when more women consider themselves beautiful, but when all women everywhere know that they have a right to live with dignity, no matter what they look like, no matter whether their body meets the strict standards drawn up to wreck our confidence and waste our time. The question is not simply what beauty is – the question is how much beauty matters, and white men have been allowed to answer both of these questions on everyone else's behalf for far too long.

The only way to win this game is not to play it, and the only way to opt out is by talking about it. There is magic in naming. By talking honestly about female beauty, we can start to redefine it – but more importantly, we can stop it from defining us. We can stop it from dividing us. We can claim space for ourselves, and hold space for one another. We can decide what we want beauty to be – but only if we're brave enough to speak its name.

Fear of female flesh is fear of female power. Of all the qualities that male culture deems unbeautiful and therefore morally unacceptable in women, the most unforgivable is the sin of taking up space in the world like you belong there, or worse, own it. Today, the ideal woman takes up as little space as possible. She is fragile, breakable, thin and hungry-looking. It's hard to hang onto the feeling of full humanity, of being a person with desires, when you are constantly reminded that your body is an object of scrutiny, a piece of public property, that whoever you are and whatever you do, as a female creature you are a body first, and you will be judged on that basis.

It is estimated that 28.8 million Americans, the vast majority of them women and girls, will have some sort of eating disorder in their lifetime.[5] That is a horrifying statistic, but the harder reality is that eating disorders occur in the context of a culture that has a horror of female flesh, that encourages women and girls and queer people to be as small as possible, to take up as little space as possible. The aesthetic that is morally, socially and financially rewarded is an aesthetic of hunger. Of lack. Of the woman who restlessly denies her body's basic demands. The ideal twenty-first-century woman looks desirable but desires nothing for herself. That ideal woman stalks the imaginations of real women, girls and femmes, chases us through our nightmares on spindly legs, telling us to want less, dream less, be less, if we want to be loved and successful and safe. And the images around us back up that narrative.

It starts young. By the age of ten, 80 per cent of young women are afraid of weight gain;[6] fear of taking up too much space begins at the preschool level, with half of three- to six-year-old girls in one 2009 study saying they were worried about being 'fat'.[7] This does not just affect women with active and pernicious eating disorders, and it does not only affect people whose way of dealing with bodily control is to starve themselves. It affects all of us, whatever our size – and for every one of the millions of women diagnosed with a life-threatening eating disorder there are dozens more who waste decades obsessing over food, frantically trying to deny their own appetites, sculpting away every inch of spare flesh in the gym, pursuing an image of perfection which, should they ever attain it, will mean they are finally lovable, finally allowed to like themselves, and if they still don't like themselves, they must not be perfect yet.

In Britain, hospital admissions for eating disorders doubled between 2011 and 2017.[8] Parents and patients have spoken of agonies trying to find treatment that even approaches adequate.

All over my home country, all over the world, women and girls are starving themselves, sometimes to death. It's a species of madness, and as Naomi Wolf puts it, 'a quietly mad population is a tractable one'.[9] People who are constantly engaged in ritual self-sabotage are easy to control.

When I was much younger, I starved myself. It was a private, violent way to recapture what felt like a measure of autonomy over my body – to place restrictions on myself before anyone else could. To punish myself better and harder than anyone else could. It felt like the closest I could come to a strike – defying what was expected of me by doing exactly what I was told, and doing it so well that I nearly died in my late teens.

When I went to hospital, the logic behind the treatment that I received was that girls with eating disorders were afraid of becoming women, and in order to be healthy they had to become reconciled to our place and role in the world of men. Nobody asked if some of us might have good reasons to be wary of womanhood. Real recovery, for me, was about rediscovering desire – about acknowledging hunger, about letting myself be a messy, wanting human thing rather than a shell of symbols in the shape of a girl. But in the decade and a half since I left hospital and built a life for myself, fear of fatness has completed its colonisation of the female imagination.

In Britain, NHS figures showed that admissions for conditions including anorexia and bulimia reached 13,885 between April 2016 and 2017, including almost 2,000 girls under eighteen admitted with anorexia,[10] which has the highest mortality rate of any mental illness. It is estimated that 1.25 million people in the UK have an eating disorder,[11] and 75 per cent of those people are women and girls. It's not just about the lives lost– it's about the lives blighted, the years spent in pointless, painful self-torture. Candida Crewe, in her memoir *Eating Myself*, calls it 'the everywoman disease'.[12] We know this is happening, and society seems more or less comfortable with it.

If eating disorders were a disease associated with men, rather than women, they would be taken more seriously and treatment would be funded properly. Self-starvation and preoccupation with thinness, with body image and with self-denial, has become so standard in our society for women that you can't help picking up on the suggestion that anorexics and bulimics have the right idea – they just take it 'too far'. We tell girls they're not allowed to take up space in the world and then we're confused when they start starving themselves. We raise our young people in a culture absolutely obsessed with controlling women's bodies and then we wonder why they want to take back some of that control in savage, intimate acts of passive-aggressive defiance. As Wolf writes, 'A culture fixated on female thinness is not an obsession about female beauty, but an obsession about female obedience. Dieting is the most potent political sedative in women's history.'[13]

The naked praise girls get for slowly murdering themselves in public is in direct proportion to the amount of shame and stigma heaped on perfectly healthy women who happen to be a few deviations away from the required standard of slenderness. That's no coincidence. There is solid workplace data backing up the fact that women are penalised financially and socially for gaining weight and rewarded for losing it – far more so than men. One study published in the *Journal of Applied Psychology* in the autumn of 2010 showed that 'very thin' women earned approximately $22,000 more than their average-weight counterparts, whereas being just 13lb overweight severely damaged a woman's chances of promotion and job security.[14] A more recent study revealed that just 15 per cent of hiring managers, when shown photographs of women of different weights, would consider hiring the heaviest for a position of responsibility.[15] Statistics like these bear out what almost every girl knows in her bones: that the world wants her smaller and thinner, that the world wants her to want less, to be less.

It's not just in the workplace that women are expected to make themselves small – unless we're honest and admit that women and girls are expected to be at work in the great unpaid internship of womanhood every waking hour of their lives. How are women and girls meant to love and care for their bodies when the world at large does the opposite – especially if they live in Black, brown or Indigenous bodies, disabled bodies, overweight bodies, older bodies, bodies that don't match the meagre stereotype of beauty that's supposed to determine a woman's worth? Teaching women and girls to love and look after their bodies is still a radical proposal in a society that both anticipates and profits from our self-hatred. But individual journeys of self-love can only take us so far when the problem, again, is structural. The problem is sexism.

But when you name the problem, the response is gaslighting. We raise girls in a hailstorm of images of unattainable perfection, subject them to a relentless show-and-tell demonstration of exactly what they have to lose by not looking a certain way, imply that whatever else they grow up to be will be of no value if they do not also conform to an image of beauty too narrow for a human body to breathe in, make them pay day in and day out for simply existing in a body that is female or queer – we do all this and then, when they become ill, when they develop body dysmorphia and eating disorders, we shrug and say: these silly girls. Why don't they just chill out and eat a sandwich?

Telling the women and girls of the twenty-first century that they have a problem with body image is a little like telling a stab-wound victim that they have a problem with blood leakage. Yes, we know. And we know it's probably our fault: we were weak and frivolous for letting ourselves get stabbed, and if we were stronger we would be able to knot up our arteries through sheer force of will and stop the bleeding, but in the meantime would it be possible, if you'd be so good, to help patch us up before we go out hunting for some justice?

That sort of anger was impossible to articulate when I was in the throes of eating-disorder hell; so often, self-denial is a way to deal with anger that feels too dangerous to express, turning it inwards against your body, controlling all the hungers for the things you're told you're not allowed to want, like food or a fuck or a scrap of respect or a safe place in the world, which is why eating disorders often strike young women in particular. Boys are more likely to act out, because boys are allowed to act out. Girls act in.

Modern society is still so afraid of female flesh, of female hunger, of women who want anything at all beyond what they're told to be grateful for, that it teaches girl children to make themselves smaller, slice themselves down, shrink their bodies and starve down their ambition until they take up less space in the world. It is shocking how comfortable culture seems to be with girls who punish and neglect their own bodies. It is stunning how much time and energy the utterly brilliant upcoming generation still seems to be wasting on hating themselves and hurting their bodies, just like we did, only rather more efficiently, because young people these days are obliged to do everything more efficiently. This is not their fault. It is the fault of older generations for not treasuring their young people well enough.

Fear of fat women is sexism at its least subtle. Fear of female flesh, after all, is fear of female power, of female desire. And so we can't speak honestly about the way we treat female bodies or the way women and girls are taught to fear their own desires without speaking about the way fat women are punished and controlled. When we talk about rape, when we talk about harassment, we often prioritise the experiences of women and girls who are not only white, cisgender and able-bodied, but also extremely thin and traditionally attractive, which is almost a tautology these days.

Fat women do not make 'good victims'. Overweight and obese women and girls are just as likely to experience rape, abuse and harassment, but less likely to be believed or treated with anything approaching respect when they speak about it. The idea, implicit or explicit – is that a fat woman should feel grateful for any male attention, even if that attention takes the form of violence, of rape. Those who understand rape as simply an exaggerated display of male desire often refuse to believe that a woman who is considered 'unattractive' could be a victim of rape. Who would want to rape her?

Fat women in particular have transgressed the patriarchal prime directive even more – they have insulted men and boys by neglecting their duty to be as hot and as thin as possible. They might even have committed the cardinal sin of placing their own bodily needs, their own hunger and desire, above what any man they meet might expect from them.

Other women, too, whether or not we are 'overweight' ourselves, are complicit in society's policing of fat bodies – particularly fat female bodies. Too many of us use the word 'fat' the same way we use the word 'slut' – as an insult that incorporates our terror of what might happen if women were ever allowed true ownership over our bodies.

If we are serious about reclaiming female desire, if we believe that every person has a right to agency over her own body, none of us should stand aside while women who are fat, or deemed to take up too much space in the world, face the most disgusting, targeted misogyny imaginable, in the street, at work and online.

The problem with an eating disorder, whether you are starving, bingeing, purging or all three, however you are managing your terror of giving your body what it wants and needs, is that the thing you are trying to control becomes an obsession. When you deny your own hunger, that same hunger swallows everything brave and interesting about you. You stop dreaming about grand adventures and start dreaming about chocolate cake. Your daily life becomes a routine of micromanaging how you're going to avoid food and what and when you're going to eat. Your body becomes an abominable roommate, the kind you can't get away from but spend your whole time resenting, communicating in nasty notes on the fridge door, convinced that they are stealing from you when in fact, it is you who should have reached out and tried to understand. Food becomes a gaping maw in your mind, with everything else that actually matters jostling for attention around it. It's no way to live.

'For a woman who has learned to make herself physically and emotionally small, to live literally and figuratively on scraps, admitting that you have an appetite is a source of cavernous fear,' writes Jess Zimmerman at *Hazlitt*. 'Women are often on a diet of the body, but we are always on a diet of the heart. The low-maintenance woman, the ideal woman, has no appetite ... She is satisfied and satisfiable ... What would it take to feel safe being voracious? What would it take to realise that your desires are not monstrous, but human?'[16]

What it takes is the courage to acknowledge your own hunger. To choose abundance. To accept risk. It's a monumentally difficult undertaking, one I expect to be working on for as long as I live. During the awful early months of 2017, as the world spiralled into crypto-fascist chaos, I broke away from a bad relationship and lost my job. I slipped back into anxious old habits, reasserting control over my corner of the world. My life was on fire and so was the planet. I wanted to need less, to be less, and so I started to eat a little less – and then a lot less. I lost weight I couldn't spare. I started to look drawn and ill. I came down with every flu that flitted by, I felt weak and sluggish, I looked vulnerable, I was too thin. And something strange happened. Somehow, suddenly, I had become irresistible to men.

I have rarely in my life had more sexual attention than in those numb, painful months. I was, unsurprisingly, rebounding like a pinball with avoidant attachment, and every single man I went to bed with commented on my thinness, approvingly, guiltily. I had one person count my ribs in bed. I had another man try to guess my weight during sex. (He guessed a strangely specific eighty-four pounds, which is around what I would weigh without any of my internal organs: I was barely registering as a person with a functioning body at all.) Sadly, one of the things they don't tell you about starving yourself is that it deadens all of your desires. I was having a lot of sex, but I was having it compulsively, chasing the juiciness and abundance and pleasure that you can only really access if you're actually at home in your own flesh.

When you're a barely tolerated guest in your own body, you behave like one: you don't relax, you don't help yourself to snacks and blankets, and you definitely don't shag with abandon on the sofa. When you're starving yourself, the fear is that you will eat and eat and never stop, that your body's demands will destroy everything around you. That's a convenient mindset to cultivate in a society that has good reason to worry about what might happen if women start asking for more.

Of course, when you're starving, 'eat and eat and never stop' is precisely what your body does want to do – but, crucially, only for a little while. Recovery only comes when you actually do let go, when you get to a place of safety and can trust that there will be *enough* in the future – enough food, enough joy, enough love. That letting go was what I was truly afraid of when, for a long time, I was afraid of being 'fat'. I even said so, at times, in front of friends who actually *were* fat, and I remain grateful for their kindness, for their understanding that I was so mired in self-doubt that I didn't realise that what I'd said was, 'My worst fear is that I'll look like you.'

For a lot of women and queer people, fear of fatness is a fear of losing the little control they were ever allowed: control over the way men measure your body. What I was actually afraid of – what I am still sometimes afraid of – was that I would lose control, that there would be no end to my emotions and my ambition and my desire, that I would uncrack an unstoppable hunger for every possible taste in life – not just for food, but for love, for sex, for power and pleasure and adventure and everything a man-sized portion of life is supposed to encompass. I was afraid I would be too much, that I would want too much, that I would scare people away, that I would be overwhelmed, overwhelming.

And in fact, that's exactly what happened. I *was* too much, and I *did* want too much, and plenty of people took issue with that, as soon as I stopped hurting and hating myself enough to own it. Like most of the interesting people I know, I take up far more space than I'm supposed to, and I've paid for it in private and in public, although not half as much as I might have paid without the privileges of class, race and cultural background I was born into. There have been so many times when it would have been easier to shrink myself, to stay small and dry and grateful and squash down every hunger and heartache and ambition I ever felt, to take tiny birdlike bites of experience and never ask for seconds. But I'm not sorry, because I'm surrounded, these days, by women and queer people who are insatiable, women and queer people of every size who want more and more from the world and care less and less if the world likes them for it, who refuse scarcity, who lick the plate of life and ask for more.

6

Labours of Love

Heterosexuality is in trouble. Over the past decade more straight women than ever before have chosen to delay marriage and partnership, exit unsatisfactory relationships or forgo them altogether. Birth rates have fallen off a precipice in developed nations that never bothered to imagine a strategy for supporting family life beyond shovelling women towards marriage and motherhood. Around the world, more and more women are refusing to be shovelled, in a mass walkout from the traditional, heteronormative couple form, with all its dangers and disappointments. The social shockwaves of that walkout will be felt for generations to come. Why is this happening?

There's one simple reason. Yes, there are complex, intricate socioeconomic factors behind this sea change in sexual politics, but it comes down to this: a great many millions of straight women are unable to find suitable romantic partners who treat them decently – and are unwilling to build their lives around men who don't. It's not that straight women and girls have given up on love altogether. But they are now freer than ever before to set their own conditions for what they will and will not accept in relationships with men – and freer to walk away if those conditions are not met.

Love is political. I have spent the past decade of my life navigating men's messed-up relationship to sex, love and status. I have watched men with money, fame and power treat women and girls as interchangeable fuck-toys, and I have watched women and girls get relentlessly devastated in relationships with men who don't feel powerful enough. I have watched men assume that along with success comes an all-access pass to the hearts and bodies of beautiful women. I have watched successful, confident straight women be crushed by their inability to connect with men. And I have watched women in committed relationships staggering under the weight of emotional and domestic labour that partnership with men so often involves. Love is political. And a new politics of love is essential if there's to be any chance of salvaging anything precious out of the sociopolitical wreckage of straight sexuality. Especially for women who are unwilling – more than ever before – to compromise their own power for a man's love.

It took me a long time to understand that pain and self-denial were not the price I had to pay to be loved. In fact, in my own life, again and again, I have had to make the choice between being seen as 'girlfriend material' and my dedication to my writing work, and that choice has been as painful as it has been obvious. There was never a part of me that considered shrinking my ambition to avoid threatening the men in my life. I knew what that would cost. I also knew that I was lucky to get to make that choice – to get to choose my freedom at the expense of a man's undependable love. My grandmother didn't. A lot of people still don't. But choice is not the same as control.

Men are almost never asked to sacrifice their fundamental identity, swallow their sexual longings or stifle their ambitions in order to have a love relationship and a family life. In fact, since the limited sexual revolution of the 1960s all but destroyed the social obligation on men to support women in marriage, men are now free to be as promiscuous as they like with their hearts, with barely any social sanction against abandoning a partner. It is no longer taboo – if it ever was – for men to walk away from their families because they have grown bored, or sexually frustrated, or tired. Straight men are routinely forgiven for pursuing their desires even at the cost of existing family commitments. But straight women who do the same are considered unnatural. This means, again, that where love exists between men and women, it is undermined by an imbalance of power, and must be negotiated on unequal terms – where for one party the stakes are always higher. There are few remaining ways for men to hurt women and continue to feel good about themselves. This sort of casual brutality is one of them.

Men have always held the power when it comes to sex – but they also hold a great deal of power in love relationships. Most of them did not ask for this power, and far too few of them wield it responsibly. Little boys looking for love and adventure did not invent the idea that a girl's life is empty, meaningless and a failure until she has found a man to love – but that ideology is horrifyingly convenient all the same.

It is important to be honest about how straight men come to use the structure of love relationships, as well as sexual violence, to suck the marrow out of women and girls. It's not just about acts of physical cruelty or abuse – it's also about the everyday assaults on women's self-worth that have become part of the love-language of heterosexuality. 'Not raping or beating your partner' has long been the standard for decent male behaviour in straight relationships, when it ought to be the baseline. The bar is low. The bar is in the floor, and a lot of straight men still fail to clear it. And for good reason: if a lack of active physical harm were the baseline of straight male behaviour rather than the gold standard, if women were entitled to expect more from their primary relationships than simply to survive them, perhaps they would feel more comfortable demanding more from the men in their lives in private as well as in public.

In the machinery of modern masculinity, the drive to systematically devastate women, to seek out sex and intimacy as sources of status, is becoming ever more frantic. That's because the traditional ways that men get to feel good about themselves are harder and harder to come by. To be raised male in late capitalism is, in so many cases, a process of psychological castration – of having all your tender desires reduced to a logic of merciless competition, of being taught to seek power, wealth and status in a culture that denies most of us most of these things, and of being forbidden any emotions beyond lust and rage. Men who have grown up expecting to be the heroes of their own stories end up having to fight for scraps of self-worth in an economy and a culture that creates far more losers than it does winners.

There can be no honest conversation about consent unless we acknowledge how much routine abuse occurs within romantic relationships – and how the stories we tell about love can normalise abuse. There's more to allyship than graciously refraining from rape, and it matters that there are a great many men who perform wokeness in public but, in private, exploit and demean the women in their lives, treating them as receptacles for their own pain. How a man treats women in private, matters. It is political. If a man claims to be an ally or a supporter of women's rights but routinely abuses the trust and hurts the bodies of the women with whom he is intimate, he is as great a peril to those women as the unapologetic misogynist.

'All too often,' writes bell hooks in *All About Love*, 'women believe it is a sign of commitment, an expression of love, to endure unkindness or cruelty, to forgive and forget. In actuality, when we love rightly we know that the healthy, loving response to cruelty and abuse is putting ourselves out of harm's way.'[1]

Love is still so often the language in which we learn to understand violence. The fact remains that the majority of rapists and abusers are in some sort of close relationship with their victims. Most rape is not 'stranger rape'. Most sexual and physical abuse occurs within the family, and this means that the people who hurt us when we are most vulnerable are often the same people who we love most – sometimes because we have no choice, because we are too young to understand that love isn't supposed to hurt like that.

Heterosexuality is a system for enforcing power hierarchies, and it is also, at the same time, where a great many people live their most raw and personal truths. That's why, in order to speak honestly about sexuality and abuse, it's essential to interrogate love. Those of us who are raised as women absorb the same lesson over and over again: romantic love, specifically heterosexual love, is the most important thing that will ever happen to us. Dating advice, as Moira Weigel observes in *Labor of Love*, tells young women 'here is how to be if you want to be loved ... which is to say if you want to be worth anything.'[2]

Finding a man to love you, and hanging on to his love at any cost, is still phrased as the final pass/fail grade for every growing girl. Regardless of context, whatever else any woman at any age accomplishes is recast as meaningless if she does not also secure her own sweetly devoted Prince Charming. The trouble is that it is very difficult to love freely when one gender has a great deal more structural power than the other. It is almost impossible to love freely when you are a straight woman who loves her freedom, who has determined that freedom is too high a price to pay for love, in a world that still makes our survival conditional on finding and keeping a man and then shames us for making marriage an economic prospect, in a world that made our sexuality a commodity and then decided the worst insult for a woman was *whore*.

Most straight men have never had to negotiate romantic relationships as equals. There is still so little in culture that teaches them to do so, and less incentive to learn. The requirement that men behave towards women like gentlemen – always a weak excuse for othering – has vanished without being replaced by the requirement that men treat women like human beings. Both sides of this equation – the ritualised treatment of women as ethereal beings of fragility and the cruel mercenary scoreboard – are ways of treating the 'opposite' sex as other than human.

Love is political because the quality of so many straight women's lives still leans – unless they are lucky – on whether or not men love them, and love them well. Love is political because love is where we live our intimate politics. A man is entitled to demand love; a woman may only be a passive love object. Men are allowed to define standards of what is desirable, attractive and worthy of love and respect in a woman. Men are allowed to demand that women meet these standards and punish them for non-compliance – and that means any woman, whether or not they've ever been intimate with her or, indeed, have ever met her. Women are not allowed to hold similar expectations about men – even the expectation of basic personal safety.

That threat of abandonment is the ultimate tool of coercion. Telling people that if they don't behave, nobody will ever love them is far more effective than threatening them with violence. Hold a gun to someone's head and you've lost the moral argument. Eventually, your victims will rebel. On the other hand, if you can convince people that if they don't act like compliant citizens, docile workers or submissive servants they will be alone for ever, there is almost no limit to the concessions you can extract.

If you make love conditional on obedience, people will find ways to obey. If you make submission the basis of self-worth, people will find ways to submit. As a younger person, feeling trapped in a body that I was convinced was socially unacceptable, I sometimes slept with men not because I wanted them, but because evidence that a man wanted me seemed to renew my right to take up any space in the world at all. I wanted love, but I also wanted to *be* loved – to be found worthy of love by some man, so that I would be allowed to love myself. Isn't that what all girls are supposed to want? To be relentlessly, unflaggingly wanted by one man, to be purified by the act of reflecting their light back into the world?

I grew up in the 1990s, the decade of stranger danger. I remember picture books with reassuring fables about children who made good decisions on family holidays. I remember visits from local police officers telling us not to get into a weird guy's car, not even if he offered us sweeties. The answer, somehow, was to practise a sort of auto-surveillance – and not to play outside alone, however nice a day it was. If a creepy man in a raincoat happened to accost us during a rare unsupervised moment, we were supposed to shout, loudly, 'I DO NOT KNOW THIS MAN.' What nobody was telling any of us was what to do if the people who were supposed to love and protect us were the very people hurting us. Nobody told us that strangers weren't the only danger.

The fact that violence, sadism and misogyny live alongside something that passes for love is a terribly difficult thing to acknowledge. When it happens to you, no matter how many horror stories you have heard, you find yourself contorting into gymnastic feats of twisted logic not to confront the damage, the danger and the waste.

It is so difficult to watch young women self-harming with love. I have a friend who is entirely obsessed with the married lover with whom she has been having an affair for years. Her life revolves around him, and so does our friendship – every intimate conversation we have comes back to what he meant by that text, or why he's not been in touch, or what the sex was like, is like, might be like, and whether she will ever be good enough, special enough, lovable enough to be *his*. Even when she's in the room with you, my friend often seems to be somewhere else. Because she is: she's with him, ruminating on it all, turning it over and over in her mind, wondering what he's doing, if he's thinking of her, what her future will look like with him. She has ceased to be able to imagine one without him. This is not his fault, except obliquely.

When you're in love with someone in that fierce, remote way, someone who will never quite be yours, it's not about them – not really. It's about you, and the drama of your own self-worth, which you've hung wholly on whether or not they will ever love you like you want them to, like you need them to. You hollow out your life around the shape of them, hoping they will step in to fill that void. With their brilliance. With their passion. With their great hair and lingering kisses, whatever it is that keeps you awake night after night thinking, wondering, wishing you knew the magic words to say so that you could belong to them, so you could be precious enough to be theirs, because you want to be owned by them, you don't want to own yourself.

The fact that it never happens, the fact that they are never quite accessible, is part of the addiction. It's the core of the compulsion. You fill their absence with everything you fear, everything about your life that hurts, everything about yourself you hate, and nothing else is quite as important any more. If you can wrap your hurt and terror around this man and what he means to you, nothing else matters.

When people self-harm, when they cut or hurt themselves, they are relying on the pain of it to ground them in their body, nail them to the present – or to take them away from everything else in their lives that is upsetting and out of their control. Or both. Love, this sort of love, does both.

I once loved a man in San Francisco: rich and brilliant, older and cruel. I smashed myself against the glamour and the danger of him, over and over, and the more he made it clear that he enjoyed toying with me, enjoyed showing me just how disposable I would always be to him, the more he hurt me on purpose, the more obsessed I was. He enjoyed reminding me that although I was clever and accomplished, none of that mattered – because I wasn't hot enough. At twenty-seven, I wasn't young enough. I wasn't vulnerable enough. If I could only break through. If he could only see that I knew him best, saw him fully. If he could only see me as an equal. None of the prizes I'd brought home in my life would matter unless I could win his heart.

When he finally told me what I had always wanted to hear – that I was special, that I was different, that he needed me – it was because he was in trouble. He needed someone to defend him. A woman with social capital to set on fire to fuel his escape from consequences. I was the perfect choice. I still loved him. I still wanted to be his favourite. But he made one mistake. He forgot that women do, in fact, talk to each other. And while he was saying all the right things to me to get me to do what he wanted, he was also saying all the right things – very different things – to others.

I wasn't special. I know that, just like I know that if, right now, he called and told me that he needed me, that he had always loved me, that I had always been the one, I can't say for sure I wouldn't go to him, and burn my life down behind me. That part of me hopes he will call, which is why the rest of me has blocked him on every possible platform. I cut that man out of my life entirely, even though it felt like severing a finger on the hand

I held onto reality with. I swore I would never make the same mistake again.

I have been obsessed, just like my friend, with unavailable men. With violent, charming men. With self-loathing, self-important predators with pretty eyes and a vacancy for a secret side-piece. With gentle artists who did nothing wrong but look at the vast array of women to choose from and chose someone else. I have been told, over and over again, that I am too much. Too ambitious, too intense, too masculine, too loud, too weird, too independent, too political; too clearly the protagonist of my own story to be the prize at the end of some man's hero's journey.

I know perfectly well that all the things I like most about myself, the things I'm proudest of, are things that make me less of a romantic prize – less of an ideal love object – for the men I'd like to date. The hardest part of the sexual revolution for me has been no longer waiting for a man to find me lovable before I am allowed to love myself.

Just months ago, a friend of a friend called me in tears; she had been humiliated, yet again, by a mediocre stranger on a date. He became cold and angry after realising that she was his professional superior – a few years ahead of him in his chosen career. He insulted her and ended the date, and that night she could not stop feeling that everything she had fought for in her own work, all of her competence and expertise, was somehow invalid if it did not win her a man.

This narrative in straight relationships is demeaning to everyone involved. It's a small-minded single story that insists that there's only one way for power to work between people of different genders: men are active creators and consumers, and women are passive objects there to appreciate men's brilliance and reward their hard work, and that's the way it will always be, for ever. Men are protagonists of their own stories, and women are sidekicks, love interests or straight-up non-player characters there to provide men with an exciting side quest, and fold up and disappear when they're done with them. In many creative communities, men with talent and fame get to assume access to a replaceable roster of young, beautiful, biddable women, and by and large that assumption is correct. Those powerful, influential men are treated as if sexual and romantic access to those women is part of the reward for success, and most of our cultural mythology supports that narrative.

'What does it mean to be lovable?' asks Dalia Gebrial in her brilliant essay 'Decolonising Desire: The Politics of Love'. 'Who is and is not deserving of particular kinds of love? How is love coded and reproduced? What, and who, is absent when love is represented?'[3] Gebrial points out the wealth of research showing that Black and brown women are routinely passed over on dating sites, and face extra challenges fitting into the model of 'dateability'. Of course, getting attention on a dating website or 'being married' are not indicators of being loved. However, what this body of data and personal narrative tells us is that race profoundly structures your experience of desire, commitment and respect. 'What I'm interested in further investigating is what it means to not be legible within even these problematic discourses of love.'

The emotional need men appear to have to 'protect' women is one of the most obvious ways the story of straight romance is shot through with racial as well as gendered prejudice. The social construct of the 'fragile white woman' – frail, precious, in need of protection – that plays out so often in modern race politics has its corollary in the 'strong Black woman', who is assumed, by definition, to be less vulnerable and therefore less lovable. Some women of colour, particularly women of African, Middle Eastern or South Asian descent, are coded as inherently less deserving of protection.

The lovability of white women – our status as 'love objects' – has been constructed in opposition to the routine relegation of Black bodies, even within our most intimate interpersonal scripts. Most of the things that are associated, in a patriarchal white supremacist culture, with 'beauty' are also associated with being worthy of love. Being young, being thin, being white, looking frail. To this we can add: lack of confidence and no more than modest professional and financial success, in a culture where independence and confidence themselves are considered ugly and unlovable.

In fact, the entire culture of heterosexual love is becoming more coercive. As Linda R. Hirshman and Jane E. Larson write in *Hard Bargains*,

> cultural conservatives and sexual libertines in concert have invoked the ideology of romance to stave off feminist moves to strategies of law and collective action in support of female sexual bargaining power. Women who are strongly self-protective in sexual bargaining are labeled unromantic, asexual, or man-hating, and thus threatened with a life of loneliness.[4]

Women, in other words, are not entitled to respect, care or consideration. Straight men are entitled to all of this, and more. Recent studies showed that higher levels of belief in male entitlement predicted greater sexism in both men and women. Men and boys often grow up marinated in the assumption that they are owed certain things from women – not individual women, but women in general. They have a right to sexual and romantic attention from at least one woman for the duration of their adult lives. They are entitled to pleasure, comfort and emotional caretaking. They don't have to do anything to earn this consideration: it is their birthright. If they don't get it, they are entitled to riot, to lash out, to punish.

As psyches and certainties shrivel in the heat of the age, gender and sex become more and more freighted with anxiety. The desire to prove oneself a real man, to become loved and powerful through access to women's bodies and the almighty fuck, becomes more frantic, more all-consuming, more blinkered. The more men believe that they must have a woman in their life, that they are owed a woman in their life, the crueller they become.

For men, romantic love has long been understood as a feeling that can be experienced by one person alone, projected relentlessly onto the scrim of another person's skin, a feeling that entitles a man to a certain claim on the object of his adoration. If he decides he is 'in love' with you, that means you owe him something. This has been happening for hundreds of years. Early in *Don Quixote*, Cervantes recreates it perfectly in Marcela's speech:

> Heaven made me, you say, so lovely that my beauty makes you love me despite yourselves; and in return for the love you show me, you claim, and even demand, that I should be bound to love you. I know by the natural sense which God has given me that whatever is beautiful is lovable; but I do not understand why, merely because she inspires love, a woman who is loved for her beauty is obliged to love the man who loves her.[5]

In her book *Down Girl*, the philosopher Kate Manne explains that the 'logic' of misogyny is predicated on the 'moral goods' that women are supposed to owe to men – including sex, care, child rearing and domestic labour.[6] Part of the unspoken bargain here is that women are not permitted to ask for these things themselves, no matter how much they may want or need them. What women are meant to get out of this is increasingly unclear, but there's usually some hand-waving about protection, provision and having someone around to get the lids off jars.

According to Manne, society separates souls along the gender binary into 'human beings' and 'human givers'. Men are allowed to be 'human beings', who can act on and in the world, and women are expected to be 'human givers' – the ones whose lives are defined in relation to what they can do, and be, for others. This is how the logic of heterosexuality is still phrased. Women owe men a range of services, including sex, attention, emotional caretaking and domestic care. Men are entitled to expect these things from women, and women are not entitled to expect them in return.[7]

From the start, whoever I was dating, there always seemed to be some reason I owed him. At fifteen it was because he was generous enough to date me. At nineteen it was because I was at a fancy college and he worked in town and drank in the evenings. At twenty it was because I was able-bodied and he was not, because I had the energy to find work and he did not. At twenty-four it was because he was working class and I was not. At twenty-six and twenty-eight and twenty-nine it was because I had a writing job and a small amount of public recognition and he did not, or because I seemed like I was coping emotionally and he was not, or because, or because, or because.

Like many young women, I spent most of my early years in relationships with men apologising for things that weren't my fault. I spent years trying to make up for the harm the world had done to the men and boys I adored, and minimising the harm it had done to me, hollowing myself out to make a home for those men in my heart. I felt like I owed them. I owed them my time, my care, my money, my body, and that didn't make me feel good, but it made me feel... *good*. It didn't bring me pleasure, but it made me feel virtuous and worthy. I was a good and giving girlfriend, and therefore a good person. Most of the young women I've been close to who regularly date men have had experiences like mine – of bleeding themselves translucent trying to bolster the men they have adored, because that's what love is meant to mean.

What is it that men, as a cohort, feel they are entitled to from women? What are women supposed to owe to men? Everything the world at large refuses to provide. Basic emotional and physical care. A sense of wholeness. Comfort, community and understanding. Someone to notice when you're struggling. Love, care and attention. These are precisely the things that the neoliberal state refuses to provide or pay for, and precisely the things that the all-caps logic of misogyny suggests women owe men as their rent on this earth.

One word for this sort of work is 'social reproduction', but it has been called many things, often as a way of distinguishing it from 'real' work done, traditionally, by men. It has often been called 'women's work'. The philosopher Hannah Arendt, in her famous study *The Human Condition*, calls it 'labour', distinguishing it from 'work' and 'action', which, she explains, are the other categories of effort that constitute human life. Labour, according to Arendt, is ephemeral, the basic work of survival, of being a 'creature in motion'; 'work' is constructive and produces tangible, lasting results, making it the sort of work you are more likely to get paid a wage for; action, the most rarefied, is the work of thinking about and constructing society and your place in it in relation to others – art, politics, storytelling. If labour is making dinner, work is making a table, and action is making your mark on the world. Arendt does not explicitly say which sort of work is better or more important, but it's also clear what she spent most of her own life doing. Only a mind like Arendt's could so deftly describe the major modes of human activity while almost entirely side-stepping the questions of profit and power, of who actually does these different kinds of work in society and who is enriched by it.

What is largely lacking in Arendt's coy summary, as it is lacking in most political philosophy, is any acknowledgement of social reproduction as valuable work.

If the Covid-19 crisis has taught the world anything, it should be that the work of sustaining human life is the most essential work there is. Forty years of neoliberal policymaking that stripped down social safety nets have meant that the work of making and sustaining life is no longer seen as public responsibility – instead it is women, usually in private, intimate settings, in romantic and family relationships, who are the first and last line of defence against the ravages of the modern economy. When men and boys teeter on the edge of the cracks in kamikaze capitalism, it is women who are expected to make nets out of their bodies. Very often they do it because nobody else will. I've done it too many times to count, and I wasted a lot of my own time and theirs before I realised you can't save the world one broken man at a time.

In recent years the phrase 'emotional labour' has passed into everyday use as a way to describe some of that work – 'girlfriend work', the work of patching up the walking wounded of the modern economy. As women struggle to fill the gaps in social provision within relationships, they find themselves blamed for the promises late capitalism made to men and never intended to keep. They find themselves blamed for the humiliation of men. They find themselves blamed, implicitly or directly, for men's lack of security, their lack of dignified and secure work, their frustration, their lack of power. That women may be suffering all of these degradations and more does not factor: women were designed for humility, for suffering. Around the world today, untold millions of men are consumed by an awareness that they've been cheated, by the suspicion that they are entitled to more out of life than they've had. They are right. But *the things they are entitled to are not supposed to come from women and girls.*

Not so long ago, straight marriage was a straightforward economic arrangement – one in which women's labour power and sexual services were provided in exchange for food, shelter and 'protection' in an economy designed to keep women dependent on men. This assumption was the bedrock of the nuclear family, a way of organising households into units of economic production. The great task of a woman's life was to be good enough to be owned by an acceptable man. This logic is taking a surprisingly long time to die.

Women's suffrage and the liberalisation of divorce laws have not taken away the implication that love is the chief task of a woman's life, and marriage a work contract in which she is both the employee and the product. Instead of counting on a job for life, however, modern women must now be constantly hustling in the precarious market of bland, managed romance.

Today, marriage and other forms of straight, monogamous partnership are no longer the recipe for security that they once were – but that lack of security has not been counterbalanced by greater personal freedom, at least not for straight women. Instead of marriage as a 'job for life' – or a significant part of your life – women find themselves bargaining for a succession of insecure, exhausting relationships with no promise of long-term commitment. Without the cultural or economic structures in place to make dating more of a choice, this is not freedom – this is gig-economy dating.

The straight 'dating market' is like any other market: fundamentally skewed in favour of a handful of wealthy old white men at everyone else's expense. It's an architecture of constrained choice and arbitrary rulemaking designed to screw the rest of us out of as much of our time and energy as possible, while dangling visions of fulfilment in front of us that are, by necessity, impossible to satisfy. This is how brute commerce captures the most intimate of human relations. This is how the unimaginative powers that be have turned our most visceral and transcendent moments together into a joyless competition for resources.

Millions of women and girls around the world are still devoted to this depressing idea of love. Who can blame them? If your day-to-day survival and the security of your children depends on making sure the men around you are comfortable, and if the comfort of the men around you depends on you squashing down your ambitions, railroading your own needs, providing endless hours of free emotional and domestic care, tolerating disrespect and violence, putting your sexuality to work for their satisfaction, and never letting them know how much they have hurt you, then you will do all of that, and more. Not because you are a fool, and not because you are naturally selfless, but because you have to.

The market in intimacy has butchered romance and sold it back to us in bloodless, bite-sized pieces, and the dating market is where most of us actually encounter the commodity logic of sex in the flesh. However frigid and joyless the dating game, however exhausting and unsatisfying straight relationships become, the cultural horror of being alone – single, independent – is urgent enough to make many of us afraid to question the rules of the game. The scarcity mentality has infected cultural attitudes to love and sex, drenching them in panic and desperation. We become like supermarket shoppers on the day before a hurricane, grabbing as much as we can of whatever looks edible, shoving and shouting at each other as we clear the shelves. We forget, until it's too late, that we are competing – among other things – to be allowed to do more work. That the role of wife, girlfriend or mother is not something women can relax into. That there is a great deal of effort and energy involved that remains invisible, because it is still part of the taxonomy of 'love'.

When you start to understand love as a form of work – necessary work, work without which the fabric of humanity unravels like wool: the work of care, of attention, of attending to the needs of another person – you begin to see the inequity at the heart of all the old love songs. The work of love – including sexual, erotic love – was not, and often still is not, work that most women can choose freely. The work of love was not and is not work where women are allowed to negotiate for protection.

Research has shown that the 'marriage benefits' – the increases in health, wealth and happiness that are often associated with the state of wedlock – go disproportionately to men.[8] Married men are better off than single men. Married women, on the other hand, are not better off – emotionally, physically or financially – than unmarried women.

No matter how many movies and mawkish dating manuals hammer home the message that a woman's life is incomplete if it is not in orbit around a man, that a woman without a husband or children is a tragic failure fated to die alone and be slowly eaten by her household pets, it is, in fact, men – consistently – who benefit most from 'traditional' monogamous marriage. This is important – because it means that more women are wondering if the whole thing is worth it.

If love is work, women need to organise collectively for better conditions. And that's exactly what's happening.

All over the world, women are on strike. There has been no great fanfare, no organised movement. It has happened organically. Women are simply opting out. Opting out of marriage, opting out of long-term relationships with men, and opting out, in particular, of having children. There are more single women living alone or without partners in Europe and America today than there have been at any other time in recorded history. This is not necessarily the tragedy it might appear. The simple fact is that – particularly for women who aren't anxious for children – singleness is often the better option.

'It is a radical upheaval, a national reckoning with massive social and political implications,' writes Rebecca Traister:

> Across classes, and races, we are seeing a wholesale revision of what female life might entail. We are living through the invention of independent female adulthood as a norm, not an aberration, and the creation of an entirely new population: adult women who are no longer economically, socially, sexually, or reproductively dependent on or defined by the men they marry.[9]

After generations of feminist struggle for property rights, equal pay, better divorce laws and welfare provision, there are far fewer women who are legally or financially compelled to be someone's wife or girlfriend. Women still earn less than men in equivalent roles across almost every industry, and women still earn less over their lifetimes, in no small part because of the lack of provision for maternity pay and child-rearing within what is considered the 'real' economy. But the gap is narrowing. It is possible for more and more women, including mothers, to achieve basic security without sacrificing their independence.

Women and girls are not just withholding sex from men who have no interest in their pleasure – they are withholding intimacy and romance from men who have no interest in relationships of equality. With a scarcity of men out there who treat women like people and have even an ounce of their own shit together, more and more of us are finding that we'd rather be single. Being single is simply more enjoyable and enriching than trailing around after some bitter, boorish emotional vampire hoping he'll improve if you open another vein.

Given the option to do literally anything else with their short time on earth, more and more women are choosing not to spend

126

it rearranging a man's sock drawer, soothing his childhood traumas and raising his kids. Women's increasing independence is profoundly threatening to male identity, and for good reason. We have educated women to be independent of men – to be, in Gloria Steinem's words, the men we want to marry – but we have not educated men to be their own wives. Straight men are finding themselves unable to cope independently of women, and it is making them furious and frightened.

The simple fact is that while there are indeed men out there who are brave and decent and looking for equal partnerships with women in love relationships and who have the maturity to carry it out, there are not as many as there are women looking. And this affects the balance of power within heterosexuality. It is worth remembering that criminal sexual assault is not the only way that men can exert power over women. In fact, many of the most damaging tendencies of straight men in positions of social power – the lying, the cheating, the systematic betrayals of trust – are not crimes are all. This makes them hard to talk about in a culture where not being an actual violent rapist is still apparently the gold standard for decent male behaviour. But that makes it all the more important, then, that we do talk about how many more ways there are for men to degrade and dehumanise women and girls.

Our romantic, gendered scripts affect the stories we tell, the art we make and the worlds we build in fiction and in the flesh. And when we repeat, over and over again, the message that women are only valuable in relationship to men, that women are most lovable when they don't know their own worth, we send a message. It's just as damaging a message, in its own way, as the attitude that women in some cultural circles are only valuable if they are young, hot and uncomplaining. In fact, those two attitudes go hand in hand: the logic of misogyny that devalues women as active, independent thinkers and creators is the same logic that measures a woman's worth by her youth and inexperience – and systematically exploits both. Powerful men make art, change the world and get the girls, and the girls appreciate the art and wait patiently to be picked. That's the way it was always supposed to work.

I'm routinely surprised by the number of decent, progressive, empathetic men, men who are totally on board the gender-equality train – in theory – who nonetheless seem to believe that the way they behave in intimate relationships with women exists in a magical sphere separate from politics. Feminist and anti-racist men who seem to think the way they treat women romantically has nothing to do with racism or sexism. Often these men are uncomplicatedly decent to women they're not dating or married to. They want to want relationships of true equality and mutual humanity with dynamic, confident, adult women; they want to want all the things they know they ought to want if they were the ethical men they know they want to be.

But human beings want all kinds of things they're not supposed to want. Human beings want status and simple adoration and someone to fill the sucking hole in their self-esteem. They want to feel safe from the risk of rejection; they want to feel strong and important; they want to feel needed without really being known. Studies back up the observation that while many straight and bisexual men like the idea of being with an older, more successful or more talented woman in theory, in practice the qualities most valued in a female partner are beauty, self-sacrifice and the appearance of 'vulnerability'.

Most people want to feel competent, important and powerful. And for men wrestling with the contradictions of modern masculinity, the impulse to treat sex and intimacy as itemisable sources to status is even more pronounced – because so few of the traditional ways that men are allowed to feel good about themselves are easy to come by any more.

Some men might baulk – and rightly so – at being told that they find independence, confidence, intelligence and professional success unattractive in women. Indeed, a lot of men loudly insist that they would love to be with a smart, witty, dynamic woman with her own money. So why, then, are almost all of my smart, witty, successful straight female friends either single or slogging through a succession of relationships with cruel, mediocre men because they feel they have no better options?

Actually, that applies to a lot of successful women, too – but successful women don't generally have access to a roster of beautiful, fragile twenty-two-year-olds to tell them they're wonderful. Successful women don't have to be told that fame, money and power don't buy you love. They find out pretty quickly, somewhere between the first round of death threats and the second time they watch their first date's face fall when they reveal what they do for a living.

This sort of calculation is almost unthinkable to straight men, who are rarely required to change anything about themselves to appeal to the opposite sex, much less to diminish themselves or narrow their ambitions to fit inside the fragilities of a potential mate.

The plain fact is that men are not obliged to choose between power, creative fulfilment, independence – and love. Women are, and always have been – but the calculations that go into that choice are changing. It is no longer so likely as it was for our grandparents' generation that a straight woman's entire well-being depends on securing male affection.

It is not strictly true that confident, accomplished straight women who are old enough to have invested in a decent mattress are entirely unable to find someone to share it. There are options, but many of them are unappealing or actively dangerous.

Nor is it the case that straight and bisexual women don't want romantic partnerships with men. Most of them do – but, crucially, not as much as the things they might have to give up to get one. Most of my single, accomplished, confident female friends have a pretty accurate idea of why they're not fighting off eligible men. The trouble is that the things that put men off are often the things they like most about themselves.

Women are now allowed to want things more than they want the love and approval of men, and that's a shift that is slowly upending society as we know it. In the meantime, I am sick of watching the most brilliant women I know expend their energy, wreck their hearts and waste their time in endless unpaid internships of straight romance, waiting to be invited into men's hearts, even though they know they'll instantly be handed a mop and bucket and told to start scrubbing. I'm sick of watching my most sensitive, empathetic friends reshape themselves around lacklustre boyfriends, pouring their care and emotional labour into propping up the walking wounded of late-stage capitalism, as if the only way a woman could ever change the world was one man at a time. And as in the rest of the gig economy, the ideal worker is young, vulnerable and easy to exploit.

Women writers, artists, creators, professionals struggle just as much as men to break through in our fields. We have to do the hustle, the hard work, the late nights and longing, and the crippling self-doubt. We have to deal with everything men have to deal with – and then we also have to deal with the men. We have to meet their expectations, be brilliant enough to get noticed, but somehow also not interesting enough to make them angry. If we are disabled, neuro-atypical, queer, indigenous or of colour, it's even more difficult to match that standard. And the more we deviate from the romantic ideal, the less leeway we have to make a single mistake in any other aspect of our lives.

Down the centuries, men have created a social, economic and political system that makes it all but impossible for women to reject them. This is why the concept that women's consent might more than fleetingly matter creates such cognitive dissonance.

It's not that men have nothing to offer women any more. On the contrary. But the things they have to offer aren't the things that they have been taught are valuable. Jon Birger's famous 2015 book *Date-onomics: How Dating Became a Lopsided Numbers Game* made the argument that the dating 'market' is skewed in favour of men because of the relative scarcity of marriageable men who are college-educated. The book, which is exactly what would happen if a statistician tried to write softcore pornography, takes it as fact that 'college-educated' is the main scarcity factor when, in fact, many women are looking for a partner with a stable personality rather than a stable retirement fund. College guarantees neither. Interestingly, in building his statistical models of dateable men, Birger factors out the number of graduates who are unavailable to women because they are gay, but he does *not* factor out the number of graduates who are undateable because they are, for example, soul-sucking, mind-fucking perma-toddlers marinated in toxic shame. These squalling men-children do not figure on the statistics because it continues to be assumed that in relationships with women, as in so much else, a man's actual character does not matter.

I know that the idea of character is adorably retro. I know we're in the future now, where every human faculty has to be flattened into the logic of the market. But it remains the case that in their struggle to be 'men', men struggle to be human. And, factoring for taste, human decency is what most people are looking for from healthy relationships. Especially because, as straight women become more and more independent, all the other things that they were traditionally taught to look for in men – financial security, the ability to defend you from any wandering brigands – aren't just less common, they're also less important.

The bottom line is that men are not obliged to choose between being powerful and independent, and being loved, and women are. Perhaps one of the reasons that so many men seem so afraid of accomplished, well-rounded women is the reasonable fear that they too will have to become more rounded. If they are no longer useful only because of their contacts and the contents of their wallet, they may have to work on the content of their character.

Refusing to settle for mediocrity in life or in partnership is a quiet, private act of rebellion for women and femmes. In fact, one trait that the women I know who are as successful, happy and confident as it is possible to be in a time of global crisis have in common is that they *do* refuse to settle – in any aspect of their lives. They know their own worth, or have learned to act as if they do. They want a seat at the table, a slice of the pie; they won't accept crumbs in the corner. Most of them spent years developing that mindset. Why would they change it, now, for a man who might one day let them down? A tenure track position cannot walk out on you because it met someone on Instagram who really listens. Your job might disappear, but it won't take the good china with it. Your savings may only be as reliable as the global financial system, but that's still a lot more reliable than a lot of millennial men.

Given the choice between men's love on the one hand, and security, independence and personal power on the other, many women are choosing the latter. It's not an easy choice. It's still a choice that invites pity. But for more and more of us, it is a positive one – and one that may change power relations between the genders for ever.

If women are no longer running on a frantic schedule, trying to find a marriageable man before the song stops in the great mercenary game of musical chairs that is modern dating, if women are no longer obliged to seek love on men's terms, if we are prepared to walk away from love that hurts and humiliates and exhausts us, that's more than empowerment. It is a new form of collective bargaining in the sphere of love's work.

It is still hard for a lot of women to walk away from men – but not as hard as it used to be. When straight women are unlucky in love, they are usually persuaded that the fault lies in their own inadequacies or their own bad choices – that they simply need to work harder on being girlfriend material and choose more wisely next time. This narrative does not allow for the possibility that it might not be entirely women's fault that a significant proportion of straight men might simply not be good enough partners, because they have been raised to think of relationships as something to acquire, not something they might need to put effort into. Sexual revolution is not about women making smarter choices. Sexual revolution is about giving women more actual options.

For some people that's a bridge too far. It's too radical to actually allow women en masse to leave lacklustre relationships when they are not loved actively in return, when they are not afforded the care, decency and autonomy they deserve. But every time a woman refuses to believe that the problem is with her, refuses to tolerate disrespect, cowardice and violence as the price of love, it becomes that much easier for the rest of us to do the same. And women and girls are already walking away from dangerous, unsatisfying, exhausting straight relationships, choosing their own freedom over the often undependable security of male love, no matter the social cost. There are more single women supporting themselves in the developed world now than at any point in recorded history. That is sexual revolution.

As marriage and birth rates continue to fall, world governments are beginning to panic, and far-right parties openly run on platforms of returning women to their traditional role as mothers and wives. Heterosexuality isn't working for women – so how can they be coerced back into the kitchen? The one obvious solution that nevertheless seems not to occur to conservatives is simply to *make heterosexuality work better for women* – with all the effort and economic infrastructure that requires. It often seems as if straight men will do anything to force women to love them apart from the one thing women actually want them to do: love them in return, and treat them with basic respect.

Instead, the only socially acceptable solution still seems to be for straight women to lower their expectations. The idea that men might actually need to work on being better partners is still taboo in modern politics, so much so that fantastic euphemisms are employed to disguise that basic failure. But women everywhere are refusing to settle for men who refuse to do that work – and every time a woman finally decides she would rather feel good than be good, the world changes fractionally and for ever.

Heterosexual love will only be truly free when women can choose to be with men not because they have to, but because they want to – when love is no longer a service that one sex provides for another, when everyone of every gender is invited instead to the challenge of love's work. That's a romantic idea, in the original understanding of romance, which has nothing to do with flowers and platitudes or a desperate, competitive game of musical chairs. Romance is the triumph of the possible over the merely probable.

What would it be like to live in a world where there was enough love, enough pleasure, enough care to go around? Where people didn't have to scheme and cheat and bully affection out of one another? Where men, women and everyone else would be able to meet as equals, to see one another face to face, with all our flaws and broken hearts and battered places, and try to work out how to be human together as the world changes? What would it be like to love one another without the straitjacket of gender? Maybe it's because I'm a romantic – but I still think we'll find out, someday.

7

BODIES OF WORK

In almost every conceivable industry, sexuality has been weaponised against women's advancement. Sexual violence in the workplace functions as a way of making sure women in male-dominated environments know their place and remember their role: shut up and smile, or else. For every famous man who has lost his job because he couldn't keep his hands off his interns, there are hundreds of talented, brilliant women and girls who never rose through the ranks, never got to make full use of their faculties or contribute to culture. That's the part that so often goes unspoken when we talk about work, and whose work matters in the world.

The #MeToo movement began as a campaign against workplace sexual harassment. First, women within the relatively rarefied worlds of media, entertainment, politics and technology spoke out about the humiliation and silencing they experienced when trying to do the jobs they'd been hired for. Then, with somewhat less fanfare, women in lower-paid, less glamorous industries began to make demands. Fast-food workers. Farm workers. Domestic workers. Members of the military. Soon, men all over the world were losing their jobs because of sexual violence – and that continues to have enormous implications.

Traditional legal systems have proven themselves utterly inadequate to the task of regulating sexual violence, sexism and institutional racism. As a result, it has fallen on employers to provide some form of restitution, and to be the standard-bearers for cultural change. In recent years, when individuals have been accused of abuse, harassment or active prejudice, they have been far more likely to lose their job or be forced to resign from positions of influence than they have been to face any legal consequences. Corporate reputation, in short, has become a substitute for collective ethics.

When a man loses his job because his company or colleagues cannot support his behaviour – particularly if he is an influential white man – it is experienced by wider culture as a collective attack. Demotion or unemployment is a humiliation on many levels in a culture that values work as the pre-eminent moral discipline and equates professional success with private virtue. The idea that men and white women might suddenly be held to higher ethical standards in the workplace provokes revulsion precisely because it signals a change in social norms.

Much of the pushback, over the last half-decade of public resignations and high-profile firings across the worlds of media, culture, academia, finance, politics and entertainment, has centred on the loss this represents, the valuable contributions that these men and white women might have made had they been allowed to continue their work unchallenged.

This argument is nonsensical for two reasons. Firstly, it assumes that a person who routinely acts on their racist or sexist values can create or contribute to work without drawing on those values. Secondly, it ignores the greater loss to industry and culture brought about by centuries of systematic prejudice.

The capitalist workplace has *always* been an enforcement mechanism for gender and racial norms. When people of colour and white women are routinely passed over for promotion, edged out of their workplaces by harassment or simply not hired at all, that is not just a loss to individuals – it is a loss to society as a whole, as talent and innovation are systematically suppressed in order to concentrate power, money and influence in the hands of white people and of men. Every year in the United States, the Equal Employment Opportunity Commission (EEOC) receives over 100,000 complaints of discrimination at work on the basis of race, sex, gender and ability – but less than one in five of these cases ever results in restitution.[1]

As polite society continues to rail against 'cancel culture', the wealthy and successful deplore dismissals on the basis of prejudice as 'mob justice', even going as far as calling such campaigns 'witch hunts' and 'lynchings'. It is significant that when the white and wealthy feel they are being hard done by, they reach for language used to describe actual, physical, murderous violence enacted within living memory on the bodies of Black and brown people and of white women.

The modern workplace is an enforcing mechanism for hierarchies of racial and gendered power. The expectation that unwanted sexual attention would be part of the work for any female person in paid employment ought to have been buried with a stake in its heart long ago. It persists, however, because sexual violence – including workplace sexual harassment – is a form of discipline. It's a tool of social control. It's a way of demonstrating who, collectively, has power – who belongs in a workplace, and who does not. It's an expression of resentment at the presence of women, girls, queer people and men of colour in what was, for many generations, coded as white men's privileged space. Of course, the idea that women are not supposed to be in 'the workplace', that they have usurped men's 'natural' status and earning potential, is at odds with the reality that women have always worked, and that work has always been necessary.

Workplace sexual harassment performs the same role as street harassment – a constant reminder that whoever you are and whatever you accomplish, you are a body first, and that body is not wholly your own. In 2009, Cornell University published a study that found that waitresses in the United States with blonde hair, smaller waists and larger breasts received higher tips than women without those traits.[2] The findings circulated among restaurant hiring teams and managers eager to jack up sales in the $799-billion restaurant industry. Like Hollywood actresses, waitresses endure endemic sexual harassment – in fact, 90 per cent of women in the US restaurant industry report being subject to unwanted sexual advances at work, and more than half say these interactions occur weekly, according to a Restaurant Opportunities Center report from 2014.[3] For the restaurant industry – which employs 10 per cent of the overall US workforce and where women outnumber men by two to one – the magnitude of sexual harassment is difficult to fathom, especially when you consider that most restaurant workers have very little protection on the job. In America, restaurant workers rely on customer tips to make up their wages – which means that their take-home pay depends on putting up with customers' poor behaviour.

Not all workers can afford to complain about mistreatment. That goes double for farm workers and domestic workers. Decades ago in the United States, domestic workers and farmworkers were excluded from the National Labor Relations Act, which gave workers the right to organise and bargain collectively, along with the Fair Labor Standards Act, which created minimum wage and overtime protections.[4] This was a direct response to pressure from Southern lawmakers, in large part because a huge proportion of those employed in agriculture and domestic service were – and still are – people of colour. Currently, there are more than 700,000 women farmworkers across the United States and more than 2.2 million domestic workers, the majority of whom are women.[5] Domestic workers are also a staggering three times as likely to be living in poverty as other workers.[6]

Domestic and agricultural work is often isolated and invisible, taking place behind the closed doors of private residences or in fields or packing sheds in rural America, so women in these workforces are particularly vulnerable to sexual assault and harassment. As many as eight out of ten women farmworkers interviewed in a recent study by Human Rights Watch reported sexual harassment.[7] Neoliberal 'choice' feminism, which phrases women's liberation as a matter of making better life choices and working harder, has almost nothing to say to women and girls who already work as hard as a human being can and still have little to no protection.

For a long time, feminism was repackaged as an aspirational lifestyle choice: work hard, lean in until you're flat on your face, fatten your lashes and dampen your personality, and you too can be that businesswoman with bouncy hair and the nanny on speed dial, eating salad alone in her twelve minutes of free time a week. Women were sold on the idea that the right to do the work of men was the only human right that mattered. In fact, the idea that paid work itself, any paid work, however punishing and poorly rewarded, is synonymous with freedom is one of the great fallacies of our age.

The annual dinner of the Presidents Club was once one of the most exclusive events on London's social calendar. A male-only, invite-only, extravagant shindig for politicians and bespoke-suited City types, the dinner has long been billed as a night of sanctioned hedonism. Until, that was, a 2017 undercover investigation exposed what was really going on. *Financial Times* journalist Madison Marriage, posing as a hospitality worker, revealed it to be merely seedy and pathetic. The event featured a charity auction, and the prizes included cosmetic surgery – to 'spice up your wife', as the host joked.[8]

The young, female hospitality workers were not explicitly told that they would be expected to serve more than food. Between the crass propositions and clumsy fondling, one detail stands out: the frequency with which Marriage reports that guests held and stroked the girls' hands. Confusing intimacy and predatory sexuality with the expectation of care that should come with power is a grim thing to have to sit through for a night's wage. Not just to laugh at rich men's jokes and put up with their pawing, but to listen to their problems too. The details cast these men in a feeble light. The event was flagged as a vision of a modern Valhalla of masculine indulgence, where the men could offset their bad behaviour with lavish gifts to charity, money buying them a moral pass.

Part of women's work in such situations has always been to pretend to find this sort of man impressive. The Presidents Club debacle had the rhythm of the work requirements for airline stewardesses in the 1960s, before the Pan Am court cases helped the world find words for sexual harassment at work. Airline stewardesses working at Pan American airlines were among the first to take their employers to court to demand less degrading treatment on the job. These were difficult and coveted jobs at a time when women's employment was still restricted in many industries – but stewardesses on American airline groups were required to wear pantomimically revealing outfits and put up with pawing, propositions and routine assault from passengers, who were explicitly informed that eroticised in-flight service was part of what they paid for with their ticket. Advertising campaigns aimed at the 1960s businessmen promised: 'Everyone gets warmth, friendliness and extra care. And someone may get a wife.'[9]

Women were subjected to regular 'weigh-ins', with any weight over 140lb being grounds for termination. That is, of course, unless they were over thirty-two, at which point they were automatically fired (according to former American Airlines stewardess Jeri Fonté, the saying was, 'Thirty-two-skidoo').[10]

When stewardesses finally organised for more respect at work, they had some difficulty explaining to arbitrators that airline stewardessing, like hospitality work, was an actual profession in its own right. Today, jobs that are 'feminised' – jobs that involve organising, cleaning, nurturing and caring for others – are still routinely underpaid, despite the fact that these jobs are precisely the ones that are most vital to the continued functioning of society.

During the Covid-19 lockdowns, when around the world 'essential workers' were permitted to continue doing their jobs as the rest of society huddled indoors, it rapidly became clear that there is a disconnect between how 'essential' a person's work is to others and how much that work is valued.

Today, many straight women still find themselves trapped in relationships, even with gentle and loving men, where the weight of centuries of patriarchal tradition smashes into the ruthless demands of the modern job market. This is not just an abstract argument. The refusal to recognise and support motherhood and domestic work within the economy has dire consequences. If there is no support for the work of parenthood and community care, that leaves people who are obliged to do it – overwhelmingly women, and particularly working-class women – dependent on men for the means of survival. Over the last decade, wages have fallen in real terms and social security has been decimated. At the same time, the cost of childcare has risen beyond the means of a great many working women – unless, like a third of working women in the UK, they choose to go hungry to afford it.[11]

What this means is that both in the paid economy and at home, a great many women are finding that their day-to-day survival, and that of their dependants, is contingent on keeping the men around them happy – on slathering on a smile and tolerating a certain amount of drudgery, whether that be as employers or as partners. How can a person with a chronic illness, a person whose healthcare is dependent on keeping her job, feel safe to come forward about harassment at work when she cannot afford to walk away? How can a person with student loans, a mortgage and small children to care for afford to leave a husband who beats her, a partner who rapes her, when she knows that doing so will mean penury for herself and her family?

More than two-thirds of survivors of domestic abuse have reported their partners withheld money as a method of controlling and mistreating them, according to a recent report by the charity group Women's Aid. '[W]omen told us that the fear of the financial implications of leaving made them stay with their abusive partner for much longer than they would have done if they had had financial independence', researchers said.[12]

Nearly half the women interviewed said they did not have enough money to pay for basic essentials such as food and bills while they were with their abusive partner, and more than two in five women were in debt as a result of the economic abuse, while a third had to give up their home as a result of either experiencing economic abuse or leaving their abusive partner.

The political economy of heterosexuality is structured around keeping women dependent on men. One major reason for the pay gap between the genders is not simply that women are paid less for doing the same jobs. Rather, it is because it's still almost impossible to combine primary parenthood with full-time work, even if you are among the fortunate minority who can afford to employ actual staff – usually other, poorer women. The ideal, for those who can achieve it, is 'work-life balance' – which, in practice, turns out to mean a precarious tightrope walk between different kinds of work, and for women who don't keep their feet, there's no safety net. Of course, women are still saddled with the minor chore of continuing the species, but now they are expected to get on with that risky, dangerous, exhausting work in whatever free time they can scrounge in between shifts in a waged economy where women and girls are concentrated into the lowest-paying, least secure jobs.

Parenthood is not provided for within the schematic of the modern workplace. In the United States, paid maternity leave is a rarity, and in almost every developed economy women are now expected to juggle the demands of 'work' and childcare. At the crucial mid-career stage, when men in their twenties and thirties are building their reputations, women who have children are suddenly focused on hanging on to what they have. This is presented, glibly, as a 'choice' – women choose to have babies, knowing that the market doesn't reward them for it.

Historically, times of economic crisis have usually triggered popular obsession with 'traditional gender roles' and panic about a 'crisis of masculinity'. It happened in the 1980s under Reagan and Thatcher. It happened in the 1930s in Europe and America. It happened in the mid-1800s, as revolutions rolled and tumbled across the Global North. It's happening now, as anxieties about class are transposed into the key of sex and of race.

Women are more often ready to take the shitty, poorly paid service jobs, to perform the 'emotional labour' first identified by Arlie Russell Hochschild in her essential treatise on the 'managed heart'.[13] Women, particularly young women, are not surprised when they are offered the chance to be chewed down, snorted up and horked over the balcony of the rich people's party at the end of the world, because they were never supposed to want anything else. Particularly poor women. Particularly women of colour. Men, by contrast, were raised to expect dignity and decency in work, respect and security outside of it, and when none of that is forthcoming, it is far easier to turn around and blame women.

Women, however, have been cheated just as much as men. They may now be legally permitted to perform the same low-waged, insecure jobs that men do, but that doesn't mean they're required to feel grateful for them. Women, too, are struggling to keep the lights on, to care for themselves and their families, and when a woman demands a fraction of the love, care and attention – even, whisper it, the pleasure that she's supposed to owe to men – the response ranges from confusion to outright violence.

Over the course of the twentieth and twenty-first centuries, the insistence that girls could do anything was repurposed into an insistence that girls should do everything, thanklessly and for free. This, for a long time, was the outer limit of what feminist liberation was supposed to mean in genteel, liberal circles – women now had the freedom to work both inside and outside the domestic sphere, and this, it was insisted, was what our foremothers had fought for, and now it was won. Game over. Go home, ladies – your kids are waiting for their dinner, and you might get on another laundry load and still grab six hours' sleep. The fact that women beyond the aristocratic classes had always worked 'outside' the home was conveniently glossed over, as was the fact that for most working people, the freedom to toil for fifty hours a week for someone else's profit had not always been the highest conceivable freedom. Few movements have marched for the right to spend less time with your family.

In just the same way, the cliche that the modern working women could 'have it all' – as long as 'it all' meant a life of dogged conformity to the triumvirate of boss, husband and children – metastisised into the obligation for women to do it all, and faster, and for two-thirds the pay. If they were unhappy, if it had been years since they could remember having real fun, if they found themselves awake at four in the morning with a sick kid and a deadline due the next day, shaking with exhaustion, well, wasn't that what feminism had fought for? Wasn't that what freedom meant? If women were unhappy, wasn't it their own fault for not leaning in enough, not working hard enough, not being better, doing more?

That's what neoliberal 'choice' feminism was supposed to mean, according to the logic of those who have confused not having had a proper night's sleep in years with being 'woke'. Patriarchy ties a woman's economic potential and activity to her perceived fertility and femininity. She can only earn well in her job if she is also doing the work of being a 'good woman' – a social standard that is constantly shifting and largely unattainable, entirely by design.

If we understand women's bodies as a site of work, it is equally important to understand that women are alienated from their bodies in the same way that all workers are alienated from ownership of their labour – and for the same reasons. Every time a woman tries to truly reclaim her body, it should be understood in the same valence as a factory sit-in or an occupation.

In that vein, it is vital that individual women abandon the idea that structural, economic injustice will pass them over if only they are only pretty, pleasant and well-behaved. That precise fantasy is what keeps workers across the world striving and slaving in jobs that erode their dignity and shatter their bodies: because they believe that it's possible to escape an exploitative system by working harder. They've read enough stories where hard work and gumption are rewarded, and even though they can see how unfair and unjust the labour market is, they still believe that they might be the ones to get lucky. In fact, social mobility – the raw chance of any individual person escaping the social class he or she was born into – has only gone down over the past decade, while at the same time, belief in the story of social mobility has gone up.

The harsher the working world gets, the more we believe we can escape it on its own terms. Work has become a religion for my exhausted generation, even as we look set to be the first cohort in living memory to earn less money, own less property and die earlier than our parents.

The only time that mainstream feminism acknowledges that work itself might be a problem is when it comes to sex work. For decades, feminists have been bitterly divided on the subject of whether sex work is inherently abusive. Many campaigners for the abolition of the sex trade argue that you can't call prostitution a free choice, because nobody can consent to work that they have to do in order to survive.

But is it possible for a person to consent meaningfully to any work at all, if they have to do that work to survive? That question is only ever asked about sex work – and it's a revealing omission. In societies that otherwise worship the free market and insist that freedom means letting people sell whatever they like, however they like, sex workers are still stigmatised and criminalised. Many public and private feminist organisations are all too eager for police to step in and stop women, in particular, from selling sex. Most organisations which oppose sex work want criminal charges to fall primarily on men who buy sex – but in practice, it is almost impossible to criminalise the customer without consequences for the sex worker, especially if she is undocumented. Anti-prostitution charities have, in fact, worked in tandem with border police to track down and deport migrant sex workers.

This collusion with the carceral state relies on a singular moral argument: that it is definitionally impossible for people in desperate situations to consent to sex when they need the money.

'The assumption of choice [for sex workers] leads to the conclusion of consent,' writes Rachel Moran, a campaigner against the sex trade and former sex worker, in her memoir *Paid For: My Journey Through Prostitution*. However, she continues,

choice and consent are erroneous concepts here. Their invalidity rests on the fact that a woman's compliance in prostitution is a response to circumstances beyond her control, and this produces an environment which prohibits even the possibility of true consent. There is a difference between consent and reluctant submission. As a lawyer and scholar Catharine MacKinnon says, 'When fear and despair produce acquiescence and acquiescence is taken to mean consent, consent is not a meaningful concept.'[14]

This is a convincing argument. But why is the question of consent on the job only posed about sex work, rather than *all* work? One reason it is so important to use the phrase 'sex work' is that it underlines both the fact that this is work, and that the work, not the sex, is the problem. Rather than being 'sex positive' or 'sex negative' – the traditional positions for feminists on this issue – I prefer a position that is 'sex critical' and 'work negative'.

If sex work cannot be consensual, neither can many other things that people are forced to do to survive. But the answer isn't to abolish sex work: it's to abolish all work, at least in its current form, whereby people are coerced into labour that wastes their energy and wrecks their bodies simply in order to survive.

It's important to remember that abolitionist feminism – feminism that seeks, as its core goal, to elimate sex work – has always had an embarrassing aspect of white saviourism. The spokeswomen are often wealthy, cisgendered white women who see themselves as rescuing sex workers, who are more likely to be trans, working class, foreign nationals, Black or Indigenous. In fact, the abolitionist narrative often specifically excludes those sex workers who are white, cis and middle class. This comes down to the racist assumption that – for example – a broke, Black trans woman cannot possibly be capable of making her own choices – so a rich, white cis woman had better step in and make them for her.

The campaign to abolish the sex industry is often quick to ally itself with law enforcement and with state immigration control, as a significant proportion of women who sell sex for a living do so because they are undocumented and unable to access the 'legitimate' economy. Rather than work to create a more human immigration system that does not terrorise refugee and migrant women with the threat of deportation and shut them out of the economy, anti-sex-work campaigners have colluded with immigration controls to detain and deport sex workers in the name of 'saving' them from the shame of prostitution.

Why is selling sex for money still seen as a shameful thing to do, the ultimate sign that a woman has 'fallen'? Why is that hoary old stigma still hanging around, standing in between sex workers and crucial protections on the job?

Here's one reason: sex workers disrupt the sexual marketplace.

It's like this. If all women are competing for better conditions by bartering their sexuality for male protection, then sex workers are undercutting that bargaining process – essentially, they are 'scabs', no better than strike-breakers. The stigmatisation of women sex workers by non-sex-worker women down the generations makes a lot more sense if one understands that for a very long time, erotic abstinence – among those who had the option – was a form of collective bargaining, one of the only ways women had to negotiate for better living and labour conditions. You held out for the best and least brutal man – and that worked only as long as you knew that almost everyone else was holding out, too. If everyone else was just leaping into bed for cash or for fun or any time they felt a panic in the loins, depriving yourself suddenly made less sense.

Emma Goldman – the anarchist organiser of the early twentieth century, who recounted her own brief, abortive attempts at sex work in her youth – wrote that, 'The wife who married for money, compared with the prostitute ... is the true scab. She is paid less, gives much more in return in labour and care, and is absolutely bound to her master.'[15]

Whorephobia is the sharp edge of slut shaming, but both fulfil the same function in our socio-sexual scripts. The anger about and at sex workers is often that they get paid for what women are expected to do for free. The great irony is that while women are still expected, time and again, to put their sexuality to work in the office and elsewhere, women who explicitly sell sexual services are still subject to social stigma, criminalisation and state persecution. Women are expected to manage predatory heterosexual male sexuality in return for a wage – that's just 'real life', there is no alternative; grow up or find a different job, sweetheart – but actually asking to be paid for sex remains taboo. 'Whore' is still an insult. Sex and love are the things one is not supposed to acknowledge as work or ask for payment for – women are supposed to provide them for free, to men, without demanding anything concrete in return. And that is, I am convinced, part of the reason sex workers are so stigmatised. They dare to ask for cash for what should be paid in kind, if at all.

Yes, sex work is a job like any other – but that's not necessarily a good thing. Like a great many jobs it can be dull, exhausting and insecure; it can be bad for your health and well-being; and it does not afford automatic dignity to the worker, who is often doing it not because they want to, but because it's the best way they've found to cover their costs. To describe prostitution as 'work' in the way that any other job done for money is 'work' is uncomfortable for anyone invested in the orthodoxy that paid employment is always an unequivocal moral good.

But sex, again, is not the problem. Work is the problem. And sex work is the only industry where the question of workers' consent is even considered. If a person has to sell sex to survive, can they fully and freely consent to that work? That's a crucial question. If that question were asked about every job in every industry, it might lead to some uncomfortable truths.

The truth is that feminised, unpaid, compulsory domestic labour is real work. Care work is real work. Reproductive work is real work. Sexual service is real work. They may be forms of work whose rewards are in kind and uncertain, forms of work that are insecure, treacherous and badly remunerated, but they are all work – and if we accept them as work, a number of important things become clear:

Firstly, that the system of labour under capitalism is fundamentally non-consensual. The relationship we have with the working world is exploitative – literally and definitionally so, because the structure of our economy exists to extract profit from our labour. This system is abusive by its nature, and because we see no alternative, we become apologists for our own exploitation. That means that any call for a better understanding of consent – real consent – is, inevitably, a call to redefine work.

Secondly, that the structure of the modern labour market acts to keep women, girls and other feminised bodies in a position of economic dependence, one that limits both their personal power *and* their political power. There can be nothing approaching economic justice in a nation that refuses to accommodate reproductive work within the paid economy, any state that insists that women and girls, particularly women and girls of colour, continue to do the lioness's share of the domestic, sexual, emotional and reproductive labour for low pay or no pay and without a whisper of complaint. This is what men and boys are least prepared, in every sense, to relinquish – the privilege of not having to think about the dishes, the day care, the dangling threads of the social fabric, the privilege of assuming women and girls will continue to sort it all out, with or without their consent.

And lastly, that this sexual revolution is fundamentally an economic revolution. It is a demand for change that reaches beyond private bedrooms to reshape the nature of work and family. Authoritarianism, by its very nature, cannot cope with a culture of consent – and the coming sexual revolution refuses to accept the authority of bosses, husbands or heads of the household to decide.

8

The Home Front

Sooner or later, every revolution comes down to who does the dishes. For all the gains women have made in the 'workplace', there is one crucial front where inequality remains entrenched: the right to equal work itself. Across the world, women are still doing the majority of the essential work that holds human society together, and they are doing it largely invisibly and for free.

It is still women, and particularly women of colour, who do most of the cooking, the cleaning, the childbearing and the childrearing without which every economy on earth would collapse overnight. It is generally women who care for sick and elderly relatives, women who devote their spare energies to organising family life, making sure doctors' appointments are made, smoke alarms replaced, birthdays celebrated, bottoms wiped and tempers soothed. Women do all this not because they are better at it, but because someone has to, and because men largely refuse.

If we want our machinery of employment, power and profit to keep running, someone has to do the hard work of looking after everyone. Someone has to have the babies and raise the kids who grow up to run the machines. Someone has to make sure we have homes to go to and hot food on the table at the end of the day. Someone has to keep communities and families from falling apart. Someone has to look after anyone who is too young, or too old, or too sick to look after themselves. And usually, that's women. Gender inequality is hardwired into the way the world economy operates. Women and girls have been required to do certain types of work purely on the basis that they are women – and then, because they are women, the work that they do has been falsely assumed to have no economic meaning. 'Housework is not work. Sex work is not work. Emotional work is not work,' writes Jess Zimmerman in the essay 'Where's my cut'. 'Why? Because they don't take effort? No, because women are supposed to provide them uncompensated, out of the goodness of our hearts.'[1]

We've already seen how public life is poisoned by male entitlement to women's services, sexual attention and emotional labour. That entitled attitude does not end at the office door or the college gates. One recent study of the value of women's unpaid labour valued it at $10.8 trillion worldwide – more than the combined income of the fifty wealthiest global companies, including Walmart, Apple and Amazon.[2] Mothers who also do paid work have been quietly drowning under the double shift of office hours and domestic duties for decades. The division of domestic labour is hard to accurately assess because it relies on self-reported data, and women – plagued by guilt at not being good enough at doing it all – tend to underestimate the hours they spend working in the home; men, by contrast, tend to overestimate their own contribution. During the Covid-19 lockdowns of 2020, study after study reported that 'most of the additional housework and childcare associated' with the crisis fell on women.[3]

Men, unfortunately, still seem to want housewives. Who wouldn't? In the past several decades, as women's employment has risen to match men's, men have barely increased their share of work on the home front. In fact, attitudes are actually regressing, as almost half of millennial men now believe that women should be primarily responsible for cooking, cleaning and childcare. Many of these men consider themselves progressive and are vocally comfortable with the idea of women's equality in the paid workplace – but unwilling, when pressed, to give up the privilege of having a woman to take care of the boring, repetitive chores. The unequal division of domestic labour is the last unfought battle of women's liberation. And it's a battle that has, in the past, been almost impossible to fight – because it plays out in private kitchens, behind bedroom doors, in individual relationships where women cannot organise collectively.

Without reliable ways of coercing women into continuing to do that work for free, capitalism as we know it would crumble. It's no surprise, then, that it is in the context of the home – in the context of the family – that sexual and economic freedom is most under attack.

Hundreds of years ago, almost everyone worked from home. Before the Industrial Revolution there was little distinction between the work that went into producing the things a family could sell – meat, grain, cloth, artefacts – and the work required to keep that family functional. Cooking, cleaning and raising kids were not separate activities. It is only in the past century and a half that the idea of 'separate spheres' of work for men and women – only one of which is valued in the economy – took hold. It is only in the past fifty years that the management of a home was left to one woman without an extended network of adults: not so long ago, if you didn't employ servants, there was a good chance you were one.[4] And it is only in the past two generations that the definition of 'liberation' for women became the dubious privilege of working full time in the paid economy alongside full-time unpaid labour at home.

This is known as 'having it all', but, again, for anyone without an army of paid staff, it feels more like having a breakdown. In practice, you can only 'have it all' as long as you're white, straight, middle class and able-bodied; you can only have it as long as what you want is an office job, a monogamous marriage, children and a house in an up-and-coming area; you can only have it all as long as you never asked if there was, or could be, anything more.

Over the course of my lifetime, the apparently radical idea that women could do anything rapidly became the command that women must do everything, faster, with perfect hair, making it all look effortless, and if we didn't manage it, that was our own fault.

Over those same thirty years, welfare programmes were destroyed, wages were cut, and spending on social care, healthcare, disability care, elderly care, education and childcare was slashed across the Global North, as economic orthodoxy demanded that bailouts for banks and tax breaks for the wealthy be financed by cuts to public spending. These are industries that already employed a large number of women workers – so after the financial crash of 2008, as austerity programmes rolled across Europe and America, millions of women working in caring industries found themselves facing pay cuts and job losses. As more and more governments refused to pay for the work of 'life-making', the burden of that work fell overwhelmingly on women – largely because men and boys refused to take it on. On top of unpaid childcare and domestic work, women and girls found themselves paying for the failure of the financial system, struggling by on unliveable wages, working longer hours and taking on more debt. This amounts to an enormous transfer of wealth from working-class women to wealthy men and their families.

Women's liberation has always been an issue of economic justice. But the only feminism in which neoliberal capitalism was ever interested was the sort that could be made to dance in a cage for money and be told it was already free: the aspirational, 'lean-in' feminism, summed up so neatly in Facebook COO Sheryl Sandberg's book of the same title, which spoke chiefly to and about wealthy, white heterosexual women in the Global North. Everyone else should, by working harder and making better choices, aspire to be as much like a wealthy, white, straight woman as possible.

As political researcher Arlie Russell Hochschild observed:

> Most women without children spend much more time than men on housework; with children, they devote more time to both housework and child care. Just as there is a wage gap between men and women in the workplace, there is a 'leisure gap' between them at home. Most women work one shift at the office or factory and a 'second shift' at home.[5]

Have-it-all feminism, choice feminism – market feminism – was and remains the only form of women's liberation acceptable to commercial society, the sort of feminism that can be made into an aspiration, something to reach for individually, something that can be slimmed down and crammed into a pair of pumps for people who sell make-up brushes and magazine subscriptions, something that leaves us smiling until our faces go into spasm, on call for a rotating shift of boyfriends, husbands, employers. This model of aspirational womanhood as constant, thankless, soul-annihilating work has been rebranded as empowering. Where are the calls for women to be liberated to work *less*?

For modern women as a political class, exhaustion and liberation are now assumed to be synonymous. This is, in part, a function of a dominant culture where hard work is a moral imperative – no self-respecting modern woman would freely admit to wanting *less* work. Instead, the 'liberated woman' of the twenty-first century works as long and as hard for pay as any man, and considers herself lucky. She stays as late as she can in the office in order to prove herself worth her wage, then rushes back to care for her home, manage the domestic chores, raise her children and check in on any friends and relatives who may need her. Any spare minutes she finds in between packing school lunches and juggling spreadsheets are devoted to maintaining her appearance, keeping her hair lush and her body tight and her wardrobe chic and appropriate, whether she is slogging up the corporate ladder or climbing stairs to nowhere in the gym. If she wakes in the night wondering when she last felt like a person, she'll soon have another appointment, another responsibility, and besides, there are always beta blockers and Botox.

'Fighting for equality is often misunderstood as simply being offered the same terms as men on paper,' writes the late journalist Dawn Foster in her book *Lean Out*. 'In many ways we already have that. What we don't have is emancipation: the opportunity to be free of social and external shackles that perpetuate inequality.'[6]

The work that is supposed to define women's lives and provide an answer to the small-hours question of whether she has earned her oxygen for the day is work that is largely unpaid and usually unappreciated. It is made invisible. It is not seen as work at all – not even when it's work that richer women pay poorer women to do for them, often with the attendant feelings of guilt at having morally failed as women. 'You're just naturally better at these things' is the universal refrain of the husband or boyfriend who can't understand why the woman he loves keeps 'nagging' him to do household chores. And one reason that it is uncomfortable to talk about social reproduction is that social reproduction is impossible to talk about without talking about race and gender.

For centuries, the work of running a great many white households has been undertaken by women of colour and, depending on the country, by working-class white women and girls. For several hundred years, in fact, Western and Western-colonised societies solved the problem of social reproduction with an army of unpaid and low-paid workers, most of whom had no better option than to facilitate the lives of the middle class and scaffold the fantasy of the self-sufficient white family. This, and this alone, is what has freed up white men to do so much of the work of 'action', in Arendt's terms – including the 'action' of defining social narratives, the 'action' of justifying these hierarchies as somehow 'natural'.[7]

That abject appeal to nature is insidious. It implies that people of colour and white women should not complain about having to do all the boring, repetitive, dirty jobs, because they are 'naturally' good at them, whereas men are 'naturally' better at fighting and setting things on fire. Women shouldn't complain about having too much to do – they're just naturally better at 'multitasking'. In fact, studies have repeatedly shown that human brains of every gender are much better at doing one task at a time – and nobody is born knowing how to clean a toilet or sterilise a bottle. But men's collective refusal to do these duller, more thankless feminine tasks – thankless precisely because they are femininised and racialised – is a learned helplessness that eventually wears down resistance. It is the domestic equivalent of a siege. If he refuses to do it for long enough, or does it badly, or has to be reminded again and again, or makes enough of a fuss, eventually she will conclude that it's not worth the trouble, and give up and do it herself.

Instead of being recognised as work, social reproduction is usually reimagined as a natural aspect of womanhood, part of the rent women and girls owe for the privilege of being born in bodies that are deemed female. It is ephemeral work, work that needs to be done over and over again. It is not work that produces profit directly. But it is as essential to capitalism – indeed, to any human economic system – as the work of building infrastructure and slaughtering livestock and short-selling stocks. It's more important than a great deal of work that gets paid for in the so-called 'real' economy – even though the majority of it is done for free. Social reproduction is invisible, but it underpins everything else. It is the messy stitching behind the neat embroidery of public life, the reason anyone has a clean shirt to wear or a family network to fall back on. It is the active work of caring for ourselves and one another.

Globalisation has created what theorist Nancy Fraser calls a 'crisis of care'.[8] In the decade and more since the financial crisis of 2008, as wages fell and rents soared, the nuclear-family model has come under more and more pressure to pick up the slack. The burden of austerity in countries like Britain has fallen disproportionately on women, as social services, adult care programmes and childcare provision were cut in the name of saving money the state had squandered on propping up the banks. In Britain, by 2021, £37 billion less will be spent on working-age social security compared with 2010, despite rising prices and living costs, according to estimates produced by the House of Commons library[9] – and 86 per cent of the burden of austerity since 2010 has fallen on women.[10]

In the United States, which has some of the least 'family-friendly' work policies on the planet, many households struggle to cover the cost of childcare, which can run to a third or half an individual parent's yearly salary. With no parental leave in place and fractured networks of social support, families have been forced to choose whose career to sacrifice – and when that choice comes down to cash, it's usually a woman's job that doesn't make the cut. In every industry women are dropping out of the workplace in droves, not by choice, but because they can't afford to stay employed and raise children.[11]

Newspapers report that women still shoulder the majority of the responsibility for childcare as if this were a morally neutral statement – as if the missing pieces were not the millions of men too lazy, sexist and selfish to take care of themselves and their families. During the Covid-19 crisis, as schools and day-care centres shut down, it was overwhelmingly mothers who took on the burden of full-time education and care for children, often alongside paid work. As a result, it was overwhelmingly women who left their jobs – sometimes permanently – in order to do the necessary work of care to sustain the species during a global pandemic. When this was discussed in the public sphere, it was in terms of how damaging Covid-19 was for women – but this was not the case. Covid-19 did not drive women out of paid work. Men did that, sabotaging women's careers by refusing to do an equal share of the domestic and reproductive work even at a time of crisis where that work was more necessary than ever.

And yet, whenever the unequal division of domestic work or the refusal to support that work within the economy are mentioned, it is always in terms of how much women are struggling – rather than whose fault it is. There is a huge taboo around asking openly for men or for society to actually do more to help. Shame and self-doubt muzzle women's collective frustration. There are so many reasons why a woman staggering under the double burden of social reproduction and paid work might decide it's easier to just get on with it. There's simple exhaustion – who has time to organise or protest when they're barely sleeping? There's the fear of being seen as a failure, of not being a good enough mother and partner. There's the enormous cultural stigma against being a 'nag'. And, finally, there are the relationships themselves, those relationships with men, which are so central to identity and security in an uncertain world.

Time and again, culture reminds us that to hold a man accountable is to become unworthy of his love. There are plenty of bad words for women who dare to enforce boundaries: bitch, nag, shrill, shrew. There are almost none for men who manipulate their wives and girlfriends into acting as their unpaid cook, maid and personal assistant.

Women pay for men's moral cowardice in many different ways, but mainly with money. Even women who are the chief earners in a family do more housework than their husbands,[12] according to data that is usually presented as if the intransigence of men were an inevitability that must be accommodated rather than a collective failure of character. Data is not available on how much more unpaid work women do if they are married to spineless throwbacks so inured against housework that they refuse to learn to work a washing machine.

When a person is coerced into doing work she did not choose, when she is not free to set her own boundaries or negotiate her own hours, that is exploitation, just as surely as the suppression of truck drivers' wages, or the theft of restaurant workers' tips to fund bonuses for their bosses is exploitation. But the traditional framework for understanding exploitation only takes into account the abuse and theft of men's time, rights and labour. When women are expected to put their hearts and bodies into service for someone else's benefit, shamed and threatened with ostracism if they refuse and punished with violence if they complain, we should understand that as an architecture of work exploitation.

The idea that feminism was ever about the 'freedom to work' at all is the greatest 'gotcha' of modern gender politics. Certainly, the fight for equal pay and for access to traditionally male workplaces is and remains vital, because the legal right to support herself is the basis of any woman's independence from men. But most women, for most of human history, have worked.

Automation and technology have not freed women from unpaid labour any more than they have freed paid workers from the obligation to toil to survive – they have simply increased the amount of work to be done. The invention of technology designed to reduce women's labour around the home – like the vacuum cleaner and the washing machine – did not lead to a decrease in the amount of work women were doing. It just led to an increase in standards – and a decrease in the number of women being employed as domestic servants in larger, richer homes.

Domestic work is neither evenly distributed nor freely chosen. Women, in particular, are pressured or bullied or passive-aggressively guilt tripped into doing the vital work of social reproduction because they know that if they don't, nobody else will. Without social reproduction, capitalism would collapse. But if social reproduction were properly acknowledged, respected and supported by the monetary system, the growth models of capitalism that we have right now would – you've guessed it – collapse. This is why universal basic income – the idea of a wage paid collectively by society to support a base-level dignified existence – has always been a feminist demand. The 'wages for housework' movement of the 1980s, which is enjoying a renaissance, was all about the demand that women's work be recognised and valued. As one of the leaders of the movement, Selma James, wrote:

> housewives are involved in the production and ... reproduction of workers, what Marx calls labour power. They service those who are daily destroyed by working for wages and who need to be daily renewed; and they care for and discipline those who are being prepared to work when they grow up.[13]

The privilege of having someone to do the boring, thankless work of keeping your household going is not one that most men, even millennial men, are willing to relinquish.

By refusing to let go of that privilege, men are directly responsible for edging their wives and girlfriends out of the paid workplace.

Since the mid-1980s, according to one recent study,[14] no more than 2 per cent of female high-school seniors (aged seventeen to eighteen) reported planning to be full time 'homemakers' by the age of thirty. But by that age 15 to 18 per cent of women have left the workforce to care for children – in part because of the rising costs of childcare. A great many women who have given up paid work, reduced their hours or curtailed their leisure time have been, effectively, coerced into doing it – coerced by individual male intransigence and an economic order that refuses to value the essential work of care.[15]

There are, as we have already seen, any number of situations where male dominance operates on a structural level – where individual men are not really to blame for women's lack of power over their lives. This is not one of those situations. When it comes to the home front, men's learned laziness is the problem. It is men and boys, refusing to give up the privilege of having someone else take care of their domestic needs, who are standing in the way of progress. Studies have shown that men who claim they have 'different standards' of cleanliness become resentful and even aggressive when women don't keep up the standards they claim not to care about. Young mothers of my generation are struggling hard to solve that impossible equation, trying to do at least two full-time jobs at once and retain some agency over their lives. The fact that most mothers of young children work incredibly hard and sacrifice more than you'd dare to conceive of doesn't mean that the hard work and sacrifice are necessary, useful or an inevitable part of a woman's lot.

The cruel and concrete consequences of all this are that many heterosexual women considering whether to start families face a choice between a family life in which they risk being exploited by those who are supposed to love them, forced to do years of thankless drudgery while trying to keep a lid on their anger – or no family life at all, in the traditional sense. This means that women are held hostage to their own relationships. It means that most women can't, practically speaking, 'just leave' a partner who is selfish and unloving.

Young women are still taught, by implication and example, that a good marriage is one in which a woman is not at risk of being maimed or killed, rather than where she is treated like a human person whose life, energy and time actually matter. The only reason that this is still tolerated within heterosexual relationships is because the bar is that low. Many of the women who have told me tearfully that they didn't expect marriage to mean years of hassling an apparently educated adult man to pick up after himself follow that up by saying, 'But he's a good person – he would never hit me.' Women in heterosexual relationships are still expected to settle for decades of disrespect, whereas men are politely asked not to commit murder. Women are obliged to put up with a certain degree of unhappiness in their marriages, while men get to walk away, and often do, as soon as things get difficult.

The one thing that would make this problem vanish is dependable, well-paid, affordable childcare, free for those on low incomes, tax-deductible for everyone else. Most states refuse to pay for this – and the problem isn't simply the price tag. The problem is that publicly available childcare would give women far more bargaining power than the world wants them to have. Women and femmes who plan to have children would no longer need to shackle themselves to lacklustre, undependable men because they cannot afford a child without a co-parent.

The greatest gap, today, between men and women in the world of work is in time spent not working either for pay or on domestic or reproductive tasks – in other words, it's in leisure time.[16] Men and boys in relationships with women, even when both partners are employed full time, still have far more hours to spend on 'what they will' – time to learn things and make things and play and protest, time to actually have *fun*. Most of the representations of unpaid domestic work in pop culture still tell the familiar story of the nagging wife or the stressed-out girlfriend haranguing her partner who just wants to have fun. She's always the villain in these stories, the killjoy who sours the mood because she's constitutionally unable to relax – rather than because she's exhausted, frustrated and with far more work and responsibility than she signed up for.

The fight over domestic work is the great unfinished battle of modern feminism. Many of us watched our mothers and grandmothers fight and lose this domestic Cold War; many of us live with the heavy remnants of generations of swallowed rage. I carry in my body the memory of my mother's directionless distress, my grandmother's towering frustration at finding herself trapped by love and circumstance and lack of options and lack of money into scrubbing the sink and serving dinner for ungrateful men who expected lifelong service as the price of their essential presence. This is not an unusual family history. It is part of what is meant when you hear any man say that his mother was a strong woman, often with an undertone of judgement. She did what she had to do; she suffered and worked and didn't complain. So why can't you?

I do not believe that women should be required to be that strong in order to be worthy, to be loved. Like so many women and non-binary people of my generation, I'm the first one in my family who hasn't had to develop that sort of strength in order to survive. From a very young age, I saw how miserable it was making the women in my family to have to summon that sort of strength every day to do work they resented, work that was never recognised, work they were not free, in any meaningful sense, to reject.

There is enormous difference between choosing to do that work and being bullied into doing it because nobody else will, because your partner doesn't 'see' the mess, because your husband expects to be told what to do and praised every time he remembers to empty the dishwasher, because he has been taught that it's not his job, and that eventually someone – ideally a woman – will come along and do it for him.

The home, for a great many women, and particularly for a great many mothers, is a hostile work environment. Neoliberal capitalism coped with the threat of the sexual revolution, of second-wave feminism, by making women's work invisible, by subsuming it within the demands of the nuclear family.

The nuclear family – a straight married couple living with their children and nobody else – does not describe my life, or many of my peers' lives. Nor does it describe our childhoods. More than half of millennials grew up with parents who divorced or separated, or in single-parent families. That means that most of us have seen first-hand how painfully the nuclear family can fail – and how hard it can be for a parent to struggle alone. We have fought to balance the expectation that a successful adult life involves living with a long-term committed romantic partner with the awareness that it doesn't always work out that way in the long run. We learned that the nuclear family was not synonymous with security – but we still wanted to be safe, to love and be loved, and to form families.

Today, in America, in Britain and elsewhere, the majority of adults are not cohabiting with a romantic partner. Millennials in particular are more likely to live with friends, flatmates, family members or alone than they are to live with a romantic partner. The reason for this is not because we've collectively decided to tear up our parents' social norms. It's economic necessity.

But the nuclear family, too, was always about economic necessity. The 'traditional' nuclear family, which really enjoyed only a brief heyday for three decades in the mid-twentieth century, was not just a social ideal but an economic strategy – a way of organising society to maximise production. A way of making sure that the work of cooking, cleaning, childcare and social organisation got done on an individual, domestic level. For many decades, a huge part of the reason that women in particular sought out traditional marriage was that it was the major way of securing your financial future, of making sure that you and any kids you had would be able to survive in a society that didn't provide for childcare, didn't allow many women to work for money, and paid them very little when it did. A major reason that men sought out marriage was to have, in effect, free labour – to have someone to organise their lives, to clean and keep house and raise the children while he, in theory, went out to win bread.

The ideology of romance, and the insistence that straight people marry and form two-adult households because they have 'found the one', is a surprisingly recent innovation. It also makes the nuclear family precarious – after all, if every household is centred on a single romantic partnership between adults, the family itself is ended in its current form. This, of course, plays another function – it keeps people tied into those relationships. In particular, it gives women, who still earn less money and are far more likely to be in part-time or unwaged work, a vested interest in staying in relationships they might otherwise leave, because their financial future depends on keeping that single relationship solid.

The traditional male-breadwinning model has been obsolete for decades on an economic as well as a cultural level – wage repression means that nobody can afford to support a household on a single salary any more. The nuclear family makes far less sense as an economic unit when two adults both work full time outside the home, and there are no other adults around to do social reproductive work. And yet there is an airless void in culture where alternatives to the nuclear family might be imagined.

As it becomes harder and harder to find responsible men to form families with, there's a growing trend of young straight women choosing to raise children together – and of single mothers doubling up to form households where they can provide mutual aid and support.

Marriage was always supposed to provide security, stability and space. For a great many people, for a great many centuries, it did no such thing, but there was no choice but to swallow your complaints and hollow out your heart. There were rooms in the House of the Father that were forbidden, where violence and terror chattered in the walls and shame skulked in the unswept corners, and to live there was fearful, and sometimes painful, but exile would be worse. Today, the nuclear family is transparently failing even on its own terms: for most married people, legal partnership no longer provides even the basic economic security that was part of the deal from the outset.

Millennials have had to learn to live without security, but that doesn't mean we have to live without commitment or community or care. This is what the theorist Sophie Lewis calls 'full surrogacy' – a radical alternative to the patriarchal family unit.[17]

Thinking beyond 'the family' as a way to organise a life of intimacy, care and commitment makes economic sense, and it makes social sense. It does not, however, make cultural sense. It is still taboo to suggest that the two-parent heterosexual nuclear family – which is how most modern societies insist on defining family – might not be the ideal way for everyone. It is taboo to mention the fact that for women, children and queer youth, 'the family' can often be a place of violence and abuse rather than the balm against an uncaring world that it is supposed to provide. The withering away of nurturing social structures outside the individual family makes it doubly uncomfortable to imagine that the family itself might be failing us.

The ideology of 'the family' is fundamentally authoritarian. In fact, the attachment to the ideal of a male-headed, straight, nuclear household is at the heart of conservative thought. The 'strict father model' of society, according to linguist and researcher George Lakoff, is the unifying metaphor that guides our collective political imagination. This is an organising metaphor or 'frame' – meaning that it shapes how people see the world, how they understand their place in it, and how they define right and wrong. This 'strict father' model is fundamentally authoritarian. For those who subscribe to it, the world is a dangerous, competitive place, and, 'What is needed in this kind of a world is a strong, strict father who can protect the family ... [and] what is required of the child is obedience.'[18]

In other words, the ideal of the nuclear, heterosexual household, ruled by a stern male figure with a woman and children subservient to his authority, is an ideal on more than merely a practical, individual level – the family ideal is a forming metaphor in human societies. Today's conservatives see themselves as part of a world which ought to be guided and disciplined by 'strict fathers' and this, quite literally, is the meaning of 'patriarchy' – the word means not 'rule by men' but 'rule by fathers'.

Lakoff points out that there is an explicit 'connection between the strict father worldview and free market capitalism. The link is the morality of self-interest, which is the conservative version of Adam Smith's view of capitalism.'[19] In a world of winners and losers, based on savage competition, strict fathers are necessary to instil discipline and protect the children from harm. This is also how the ideal government should behave, which is why conservatives are not against government per se – they tend to support lavish spending on policing, the penal system and the military. What conservatives are against, according to Lakoff, is 'nurturance and care. They are against social programs that take care of people – early childhood education, Medicaid for the poor, raising the minimum wage, unemployment [benefit] … that is what they are trying to eliminate on moral grounds.'[20]

Patriarchal morality is still a governing ideology in the modern world – and it has led the modern world into terrible danger. In recent decades it has become more and more clear that the 'strict father model' does not serve the interests of human flourishing on a metaphorical or a literal level. Without systems in place to encourage mutual care and nurturance, human societies cannot flourish; a society based on dominance, violence and short-term competition will tear itself apart.

The strict father worldview is failing on its own terms, even as the world trembles in the unstable fists of authoritarian strongmen we elected to run the planet off the rails. The West, terrified by the future, chose 'strict fathers' to lead it into the frightening, febrile adolescence of the twenty-first century, but those strict fathers turned out to be faithless, boorish brutes, utterly unfit for the responsibility that came with the power. Men like Trump, like Pence, like Johnson and Bolsonaro and Modi, and before them men like George W. Bush, like David Cameron and Scott Morrison – these are men who are and were masters at the moral logic of self-interest, who knew nothing but how to lie and cheat and bully their way to power they believed themselves born to. They were as brutal and untrustworthy in their private lives as they were as leaders of nations, and the millions of citizens living under their unpredictable savagery saw a language of private shame and terror repeated on a global scale. The way 'strict father' leaders treat their citizens is the way that abusive men treat their wives and children – with brutal, entitled contempt. And the way that women, immigrants, working-class people, young people, disabled people, queer people and people of colour are forced to live under 'strict father' systems of governance is the way abused women and children learn to live under the aegis of an unpredictable father figure – negotiating, retreating into shame and self-blame, wearing themselves out to appease a cruel and volatile power structure. Learning to mistrust our own desires, to fear the small and howling human core of us that says that we are worthy, that we are allowed to want things.

There is another alternative, of course. You can leave the house of the father. You can walk out of there and not look back. You can refuse to obey the diktat of compulsory domesticity, refuse to be an obedient daughter or a long-suffering wife. You can pursue forms of family that do not require you to suffer in silence and squash down your selfhood. 'If the family you came from sucked, make up a new one,' writes Lidia Yuknavitch in her searing memoir of survival, *The Chronology of Water*. 'Look at all the people there are to choose from. If the family you are in hurts, get on the bus. Like now.'[21]

'Womanhood' is coded as work, and like any work, those with the least control are taught to believe that freedom to choose one's own oppression is the only freedom worth imagining. If womanhood is work, then under late-stage capitalism that work has become more insecure, more precarious and more dangerous. If womanhood is work, then women need to organise and strike for better conditions.

And that's just what is happening. As I write, something is changing. The Covid-19 crisis has laid bare just how essential 'women's work' is to the day-to-day functioning of society, as worldwide quarantine orders forced individual families to take on the full-time burden of education and caring for children, the sick, the elderly and isolated. Women have been forced out of the paid workplace in their millions as, even in a global pandemic, male partners simply refused to roll up their sleeves and do their part. In the UK, by some measures, women with children were doing two and a half times as much domestic work as men. In the USA, hundreds of thousands of women have been forced to abandon their careers by husbands and fathers who would not consider taking on the childcare, and governments who refused to subsidise it. Women have been required to replace the social safety net for too long.

And they have had enough. On forums, on Twitter, on Facebook, in message threads, women and girls are being honest about how exhausted they are and realising that they are not alone in that exhaustion – and that something can, and should, be done.

Social media has shattered the illusion that what happens in private homes cannot be political. Suddenly, pretending to cope seems very last season. The million glossy-maned mothers of Instagram have permission to relax their rictus grins and be honest about how they're barely holding it together. For the very first time, women have the technology to compare notes and share experiences, and that could change everything, just as it did with the #MeToo movement, where women began to speak with unprecedented unity about the private, intimate injustice of sexual violence. The street, as novelist William Gibson once observed, finds its own use for technology – and so does the home. It's time for domestic work to have its #MeToo moment. It's time that this private injustice became public concern.

Firstly, men must be called to account, individually and collectively, for refusing to do the basic work of care that living in a community demands of everyone. Society must accept that there is nothing in nature that makes women better suited to wiping bottoms, and that love does not require any person to be an unpaid drudge. That an adult man who can't run a dishwasher without being asked has no business running anything more complex, like a company, or a country. That expecting your partner to shoulder the majority of the domestic work for free, without complaint, is not just disrespectful – it is morally unconscionable. That the problem is not simply that women have too much work to do, but that men are refusing to do their share, and they need to start doing it, and if they don't know how, they need to learn.

Secondly, governments must begin to treat domestic and care work as work, to recognise that work within the economy and back that recognition up with cash. The infrastructure of education, healthcare, social security, elder care and childcare that has been privatised and defunded over the past forty years must be revitalised and properly funded, so that the burden of reproducing life is no longer foisted onto Black, brown, immigrant and working-class women. The work of care, the work of common survival, has never been more critical than it is now. And like all monumental tasks, the work of keeping the species alive through the coming century will be more manageable if we can find a way, finally, to share it.

9

The Means of Reproduction

Are women people, or are they things?

Pregnancy is brutal. Every year, in Great Britain, 10,000 people are treated for post-traumatic stress disorder as a result of giving birth,[1] and tens of thousands more are injured in the process of delivery. One study of women several months after giving birth found that 29 per cent had fractures in their pubic bones and 41 per cent had tearing and severe damage to their pelvic floor muscles.[2] For human beings, pregnancy and childbirth are dangerous, risky, exhausting, terrifying and painful. Even with modern medical advances, about one woman in 10,000 still dies in childbirth, and many more will be permanently and seriously injured.[3] Women frequently emerge from pregnancy and childbirth with permanent nerve damage, lifelong pain or PTSD. In context, that's about the same risk an American soldier takes on when he or she signs up for a tour of duty in a foreign war.[4]

The question of reproduction, and the right to choose abortion, the heart of the sexual revolution. Without the absolute right to safely and legally terminate pregnancy, there can be no equality between the genders. Without abortion and birth control, women will never have sexual, social or economic freedom. That's why the movement to confiscate abortion rights is the moral centre of the backlash against women's freedom.

As the debate about a woman's 'right to choose' to terminate pregnancy rages around the Global North, as sadistic restrictions on abortion access continue to be written into law by all-male committees around the world, the physical realities of pregnancy and birth are almost never discussed. The public conversation around abortion still centres on the question of whether a foetus has human rights, whether a foetus can feel pain, whether a foetus is a person. The question of whether a foetus is a person is unanswerable by science. The question of whether a woman is a person, however, is not up for debate – and it is female personhood and female pain that ought to decide the issue.

Sometimes, though, men get together in a room to decide otherwise. In June 2019, twenty-five white men and zero women made up the legislative team that effectively banned abortion in the state of Alabama. In the same month, draconian new anti-abortion measures also won wide margins of approval in Georgia, Ohio and Missouri. As I write, more such laws are being debated, right the way up to the highest courts of the world's leading superpower, in a sadistic pan-American nationwide binge against women's basic reproductive rights with the ultimate aim of overturning the landmark 1973 *Roe v. Wade* ruling upholding abortion access as a constitutional right in the United States.

These laws are not about the 'right to life'. They are about enshrining maximalist control over women as a core principle of conservative rule. They are about owning women. They are about women as things.

Here's what it comes down to. In that same month in 2019, in Ohio, an eleven-year-old child was abducted, raped and made pregnant. Under the state's new abortion laws, that child would have been forced to give birth. It's easy to see, by any sane moral measure, how a regime that coerces a child to carry that pregnancy to full term and give birth is monstrous, heartless and immoral. And it's just as clear that a state that threatens to kill or imprison that child unless she bears that pregnancy to full term and gives birth is morally equivalent to the rapist – taking away that little girl's agency, declaring that her pain is unimportant, that she has no right to decide who has access to her body.

But the crucial connective point, the point that gets shunted to the side in the culture-war rhetoric of abortion outrage, is this: it is equally monstrous to inflict the same punishment on a woman in her thirties who doesn't want to be a mother just because the condom broke on a Tinder hook-up. She, too, deserves bodily autonomy. She should not have to beg for it just because some religious extremists and Viagra-addled Republican lawmakers are frightened of women who fuck freely and without remorse. Seen in this light, forced-birth extremism is the logical extension of rape culture.

There is nothing 'pro-life' about the anti-abortion backlash. I refuse to dignify a movement that makes a mound of women's bodies and calls it the moral high ground. Most of all, I reject the moniker 'pro-life'. The forced-birth movement has far more interest in managing and controlling human lives than it does in saving them. 'Abortion kills babies' is, of course, a foundational belief among a global pro-choice movement, and the millions of voters who have grown up hearing nothing else are not lying when they say they believe life begins at conception. They are entitled to that belief, as long as they don't weaponise it to punish strangers.

Arguing with facts against articles of faith is a waste of everyone's time. No scientific study, no matter how sensibly explained, will ever convince a true believer that a foetus is not a human being with a soul. It is more useful by far to consider what else we know. Instead of asking whether abortion is 'really' killing, it is more productive – and more honest – to ask whether the violence of abortion is justified.

Because the answer must be – yes. Yes, it is. The mere fact that an abortion is taking a life – if that is truly what you believe – is not, cannot be, a good enough reason to justify jailing a little girl for getting one. There are plenty of situations where American law permits one individual to take a life: home invasion, self-defence, membership in the armed forces. Now, I happen to believe, along with 58 per cent of Americans[5] and most medical professionals, that terminating a pregnancy in its early stages is no more murderous than a biopsy. I happen to believe that a six-week-old foetus with a heartbeat but no limbic brain activity is less sentient than what most Republicans eat for breakfast in any of the constitutionally carnivorous states of the American South.

But that doesn't matter. Nobody's personal feelings about the nature of life matter here. As the philosopher and legal scholar Judith Jarvis Thomson put it, what matters more – far more – is women's freedom to control their *own* lives. She argues that pregnancy is consistently the only circumstance where anyone is legally obliged to sacrifice their health, against their will, for somebody else. 'No person,' Thomson argues, 'is morally required to make large sacrifices to sustain the life of another who has no right to demand them.'[6]

In other words: even if abortion ends a human life, forcing someone to give birth is worse. No state should be empowered to do so at the point of a gun, just as no state should be empowered to kidnap a person and drain off pints of their blood so that someone else can get a transfusion.

In the United States, the Trump regime was given the keys to the nation's capital by white evangelicals mostly on the basis of a promise to criminalise abortion and confiscate basic human rights from pregnant people. I say 'pregnant people' here because, of course, trans men and non-binary people can also become pregnant – but to traditional conservatives, everyone who has a uterus is a woman, and therefore someone whose sexuality is by definition subject to state control.

Even after Trump left office, the anti-choice conservative feeding frenzy continued in the USA and elsewhere. In 2019, Tony Tinderholt, a Republican Texas state representative, sponsored a bill to make abortion a crime punishable by death. So much for 'pro-life'. Tinderholt admitted that the point of his proposal was to 'force' women to be 'more personally responsible' in their sexual lives.[7] The goal is – and remains – explicit state control over female reproduction.

The same thing is happening across the world – in Poland, in Austria, in Spain, in Brazil; in every polity where strongmen are elected by a population easily swayed by implicit promises to put women and people of colour in their proper place. They blanket their bloodlust in affected piety, soothe their base's sentiments with concern-trolling about how all life is sacred – far too sacred to entrust to stupid women, or poor women, or women of colour. Forced-birth extremists are not yet brave enough to make their position clear. So it's up to the rest of us to say what we mean.

I believe there should be no legal restrictions on abortion whatsoever. None. Abortion should be easily and freely available to whoever wants one. I don't believe any person, ever, should have to give a good reason – or any reason – for wanting to terminate a pregnancy. This should not be a controversial stance. There is nothing unreasonable about regulating abortion like any other medical procedure – if we work on the basis, again, that women are not things.

Criminalising abortion makes female sexual agency a crime. That is what it is designed to do. It is very much the point. Give the Tony Tinderholts of this world some credit for candour: they've openly said that what they care about isn't protecting babies but punishing sluts who think they can just have sex without social consequences. And the consequences will be nine pounds of raw, screaming need, delivered at gunpoint in the shadow of the electric chair. If such measures weren't about punishing women for having sex, the rank hypocrisy of the few remaining 'exceptions for rape and incest' would ring out even to Republicans pickled in their own self-regard.

We live in a culture that is comfortable letting men get away with sexual violence but determined not to let women get away with consensual sex. This is why there are vast swathes of society that are comfortable giving vast executive and judicial power to men credibly accused of sexual assault – on the condition that those same men promise to confiscate women's power to sexually self-determine.

Female sexual freedom is the moral outrage that unites the religious right with neo-conservatives who want to shrink the welfare state until it's small enough to slip into a woman's underwear. Modern conservatives centre the idea of personal freedom, and freedom from state interference, in their rhetoric – but that personal freedom was never supposed to apply to women. The appeal to the importance of 'choice' does not work on people to whom women's freedom of choice is a fearful thing. A centrepiece of anti-abortion campaigning is the wickedness of women who choose to have abortions for 'social reasons' – i.e. because they simply don't want to be pregnant. Those women are framed as irredeemably selfish. And yes, some of them are selfish, if 'selfish' means actively choosing to prioritise your own needs and desires above those of a potential child. Selflessness should not be a legal duty imposed on women on pain of death or jail. Choosing to have a baby you don't want to raise might make you a nice person, but nobody should be threatened with jail for not being nice.

The biggest lies about women's rights are told by people who are trying to take them away. In anxious, violent times, when oppression is enacted under a deafening barrage of propaganda, it's important to listen out for the silences. It's vital, in other words, to listen to what's not being said by those who are making the most noise. The cacophony of outrage shapes itself around a painful silence, one that prevents us from pronouncing the actual stakes at play.

The plain fact is that there are no circumstances under which it is acceptable to force pregnancy on a woman against her will. But somehow regimes of male supremacists and religious extremists around the world are now in agreement that a six-week-old clot of cells is more of a person than any adult woman. After all, that clot of cells might be the next Mozart, the next Mandela. The idea that a pregnant woman might be the next Mozart or the next Mandela, of course, does not seem to feature in their calculations.

This mind-bending determination to bring women's bodies under maximum control helps explain why the North American abortion backlash has been so coordinated, swift and brutal. In 2018, after Alabama's all-male Senate majority voted to force women to give birth against their will, their counterparts in Georgia went further still, arranging to institute effective life sentences for abortion providers.[8] In 2020 Texas used the Covid-19 crisis to effectively shut down every abortion clinic in the state – even as conservative voters organised protests against 'social distancing', on the basis that Americans have a constitutional right to freely assemble. Again, only men's constitutional freedoms are recognised as worth defending.

The anti-choice movement is also about race, and it always has been.

Controlling abortion and contraception has always been part of the white supremacist drive to reshape the species by force – to decide which bodies are protected and which allowed to die. It was anti-choice evangelicals in 2018 who – together with some carefully timed voter suppression – gave Georgia governor Brian Kemp his razor-thin, contested victory over Stacey Abrams, his Black, female Democratic opponent. Kemp simply delivered on the promise he made to white evangelicals – and former President Donald Trump, who made manic mouth-sounds about babies being executed at birth on his campaign trail, did the same. Across America and Europe, conservatives have been happy to trade away women's freedom for a chance at power.

It wasn't always this way. As is so often the case in the murky, smudged understanding of women's history, many of us assume that before the 1960s abortion and contraception had always been tightly controlled – that the age of *Roe v. Wade* and the loosening of restrictions around the pill that brought unprecedented liberalism was a historical aberration, as women were briefly, graciously allowed to make a few of their own choices for a few decades.

Most of us imagine that abortion is now more legal than it has ever been. In fact, the opposite is true. Today, abortion laws are more *restrictive* than they have ever been. What is unprecedented today is the level of state control over women's reproductive choices. This is because until relatively recently it was not technologically possible to identify a pregnancy before the second trimester. Nor could pregnant people be forced into having trans-vaginal ultrasounds, as is still mandatory in several American states for all of those seeking abortion. Sadistic, state-sponsored surveillance of female sexuality has not existed before on this scale in human history.

Before the 1920s, accurate medical testing for pregnancy was largely unavailable. Even doctors had to rely on educated guesses. As such, where legal restrictions on abortion existed, they usually cut off at the time of 'quickening' – the stage at which a woman could feel the foetus moving inside her, a stage that many religions agreed on as the time at which the unborn child was 'ensouled'. This could be anything from sixteen weeks to six months or more – but it relied on the pregnant person to define her own experience of what was happening in her body, and women seeking termination were often allowed a good deal of leeway.

In the United States, before the Civil War era, abortion and folk contraception methods were largely unregulated and tacitly accepted – for free white women. In fact, the earliest case law regarding abortion was not designed to protect foetuses, but to protect women from shady doctors operating without licences or a working knowledge of germ theory. Unsurprisingly, there have always been different standards in play for control of white women's reproductive choices and those of Black, brown and migrant women. Enslaved women were forbidden to terminate pregnancy[9] and often punished if it was suspected that they might be attempting to avoid it, as their white slave owners were anxious that new slaves kept on being produced – especially after the end of the North Atlantic slave trade, when the production of Black bodies for servitude became more pressing.

White male slave owners, meanwhile, had absolute right to the bodies of Black women, who were routinely raped by slaveholders and forbidden to prevent pregnancy.[10] Any child born to a slave, after all, was a valued capital asset, the uncontested property of the mother's 'master'. All of that changed after abolition, when white Americans suddenly began to panic about being outbred by non-white people. Suddenly the great concern was that free Black women were having too many babies – and that white women, by not having enough, might be committing 'race suicide', a phrase that resurfaces among the far right and racist factions of the mainstream throughout the industrial age. The mid- to late nineteenth century was the period when abortion restrictions began to be formalised across the developed world, placing women's health choices in the hands of the state – along with experimental eugenics programmes designed to keep the non-white population down through the early twentieth century. Laws regulating abortion and contraception – especially for white women – were instituted, along with programmes of mass, enforced sterilisation of Black and immigrant women. Eugenics is now a term that conjures instant outrage – and rightly so. But it is easy to forget that before the Second World War, eugenics was considered a reputable scientific and political practice in many nominally liberal democracies. Early birth-control campaigners like Margaret Sanger famously resorted to eugenic language to persuade the white men in power that making birth control widely available was the only way to guarantee a healthy, strong – and white – citizen 'stock'. And one of the first public figures to use the term 'race suicide' in this context was Theodore Roosevelt.[11]

Since the early days of colonial expansion, the history of abortion and birth-control policies have been associated with racist ideas about nationhood and demographic control. Far-right movements have always been obsessed with sexually controlling 'their' women. One of the few common ideological refrains among almost all repressive regimes is the insistence that women's bodies are the property of the state, and that reproductive choice is not a right but a luxury that women should willingly sacrifice for the good of the nation – or else.

The same demographic panic has metastasised across Europe and America today. In the modern age the phrase 'white genocide' has become current, incubating in the cesspools of online hate speech, where it is used to mean, simply, 'not enough white babies being born'.

'The US subtracts from its population a million of our babies in the form of abortion,' Republican representative Steve King told a far-right Austrian magazine. 'We add to our population approximately 1.8 million of "somebody else's babies" who are raised in another culture before they get to us. We are replacing our American culture two to one every year.'[12]

It bears repeating: there is little moral difference between a man forcing a woman to have sex against her will and the state – or a controlling partner – forcing her to be pregnant against her will. At least rape apologists are slightly more honest about it. And this level of state control is a new and historically unprecedented attack on women's bodily autonomy.

Ideas of race, nation and territory have always been embedded in the anti-choice movement – as has a pernicious double standard about whose lives matter. The state of Alabama, for example, cares so much about life that it executes more prisoners per capita than almost any other state; it had an execution scheduled for the day after Governor Kay Ivey signed the state's abortion ban into law.[13]

That's not the only thing about the forced-birth movement that seems to stink of hypocrisy. People who believe that motherhood is precious do not rip toddlers away from their parents and keep them in sweltering cages at the borders.[14] People who are concerned with the sanctity of life do not advocate for lethal firearms to be sold at every strip mall. People who care about the unborn do not torpedo legislation designed to ensure that the planet those kids inherit is not wholly on fire.

Despite all of these crushing moral contradictions, forced-birth extremists are not hypocrites. Quite the contrary. Underlying all of the pious and disingenuous cant of their crusade is a terrifying logical consistency. There is a common thread that cinches together border paranoia, military fetishism and obsessive state control of women's bodies. It is chauvinism in nightmare mode: a dark story told by frightened child-men about the right of strong fathers and stern paternal leaders to protect resources. And in that story, women's bodies are a resource, one that men should be able to access freely. Women should not have the right to refuse men sex, or to abort the baby a man put inside her.

Women are not supposed to get angry when we talk about abortion. An angry woman, more or less by definition, is a crazy woman and a crazy woman can't be trusted with bodily autonomy, although apparently she can be trusted with a baby. What we're supposed to do instead is quietly and politely explain, even to the fanatics hijacking the agenda of world governments, that banning abortion takes away autonomy – as if they didn't know.

Of *course* banning abortion takes away women's autonomy. That is the point of banning abortion. That's the whole point.

Making abortion illegal, after all, doesn't stop it from happening. In nations where abortion access is restricted, they don't have fewer dead babies – but they have a lot more dead women. Around the world, 5 to 13 per cent of maternal mortality results from unsafe abortion.[15] The point is to send a clear message that uppity hussies have been having their own way for far too long, and that there should be consequences. The point has never been that babies matter. The point is that women don't.

We're supposed to smile and be polite while our basic humanity is stripped away by men who think little girls should be forced to bear children in pain and terror. If you want to survive patriarchy, you mustn't talk about how much it hurts to survive patriarchy. If you must speak of it, you speak softly. You don't talk about anger. And you definitely aren't supposed to talk about pain. Women's pain, particularly Black and brown women's pain, is invisible by design.

The strategy of patriarchal revisionists, especially on the politically influential evangelical Christian right, has long been to strip women and girls of dignity and force them to bear unwanted children in the name of religious obedience. Obedience to religious authority – to the father as head of the family, to God and to the state – is the very essence of evangelical thought, and in all of these models of obedience women are obliged to accept suffering as part of their natural lot. Even in non-religious contexts, women are expected to put up with pain – particularly women of colour, whose pain is routinely dismissed by medical authorities around the Global North, and this has serious consequences – including for maternal health. In the United States, Black women are three times as likely as white women to die in childbirth, and Black children are twice as likely as white children to die in their first year of life.[16] Part of the reason for that, as Professor Tressie McMillan Cottom writes, is that Black women are not considered reliable narrators of their own experience. When McMillan Cottom was in labour, she was ignored by team after team of medical staff, until:

> After several days of labor pains that no one ever diagnosed, because the pain was in my butt and not my back, I could not hold off labor anymore ... I begged for an epidural. After three eternities an anesthesiologist arrived. He glared at me and said that if I wasn't quiet he would leave and I would not get any pain relief. [...]
>
> When I awoke I was pushing and then my daughter was here. She died shortly after her first breath. The nurse wheeled me out of the operating room to take me back to recovery. I held my baby the whole way, because apparently that is what is done. After making plans for how we would handle her remains, the nurse turned to me and said, 'Just so you know, there was nothing we could have done, because you did not tell us you were in labor.'
>
> Black women ... are superheroes when we conform to others' expectations of us or serve someone or something else ... when we perform some existential service to men, to capital, to political power, to white women ... we are fulfilling our purpose in the natural order of things.[17]

Black and brown women are obliged to tolerate reproductive injustice that puts their lives and the lives of their children in danger, just as women of all backgrounds are obliged to keep their silence about the ugly, upsetting details of reproduction: the pain, the blood, the tearing, the exhaustion, the insecurity, the poverty. We're not supposed to talk about all the bitter, degrading things that go along with pregnancy, childbirth and motherhood in an economy designed and run by men.

When I was younger, I believed what I was told by teachers and adults – that although childbirth was very painful for a little while, women quickly 'forgot about all that'. This remains a common delusion – that there's some sort of natural amnesiac that means that the agony and trauma of even a straightforward pregnancy and labour are somehow erased from the psychological record. I understood that there were some things you just didn't talk about, things that should remain mysteries, things to do with labour, pregnancy, abortion and, especially, miscarriage.

Between 10 and 20 per cent of pregnancies end in miscarriage, and the experience can be profoundly traumatic for the person who loses the pregnancy – and yet there is still a social taboo around discussing miscarriage or even mentioning a pregnancy before the second trimester, when the risk of miscarriage drops dramatically. This taboo is supposed to protect the feelings of women and girls who lose wanted pregnancies – but the actual effect is to isolate people who experience miscarriage, protecting everyone around them from the discomfort of actually acknowledging the everyday tragedies of human reproduction.

The taboos associated with talking about pregnancy are not designed to protect women – they are designed to protect society from having to think about women's suffering. People who go through pregnancy are meant to stay quiet about the pain, the trauma and the fear associated with pregnancy and labour. They're supposed to meekly wipe up the blood and the shit and spend months sweating in the gym to 'get back' their 'pre-pregnancy bodies'. If they miscarry, they must not mention it – best not to make a fuss. If they commit the cardinal sin of having a pregnancy terminated, they are supposed to be ashamed, to whisper it, to make a show of shame – just as they are supposed to be ashamed of consensual sex, just as they are supposed to be ashamed of surviving rape.

But women's personhood is not conditional, and female sexuality is not shameful. The only shameful thing, the only thing that no citizen who believes even fractionally in freedom should tolerate, is a world in which women are treated like things.

10

White Lies

There is one circumstance in which white supremacist patriarchy claims to care about sexual violence. There's only ever been one. Today, all over the Global North, far-right movements are using the age-old myth of the 'outsider rapist' to attract followers. Yes, they say, women are under threat – but not from us. 'Our' women – white women – are under attack by Black men, migrant men, Muslim men – and 'we' must protect them.

The woman was screaming. From all sides, Black and brown hands – men's hands – grabbed at her body and twisted in her long, strawberry-blonde hair. The woman was a model, and the photo was posed – and this was the image that the Polish magazine *wSieci* put on its cover in the autumn of 2015. The topic was the Syrian refugee crisis. The title was 'The Islamic Rape of Europe'.[1] Again and again, wherever racism is weaponised to shore up the power of strongmen, the presence of immigrants or communities of colour is imagined, symbolically, as rape.

Why are white supremacists so obsessed with rape? How can a movement so profoundly misogynist – a movement that, as we have seen, recruits from the same sleazy forums where furious keyboard-mashers gather to vent their sexual frustration, a movement that radicalises its young male recruits with the promise of a future where white women will belong to them again, a movement that utterly denies the humanity of women of colour – be so preoccupied with preventing rape? From the 'Mexican rapists' hunkering behind former president Trump's still imaginary wall to the urban legend of 'no-go zones' for white women in northern Europe, today's neo-nationalists are obsessed with protecting 'their' women and girls from the sexual violence they spend the rest of their leisure hours threatening feminists with on the internet.

Today in Europe young women of colour are just as likely to be victims of sexual assault, rape and exploitation as white women – and Muslim women who wear religious dress are significantly more likely to face gender-based harassment in public.[2] But still the fantasy persists that migrant and Muslim men are mustering at every border ready to prey on the virtue of innocent white girls. Events like the assault of partygoers on New Year's Eve 2015 in Cologne[3] have taken on an iconic status in the public imagination. Meanwhile, the two women a week of every background who are murdered by their own domestic partners are apparently beneath the attention of today's defenders of feminine virtue. The logic is one of ownership and it runs as follows: foreign or minority men are a danger to white women, who are the common property of white men, but white men may brutalise, murder and maim their own women as they see fit.

This new chauvinism has nothing to do with women's interests and everything to do with white male fragility. In the United States, the spectre of Black rape has long been used to justify centuries of racist attacks. On 28 August 1955, in Money, Mississippi, fourteen-year-old Emmett Till was tortured and murdered because it was falsely rumoured that he had whistled at a white woman. Fifty years later, as Dylann Roof, the white supremacist terrorist, murdered nine Black congregants at a church in Charleston in 2015, he was heard yelling at them: 'You rape our women, and you're taking over our country, and you have to go.'[4] That 'you' was not a specific charge. Even a mind as mangled as Roof's cannot have entertained the idea that the churchgoing grandmothers he slaughtered were sex offenders. That same incoherent accusation was levelled against victims of barbaric racist lynchings, which makes it doubly abhorrent when abusers called out by the #MeToo movement repeatedly described what was happening to them, as they were finally asked

186

to answer for behaviour, as 'lynchings'. Within living memory, lynching in the United States was anything but metaphorical.

The drive to protect white womanhood from sexual predators of colour has deep roots, but they're not grounded in fact. Statistically speaking, those most at risk from interracial sexual violence have historically been women of colour, because white men down the centuries have rarely faced consequences for assaulting women of colour, even those who were not understood to be their legal property. The fantasy of protecting white women from dangerous outsiders, however, is a tried and true tactic for passing off structural racism as progressive – including to its perpetrators.

The story of whiteness is worm-eaten with plot holes. Whiteness, of course, like masculinity, is a political rather than a biological category. The gender binary is a power system which is based on political categorisation rather than chromosomal or epigenetic truth; in much the same way, there is no identifiable gene for whiteness, and down the centuries different ethnic groups have found themselves dumped in and out of the broad social bucket of 'white'. Whiteness is an idea, an idea that is no less real and no less dangerous for the fact that it's not technically true. It's a grand story of dominance that frightened people tell each other to make their own violence less fearful. And the fragility of white womanhood is the romantic subplot of that story.

At first sight, there seems to be a disconnect between neo-nationalists' stalwart defence of white womanhood against the external threat of 'outsider' rape and the amount of time these same reactionaries spend debunking 'rape myths' and claiming 'rape culture' does not exist. As anxious as they are to stop foreign men from violating 'their' women, they are just as anxious to make sure that they themselves can continue to exploit those women with impunity.

This disconnect is, in fact, no disconnect at all. It's about entitlement. It's about male ownership of women's bodies. It is the eroticisation of white male power – the recruitment of human sensuality and intimacy to serve an agenda of dominance. In this understanding of sexuality, of course, there is no room at all for pleasure, desire or consent. This understanding of sexuality does not know the meaning of those words, because it speaks no language other than ownership. Sex, here, is explicitly an act of possession, as it was when rape was first outlawed in the West – not as a crime of violence against a fellow human being but as property damage, as an act of trespass upon another man's territory.

When white supremacists talk about 'rape', they do not mean non-consensual sex. They mean *any* sex that would be unsanctioned within their fantasy white ethnostate. The unifying idea, as Ta-Nehisi Coates deftly pointed out in his book *We Were Eight Years in Power*, is that white men of all classes and backgrounds can be brought together to defend the one kind of property they all believe they ought to have in common: white women. That's why modern fascists talk about women's bodies in the same way that they talk about the nation state: corrupt, decadent and needing to be brought to heel with violence.

Crucially, men like this understand 'feminism' as an exclusively white idea. To them, feminists are white women who have betrayed both their race and gender. The concept of a Black feminist does not compute for these men. Black feminists challenge the simplicity of the bargain placed before their white sisters: the patriarchal bargain where you get to swallow your own subordination as the price of your share of whiteness.

Plenty of white women have been prepared to take that deal. White women absorb a great many racist ideas along with the sexism they internalise from birth, and when they buy into the myths white patriarchy has created for and about them, when they indulge in the special sort of narcissistic self-loathing that society reads as femininity, they are also enacting a specific idea about what white women are and what sort of protection they can expect from white men. Let's look again at one of the best-known quotes of early Black feminist thought, reported as the speech of former slave and abolition activist Sojourner Truth:

That man over there says that women need to be helped into carriages, and lifted over ditches, and to have the best place everywhere. Nobody ever helps me into carriages, or over mud-puddles, or gives me any best place! And ain't I a woman? Look at me! I have borne thirteen children, and seen most all sold off to slavery, and when I cried out with my mother's grief, none but Jesus heard me! And ain't I a woman?[5]

For many centuries, white women have been taught to aspire to precisely this asinine vision of coddled, protected femininity – a vision that necessarily excludes most of the actually existing female people on earth. The fantasy is of being that white woman, sitting in the best place, lifted over ditches, helped into carriages, the fantasy where you don't have to die early of overwork, the fantasy where you know your children will be safe – and with a few updates, that's the fairy tale still being flogged to white women everywhere. Do this and you will be saved. Do this and you will be safe. All you have to do is side with white men over everyone else – and then they'll protect you. But who will protect you from them?

When I read about Sojourner Truth as a schoolgirl, her story was stripped of context. That famous speech was given to an audience of white female campaigners for voting rights who had not invited Black women to their convention. In America, the mass movement for women's rights came, originally, out of the abolitionist movement. Early feminists from every background and walk of life were adamant that the fight for women's liberation could not be won without the abolition of chattel slavery. After the Civil War, however, a new form of white supremacist anxiety swept the young republic. White colonists began to panic about being overtaken by freed slaves and their descendants, about losing their status and sovereignty in a nation which still struggles to face its own guilty history.

White, male-supremacist America is so anxious to think of itself as good that it cannot face its own original sin. And white femininity has always been a story told by and for white men – a story about protection, about fragility, and about property. It still is. A short century and a half after the official end of chattel slavery in the United States, the same people are still telling the same story.

I have noticed, with some confusion, that whenever I speak in public about women's liberation, I am immediately told by a number of far-right strangers not just that I am lying, but that there's a specific punishment for my lies: I deserve to be raped, brutally, by migrant or Muslim men. The attempt to silence women's voices with rape threats and fantasies of sexual violence is nothing new, but the form that fantasy currently takes deserves attention. I am, after all, a white woman, at least according to those corners of the alt-right granfalloon that have yet to fully embrace anti-Semitism. Technically, I'm in the demographic they're supposed to be protecting – but part of the violent heterosexuality of white supremacy involves deciding just who does and does not merit that protection. Whether a particular white woman gets inside the notional perimeter fence depends on how well she plays her part – is she well behaved, respectful and, crucially, hot? If she's not, well – throw her to the outsiders and see how she likes it.

The fantasies of feminists and other unruly females being violated by 'outsider' men are so common and so detailed that one can only conclude that someone's getting off on them. None of this is to say that rape and sexual violence do not exist outside white-majority communities – but white supremacists are hardly queuing up to set up outreach projects for women and LGBTQ youth of colour, or lobbying for more refugees fleeing sexual and homophobic abuse to be given asylum.

The idea of outsider rape is symbolically useful to white supremacist patriarchy. If the bodies of white women are still the one territory all white men are supposed to have in common, defending white women from outside attack transforms white men into a class defending their common interests. White women don't get a say in whether or not they want this protection – they're property, after all, not people. Property isn't supposed to talk back.

I've never seen so many men worked up about women's rights as at the Rally to Defend the Women of Europe. It was a cold April day at Speaker's Corner in London in 2018, and the neo-nationalist group Generation Identity had called a public protest against sexual violence – specifically, sexual violence by Muslim men against white women. And the attendees were almost all men, dozens of them, on a cold Sunday morning, in suits and ties and bomber jackets, bristling with half-formed febrile opinions and alarming facial topiary.

I have, in my time, shuffled and stomped and plodded and wondered anxiously where the bathrooms were on many women's liberation-inflected acts of public assembly. I have been one of an incandescent million-strong mob marching against the malevolent new world order in Washington; I have traded placards and snacks and barbed comments with hundreds of the usual suspects on anniversary marches; I have worn out my best boots on the Slut Walks; and I have been part of weary little straggles of public defiance getting rained on outside government buildings in the dark. The only feature that these women's protests have had in common is that most of the people who go to them are women. But on this protest men outnumbered women by ten to one. A young white woman read a printed speech in the middle of concentric circles of angry men who would do anything to protect her from harm – anything except look in a mirror.

The white women that modern neo-reactionaries claim to want to protect are largely fictional. In fact, most of the actually existing white women these men have actually met are despised specifically for not being the blonde, submissive helpmeets of their tragic daydreams. This is a special sort of hatred, distinct from the ritual dehumanisation reserved for women of colour. The hate white supremacists nurse for white women like me is milder and more personal: they don't want us wiped out, they just want us whipped into line, barefoot and pregnant in the kitchen of their crypto-nationalist daydreams. In a world where women only exist as supporting characters in male adventure stories, it is apparently impossible to fathom any reason any woman might want basic human rights other than to piss men off. Our stubborn, bitchy insistence on having suffrage, sexual agency and subcutaneous fat is interpreted as a personal insult to every straight man, everywhere. White women who don't make the grade deserve to be punished for not performing white femininity well enough to deserve their sexual protection – which, of course, is also about erotic dominance.

It is vital to remember that this sort of white woman has never really existed. She is a story white men tell each other about womanhood, a sexual fantasy soaked in racist paranoia. The fact that she is fictional, however, does not make her any less dangerous. There are men out there committing murder in her name – and there are women, too, many millions, trying to be her.

The fact that white women, too, are harmed by the inhumanity of neo-fascism should not be the deciding factor in getting anyone off the couch and into the streets to stop it. If white women were never directly victimised by neo-fascism, stopping neo-fascism would be no less urgent. It happens, however, that bodies of white women are of huge symbolic importance to white supremacy – so it is symbolically significant when actual women who happen to be white put our actual bodies on the line to resist racism. Why, then, do so many do the opposite?

Anti-feminism has been part of the white supremacist imagination for as long as the far right has existed. For as long as the far right has existed, too, women have been part of it. And for as long as women have been part of the far right, they have acted as its decoys, as soprano soloists for the baritone chorus of bigots making special claims for white womanhood as a protected category. The far right has never been a feminist movement, and women are invariably in the minority among the leadership and membership of movements for whom they provide plausible deniability.

Why would any woman cast in her lot with men who deny her humanity just to attack the humanity of others? Racism is the reason for this, of course, but racism comes in a range of unhealthy flavours. When white women cast in our lot with white supremacy, when white women choose to side with racist patriarchy at the cost of our own personhood, when decoys like alt-right poster-girl Lauren Southern claim that 'there is no rape culture in the West',[6] we are making a specific choice about what side of the line to put our precious white bodies on. In the United States more than half of white women voters chose Donald Trump in the 2016 presidential election[7] and in the 2018 mid-term elections, and the pattern was repeated in 2020. Why did they do it?

They did it to survive, and they did it because of cowardice. In her book *Right-Wing Women*, Andrea Dworkin writes that conservative white women side with the men around them as a strategy of self-protection – hoping that they will be spared violence. 'Most women,' Dworkin writes, 'cannot afford, either materially or psychologically, to recognise that whatever burnt offerings of obedience they bring to beg protection will not appease the angry little gods around them.'[8] Conservative women are raised with the belief that their womanhood and their whiteness make them worthy of male 'protection' – even if that protection comes at the cost of living out sexist stereotypes. There is a long tradition of women accepting their own sexual subordination as the price of whiteness. Just as male white supremacists worship an unreal fantasy of white womanhood, many actual white women aspire to embody it – to become that princess who will finally be deserving of the care and comfort she was promised. If she still suffers violence at men's hands, she of course has only herself to blame – she failed to adequately embody that fantasy.

Any honest conversation about rape, sexual violence and consent must be had on terms that are explicitly anti-racist. Rape has always been a weapon of white supremacy, just as the fantasy of 'outsider rape' has been a tool for justifying its existence. Racism is not just incidental to rape culture. It is central to the cod-patriotic logic that sees women's bodies not just as property but as territory. Time and again, when self-professed patriots engage in post-Oedipal masturbatory fantasies about the motherland, the land is imagined as female, to make it clear that they own her, not the other way around.

White women cannot escape white womanhood or the history of complicity they were born to, but we can and should actively attempt to reclaim it from the racist anti-feminism of the modern age. White supremacy is an open invitation to white women to moderate their demands for liberation, to accept a place on the pedestal built by and on the bodies of women who never get to be considered victims worthy of protection.

For all their talk of protecting women, the modern far right is just as clear as the slave owners of the antebellum American South on what sort of woman actually deserves dignity, protection and respect. For the past several years, Muslim women have been the most common targets of racist street violence in the UK – especially those who wear visible markers of Islamic faith like the hijab or the niqab. In Germany, where the 2015 Cologne attacks led to a national panic about immigrant men preying on white German women, attacks on Muslims have soared – the majority on lone women or women with their children. German authorities registered at least 950 attacks on Muslims and Muslim institutions such as mosques in 2017,[9] with hijabi Muslim women, in particular, being harassed, threatened, shouted at, spat upon, humiliated, choked, slapped, groped, punched, stabbed, beaten and run over, overwhelmingly by members of far-right groups. Many of the perpetrators, according to authorities, are associated with far-right and racist organisations – but there was no proportional national panic about the safety of migrant women who had fled war and civil unrest hoping to find safety. The very same political groups who are so very keen for us all to recognise the apparently unique threat posed by Muslim men to white women are not simply unconcerned about any woman who isn't white – they are actively committing assaults on any woman or girl they think is inferior.

So much for the brave defenders of womanhood. One of racism's salient historical features has always been the assumption that white men – especially those who wield economic power – possess an incontestable right of access to Black women's bodies. It's an old song, and most of the men who have mouthed it down the centuries have felt like heroes on their own terms – and all of them have lived in fear of being confronted with their own hypocrisy.

Angela Davis wrote about this dynamic in her seminal essay 'the myth of the outsider rapist', explaining that 'In the United States and other capitalist nations, rape laws as a rule were framed originally for the protection of men of the upper classes.' While white men were rarely brought to justice, 'the rape charge has been indiscriminately aimed at Black men, the guilty and the innocent alike. Thus, of the 455 men executed between 1930 and 1967 on the basis of rape convictions, 405 of them were Black.'[10] This was not because Black men are more likely to assault women. Laws around rape – as we have already seen – are framed not around women's actual experience, but around the level of coercion that men – almost always white men – deem appropriate.

Resistance to the vicious new politics of wounded white patriarchy must be anti-racist as well as anti-sexist, because the logic of misogyny that sustains sexual oppression is grounded in white supremacy. Women of all races and backgrounds are subject to sexual violence and harassment, to the threat of rape, to the mechanisms of white supremacist patriarchy as they are enacted on our real bodies. In this story, women are human beings with agency, and no man has the right to ownership over our bodies, no matter how rich he is, how white he is, or how much power he has. The heroes of this story are women, and they become more heroic in proportion to how far they are able to reach out and work together.

The far right is hardly alone in prioritising the safety and dignity of white female bodies. Of course there's a difference between the sort of racism that seeks consciously to hurt and destroy and the well-intentioned racism of omission that arises from learned ignorance – but that distinction is less relevant to those on the receiving end. Sadly, there remains a current of racism in the feminist movement – a current that seeks to win concessions from white patriarchy at the expense of women of colour. A current that relentlessly centres the experiences of white, Western women. A current that began centuries ago when the early suffrage and reproductive activists drew away from the abolitionist movement, and tried to argue their case by appealing to eugenics, and continues today as countless movements like Generation Identity co-opt women's liberation to burnish their own bigotry.

As Reni Eddo-Lodge writes in *Why I'm No Longer Talking to White People About Race*: 'In the analysis of who fell through the cracks in competing struggles for rights for women and rights for Black people, it always seemed to be Black women who took the hit ... The white feminist distaste for intersectionality quickly evolved into a hatred of the idea of white privilege – perhaps because to recognise structural racism would have to mean recognising their own whiteness.'[11]

It is uncomfortable to recognise one's own complicity with whiteness, and white people's comfort has historically been purchased at the cost of Black lives. Every white person who writes about politics is intellectually blinkered by their own whiteness, and I can guarantee that this book, despite my best efforts, is full of oversights, full of moments when I have spoken of women's experience and seen, in my own mind, only white women. In this book I have asked men to make space for discomfort. White feminists must do the same when confronted with their own violent ignorance: learn as fast as possible, identify and atone for their mistakes, remember that their feelings are not the centre of every discussion, and remember that while having your own prejudices pointed out is deeply embarrassing, being a victim of prejudice is far worse.

The world will not be worth rebuilding if individuals can't make room for the discomfort of being wrong, and this sexual revolution will be impotent if it is not also intersectional. Race and gender as vectors of oppression are neither the same – nor, however, can they be considered separately. Quite apart from being ethically suspect, any movement to end exploitation that fails to centre race is intellectually useless.

11

Angry Young Men

When the real fascists show up, will you be ready?

In the past few years, far-right movements have swept to prominence and to power around the world. And a lot of well-meaning, non-fascist people are still convinced that when the baddies in black start knocking down doors and dragging away their neighbours, they'll do what's right, just like their grandparents and great-grandparents did before them. They'll wait until they're called on, and then they'll take a stand. The problem is that the time for waiting is over. It was over long before 6 January 2021, when hundreds of heavily armed white supremacists stormed the US Capitol.

None of us have to wonder any more about how we'd react when the new Nazis march down the street, because it's already happening. This time around, though, they're not all in jackboots and uniforms. They're not all members of a dedicated party, and many don't have a clear leader to rally behind. They don't need one. The new far right is distributed, networked and entrepreneurial. The new far right is gig-economy fascism – and sexism is one of its key recruiting grounds.

Misogynist extremism is the elevator music of the age. At first, it started as a subtle whine, almost on the edge of hearing; an undertone of vengeful male despair audible to those who happened to be standing closest: online activists, anti-racists, women, people of colour in the public eye and feminists.

In 2017, in Charlottesville, Virginia, the world watched in horror as young men in white polos and khakis marched through the town with flaming tiki torches, chanting that 'Jews will not replace us'.[1] That chilling slogan echoes a key theory of the hate-addled online far right: that an international conspiracy of Jews and bankers are determined to destroy the Aryan race by encouraging, among other tactics, 'feminism and gender ideology'. This theory, known as the 'great replacement', points to the declining birth rates among wealthy Western countries like the United States and Britain, the high rates of immigration from non-white countries, and the high birth rates among immigrants from those countries. Modern extremists point to the fact that women across the West are having fewer children as evidence of the success of this 'great replacement' project.

In the week that I began writing this book, thirty-one people were massacred in the United States in two separate mass shooting incidents. Both shooters were white men in their early twenties with a history of extreme sexist and violent behaviour; one was also a militant racist who posted a 'manifesto' on a gaming site railing against the 'Hispanic Invasion' of Texas (a state that was, just two centuries ago, part of Mexico). Most of the men who carry out these murders are recruited online and have a history of violent misogyny. The man who massacred forty-nine people in an Orlando nightclub in 2016 beat his wife while she was pregnant. The man who killed twenty-six people in a church in Sutherland Springs, Texas, in 2017 had been convicted of domestic violence.

There is a pattern to these killings. They are not random. 'In at least 54 per cent of mass shootings between 2009 and 2018,' according to the gun-control advocacy group Everytown in America, 'the perpetrator shot a current or former intimate partner or family member during the mass rampage'.[2] In addition, 'in at least 61 mass shootings, the shooter had a known previous history of domestic violence.'[3] These domestic violence-related mass shootings led to 532 deaths in those nine years.

The Anti-Defamation League issued a report in 2018 titled 'When Women Are the Enemy: The Intersection of Misogyny and

White Supremacy', one of the chief findings of which was that hatred of women is often 'a gateway into the white supremacist world'.[4] Anti-feminism is not peripheral to the alt-right: it informs its entire critique of the modern world. Its basic tenets are that the world is in peril and can only be saved by strong men who are prepared to do violence; that feminism is destroying civilisation by undermining women's natural role, which is to have children, and to serve and be submissive to men.

In this narrative, straight white men are uniquely the victims of the emergence of identity politics: so while women, LGBTQ people and ethnic minorities have clear identities, giving them formal and informal rights, straight white men do not. In response, they have constructed their own oppressed identity: the 'beta male', the young man who cannot find a sexual partner because women are too busy having sex with so-called 'alpha males'. It should go without saying that the whole thing is a laughably adolescent take on heterosexuality. But it is simply one of neoliberalism's fundamental tenets pushed to its logical extreme: that human beings are biologically unequal and that the market will reflect such inequalities by rewarding the strongest with success.

In 2018 a study showed that alongside being white and male, one of the strongest predictors for those who agree with basic sentiments of the alt right was divorce.[5] Race and nation are, of course, the unifying ideas among the modern far right, but the entry point is often aggrieved entitlement based on a sense of having been denied one's masculine birthright, and the authority it entails over women and children. These were men whose wives and partners had left them, or younger, never-married men who felt cheated of what Ta-Nehisi Coates called the one commodity that all white men are supposed to have in common – the bodies of white women.

There is nothing fringe about this movement of affectless patriarchal vengeance, this army of feckless fathers whose entire argument for authority is a tautology: we are not losers, therefore we deserve to win, no matter who we have to cheat and crush to do it.

There is an apocalyptic overtone to this logic. These men, and the women who are part of their cult, are actively preparing for the dissolution of modern civilisation – preparing for it eagerly as a time when the decadence and depravity of the modern world will be swept away. In fact, one of the most common collective fantasies on 'incel' (involuntary celibate) and 'pickup artist' forums is that of the coming collapse of civilisation – when men will be real men again, and women will be grateful. There'll be no more abortion, no more divorce, no more uppity women whining about equal pay – when the zombie hordes approach, when the raiders are at the gates, when the flood and the fire and the plague ravage all our certainties, women will remember that they are weak, and that they need men to protect them. We've seen it on TV a hundred times. Decadent modern societies will disintegrate, leaving space for men to be the type of heroes they have always dreamed of being. In the meantime, though, some have determined to be villains.

The violent misogyny of the alt-right draws on a set of ancient prejudices given a new economic content and shaped into a new victim mentality by the far right in conditions of economic stress. The community is pickled in violent, racist and anti-woman propaganda, replete with fantasies of rape and murderous revenge. Hannah Arendt, surveying the rise of the Nazis, warned that it would be a mistake to confuse modern anti-Semitism with its medieval form. The same is true of the paranoid tendencies of modern misogyny. According to a study from the Institute for Family Studies two traits in particular are most likely to make white nationalism appealing to white men: they have low incomes and they have been divorced.[6] These men feel like losers – and by the crushing standards of masculinity they grew up with, they might be right.

Feeling like a loser makes modern men vulnerable to alt-right recruitment. That recruitment often starts with a sense of aggrieved entitlement – specifically, of entitlement to the time, attention and affection of women. Lonely, insecure young men who just want a girlfriend or, failing that, a fuck, are suckered in by hustlers who tell them that sex is a game, women are the prize, and a real man plays the sexual marketplace like any saucer-eyed short-trader, tricking women into giving him what he knows he deserves. Then when that strategy doesn't work, or when it works and leaves them feeling empty and cheated, or when they're too caught up in their resentment at not being delivered the female helpmeet they feel they deserve, they're easy prey.

Entry into these communities is often innocuous enough. It has to be: very few people actually sign up to be violent woman-hating white supremacists. That sounds way too much like being the bad guy, and the last thing any of these men want to be is the bad guy – they're nice guys, good guys, or at least not evil guys. They're drawn instead to vague conversations about pride, about rights, about restoring order and justice to the world – the lightning-bolt flags and red laces aren't brought out until later. Hussein Kesvani from *Mel* magazine explains it like this:

> The 'manosphere' consists of a large number of groups – whether it's incels, 'Men Going Their Own Way', or 'pick-up artists' – that all push the same message that the men who go to their pages are being hard done by women and society at large, says Annie Kelly, a PhD student at the University of East Anglia, who researches the impact of digital culture on the far right.
>
> She adds that while there isn't a single reason why men would be attracted to 'Red Pill' communities, as a hyper-networked online subculture [the 'manosphere'] is able to transmit its messages and philosophies to a much wider audience. All of which means that grievances related to lack of sexual and romantic partners are located in the same spaces as right-wing propaganda around, for example, the refugee crisis and trans issues. When they're reinforced in these groups, as well as by mainstream media outlets on Facebook and YouTube, people are more exposed to them, and they end up buying into some

of the maxims without realising it. The online world becomes part of their lived world.[7]

Soon enough, the language becomes darker. Racist memes and homophobic propaganda slosh together in a fever dream where young men cast one another as soldiers in a ceaseless bloody struggle against everything uncomfortable about modernity. Although sexual frustration is the bristling centre of this ideology, incel men do not hate other, more sexually successful men – at least, not if those men are white. Instead, they respect them for their prowess, nihilistically accepting their own place as 'beta' males, doomed to die unsatisfied, with nothing to look forward to except revenge. Donald Trump, of course, is or was the ultimate 'alpha' – the sexual and political silverback who dominated his enemies with violence and threats, who lied and cheated and took what he wanted, no matter who got hurt. That, for extremists in the death cult of modern masculinity, is precisely what it means to be a real man.

The concept that women's consent might actually matter is blasphemy to these extremists. Many reject the notion that rape is a 'big deal', claiming that being forced not to have sex is an equivalent or greater injustice than being forced to have it – or, rather, to endure it. That frigid sexual philosophy is central to the mindset of the 'manosphere': women have no real sexuality of their own, and seek only to extract the maximum amount of resources from men in exchange for 'vaginal access'.

When you've finished dry-heaving, pay attention to the language here. There's an uncanny family resemblance to the rhetoric of spin doctors, politicians and pollsters – and no wonder. Pickup artists, like salespeople in most electoral machines, treat the agency of other humans as an obstacle to be overcome. Young men on forums like these are encouraged to marshal their resources and wear down the target until they get what they want. And what these young men want, and seem to feel they deserve, is unimpeded sexual and emotional access to the women they deem 'hot' – usually young, slender white women. The question of what women might want never enters the equation. According to the logic of 'pickup artistry', women's desires and boundaries are just obstacles to be overcome as the aspiring alpha male learns, often by paying for private instruction, how to break down 'last-minute resistance' and break through a target's 'bitch filter'.

Some of the most poisonous misogyny comes out of the 'incel' forums, where young men united by a common resentment of womankind for not sleeping with them rail against the entire gender for their 'involuntary celibacy'. Like any recruiting ground for extremists, the incel movement preys on loneliness and despair. Its spokespeople fetishise suicide and reach out to those seeking an outlet for their darkest, most self-loathing impulses.

It happens in stages. Lonely young men looking for advice and guidance stumble across new friends promising to help them build confidence or offering tips on how to talk to girls at parties. But it quickly becomes something darker. On one now-banned incel forum, a user complained that his fourteen-year-old brother had brought a girl home while he himself was busy watching porn. Commenters immediately suggested rape and murder.

On 22 April 2018, Alek Minassian drove his van into a crowd in Toronto, killing ten people. Minassian, who was convicted of mass murder in March 2021, had posted hours earlier on his Facebook wall: 'Private (Recruit) Minassian Infantry 00010, wishing to speak to Sgt 4chan please. C23249161. The Incel Rebellion has already begun! We will overthrow all the Chads and Stacys! All hail the Supreme Gentleman Elliot Rodger.'[8]

Elliot Rodger was a terrorist who slaughtered six people in Santa Barbara's Isla Vista neighbourhood in 2014 as 'revenge' for the fact that women would not have sex with him. Rodger is a hero and a martyr to the incel community.

Over and over again, a young man with links to the poisonous trough of misogyny that is the incel community committed mass murder, and yet again the public was inexplicably asked to show some understanding, asked whether these angry young men might not have legitimate concerns, even though this one went a little too far when he decided to murder ten people in cold blood.

When the 'r/Incels' subreddit was finally taken offline in 2017, it had 40,000 active members. All the evidence suggests that this is the community that radicalised Minassian, and shortly after his rampage, the most popular incel forums claimed him as a soldier in their bloody battle with reality. That this toxic subculture has only lately begun to be taken at all seriously as a spawning pit for terrorist violence is an indictment of all of us. It is an indictment of our society and its interminable parade of excuses for any violence that it does recognise.

I have spent years researching and attempting to understand the mindset behind the incel, 'men's rights' and 'seduction' communities. The forums, frankly, are a dangerous trench of deluded self-pity, where young and not-so-young mostly white men circle-jerk one another into collective ragegasm, and egg each other on to acts of violence against themselves and others. The problem is getting worse. And because we are apparently culturally incapable of holding young men accountable for their actions, this, too, is blamed on women.

According to Robin Hanson, a conservative blogger and professor at George Mason University, it's actually incels who are oppressed – because women won't have sex with them. Hanson suggests that sex could be 'directly redistributed, or cash might be redistributed in compensation'.[9] What he means is that women should stop being so stuck up and agree to fuck violent men.

In other words, this could all have been stopped if someone had only shown these young men love and empathy and kindness and possibly their genitals. If women and girls had just stopped selfishly insisting that their right to basic human dignity was as important as men's sexual access to their bodies. If they had just been a little bit more polite about asking people to stop battering and raping, groping and harassing them. If they'd done their duty as women, nobody would have had to get hurt. If men are broken, it's women's job to fix them.

Being messed-up and miserable is no excuse for violence, and recognising the special sort of despair that might drive a person to political extremism is not the same as an excuse. These individuals have already had more empathy and understanding than they deserve. Whether they're marching in racist rallies, voting for neo-nationalists, serially abusing women, or egging each other on to acts of violence against any 'thot' or 'Stacy' who has savagely denied them 'vaginal access', I have heard all the arguments about how their loneliness and frustration and depression drove them there, and I've found I don't care. I don't care, because people are dying.

When will it be someone else's turn for concern and understanding? When will the frustrated man-children and hysterical racists clamouring for someone to entertain their 'legitimate' concerns offer anyone else a solitary shred of the empathy and respect they demand on pain of violence?

Right now, as the body count continues to grow, we are well past the limits of what empathy and understanding can achieve with young men who have gone down the rabbit hole of racist, sexist revenge fantasies. Zero tolerance is the only possible response. I wish empathy and understanding had been enough. But I've known enough women who have worn themselves to rags trying to empathise with men who continue to hurt and harass and abuse them. *He's a good boy really. He does wonderful work. He had a terrible childhood. He's lonely and depressed. All he needs is love. It's our fault for not showing him enough love. Maybe if we tried harder.*

If that worked, we'd have a very different world right now. I've been there. I've tried it. I've pleaded for tolerance and understanding for violent men I have loved, and watched those violent men move on to the next victim, and the next. Just as happened with the #MeToo movement, the only thing that changed behaviour was creating a climate where that behaviour was unacceptable.

Excusing violence on the basis that the people entertaining it are lonely, shy, frustrated weird nerds is an ineluctable slur on all the other lonely, shy, frustrated weird nerds out there. There are a lot of us. Most of us do not consider our loneliness or frustration a logical prelude to acts of bloody violence. Some of the kindest, sweetest men I have ever met truly do live in their parents' basements, play a staggering quantity of video games, and rarely get out, or indeed laid. They would no more consider committing mass murder than they would voluntarily lop off a limb. Stop making excuses. Stop coming up with ways to recast this epidemic of misogynist extremism as something other than it is.

Who out there isn't lonely and depressed? Who doesn't feel angry and cheated? What I've seen over years of research in these communities is an absolute inability to consider the remotest possibility of the vaguest notion that anyone else might have those feelings. That anyone else at all might have any sort of inner life. That women and girls, too, might feel lonely or depressed or angry or cheated, that we might have things to complain about, of which not experiencing enough pleasure and respect in this world is the very least.

That's not to say that these bitter, spittle-flecked hate-nerds aren't entitled to their own feelings. Their feelings are valid, just like yours and mine. Their fear is valid, their pain is valid, their frustration is valid. All of these feelings are valid – and none of them excuses a single instance of violence towards another human being for a solitary second.

The plain, unalloyed truth is that while you can bully and brutalise and threaten people into showing you obedience or even fucking you, you cannot bully someone into loving you. Or respecting you. It doesn't work that way. Nobody is entitled to sex. Nobody is entitled to anyone else's time and attention. I know that the utter emotional illiteracy our culture encourages in men and boys might make that confusing, might make it hard to distinguish between something you want very badly and something the world owes you, but trust me, there's a difference, and it's high time the rest of us started making that plain. Not just because it's the basis of a braver and more humane culture, but because toxic, murderous entitlement is not the sole province of terrorists, and it never has been.

The reason it's so hard to acknowledge that entitled misogyny leads to acts of terrorist violence is that entitled misogyny is not a rarity in our culture. Most people would agree that incels' views are extreme and their proposed solutions violent and disgusting, yet the basic premise – that women owe men sex, and men have a right to take it – is inculcated into society.

For many years, the growing threat to public safety from far-right extremists was largely ignored by police in Europe and North America, who preferred to concentrate, predictably, on 'outsider' violence – where the only terrorism that mattered was the terrorism of Black, brown and foreign-born men. The far-right threat wasn't just overlooked because it was a domestic issue, but because the logic that sustains its philosophy is also the logic that sustains the white supremacist, patriarchal state – just taken to its logical conclusion. The state is not designed to protect women and people of colour from violence that perpetuates their oppression – the state is, in many cases, simply a more polite way of dealing out that violence, whether it be through the law courts, the housing market or the prison system.

Entitled misogyny is everywhere. What I've seen on incel forums is merely the extreme iteration of a mindset shared by many apparently normal, non-terrorist men today. That mindset operates as follows: women owe men their time, love and erotic attention. When men are denied these things and have to deal with feelings of rejection or loneliness or sexual frustration, that denial is an act of violence, and it ought to be punished. Women who aren't sexually attractive are unworthy of human dignity, but women who actually have sex are sluts. If a 'femoid' won't fuck you, fuck that bitch. She'll get what's coming.

The assumption that oozes from every open pore of straight patriarchal culture is that women are expected to tolerate pain, fear and frustration – but male pain, by contrast, is intolerable. The loneliness and depression and frustration of men, particularly white, straight men, is experienced as a revelation, treated with reverence, summoned to excuse and justify the worst excesses of violence and bigotry. The mere fact of a man's pain is considered a complete answer to the question of why he chose to inflict pain on others. A man's pain, in fact, *entitles* him to inflict pain on others.

The noise is coming from inside the house. Just because the logic of this violent extremism happens to come from the clogged heart of Western culture does not mean that it is not terrorism. Just because these particular lonely, frustrated murderers look and sound and talk disturbingly like some of the white population's sons and brothers and partners and colleagues does not mean their poisonous propaganda should be tolerated. And just because they have mainlined their own fantasies of a world where women will be once more be subservient to men, doesn't mean that that world is inevitable, or desirable – or even likely.

In March 2020, Covid-19 brought the world to a standstill, and the angry young men of the internet finally got the world-inverting crisis of civilisation they had always been waiting for. But something went wrong. This was not the apocalypse they were looking for, not the return to a better, simpler time, when men would be real men again and women would be grateful. In a global pandemic, the heroes were not fighters or soldiers – they were doctors, nurses, care workers and community leaders. They were the people doing the exhausting daily labour of kindness, of keeping other people healthy and safe. The modern far right cannot understand its place in a world that is not tearing itself apart – and while hurting other people is the best way to get attention, building a movement on that basis is building a monument to your own irrelevance.

12

No More Heroes

What does it mean to be a good man?

Right now, nobody seems to know, and that's a problem. It's a problem for every society founded on ideas of masculine infallibility. Can men be good? Are they inherently violent? If so, can they be held responsible for their worst instincts? And if women are driving social change, are men now the enemy – whether they want to be or not?

Somehow, a conversation about women's lives has been repurposed into a referendum on the souls of men. The source of the anxiety isn't simply that the notion of a 'good man' is being redefined. What's scarier is that men are no longer controlling the narrative. Not entirely. And that's new. Very new. It used to be men who got to determine the meaning of morality, to define what it meant to be a decent guy or a nice girl – and nice girls weren't supposed to question that arrangement.

But once a pattern of violence has been made visible, it's hard to unsee it. All around the world, women and queer people have begun to unpick the locks on their own agency and acknowledge the depth of the harm they have suffered and seen. The conversation about sexual violence and male privilege is not about what men *are*. It is about what men *do*, and what they might do differently. And it is also about courage. The courage that modernity requires of men and boys is deeply untraditional.

For ten years, ever since I became a feminist writer, I have received a great many emails from men I don't know, or don't know well – questioning, confessing, angry emails. Most women

I know who write in public have inboxes similarly stuffed with missives from strangers, anguished stories soaked shame and pain and rage at the way the world is rewriting itself without white men as sole protagonists. Men write to me all the time, telling me that they feel trapped inside their own toxic masculinity, that they feel like losers and failures, that modern feminism feels like a vivisection of their own inadequacies, and they're not sure whether they're supposed to hate feminism, or themselves, or both.

Many of these men struggle to distinguish between the way they feel about the world and the way the world is. They feel like failures, so they are failures. They feel like feminism is destroying the world, so feminism is 'destructive', because now more than ever, it is rugged and masculine to experience your feelings as proven facts. In this maelstrom of conflicting messages, men and boys don't know what to do. They don't know how to be good. And men are supposed to know these things. A strong man is never unsure. A real man doesn't need to ask questions. A good man never wonders what it means to be good. He simply is.

The more modern culture buckles under its own contradictions, the more attached we seem to become to the notion of male goodness as something sacrosanct, something that exists independently of actual behaviour. *He's not usually like this. He didn't know what he was doing. He couldn't have done that. He's a good guy.* It's uncomfortable to acknowledge that people we know, people we love, might have been violent, sexist or cruel. The work of confronting your own complicity is always uncomfortable – and many men and boys are now looking at their own sexual and social history and wondering how they can truly see themselves as good people.

In the past five years, and particularly since the #MeToo movement began, I have spent a lot of time sitting across tables from men who have been accused of sexual assault and rape – men who are angry, and afraid, and have no idea what to do. Men who are drowning in guilt, understanding that feeling terrible because you hurt someone is in no way equivalent to feeling terrible because you have been hurt. Men who have been called out and condemned and are wondering what the rest of their lives will look like. But good – as Ms Marvel says[1] – is not a thing you are. It's a thing you do.

In any oppressive system, any system where someone's freedom comes at the expense of someone else's servitude, members of the dominant class have to find ways to live with themselves. When something can't be unseen – like sexual violence, or structural racism – alternative explanations are seized on so that the sort of people who think of themselves as reasonable and sensible can go about their daily lives.

The shock of seeing violence and injustice acknowledged for the first time stops up the mouth, settles around the heart. The transition from one reality to another is sharp and shocking. Everywhere I look, the work of helping men through that transition to a better and less brutal way of living and loving is being done by women. It is exhausting work. But it is not recognised as work. Instead it is resented. Women and girls who take on the thankless chore of trying to help men change for the better face angry accusations that they are going too far, being too cruel, pushing men to lash out or break down. Modern masculinity is apparently so fragile that it shatters under the merest suggestion of change.

The idea that men are too weak to cope with change is frankly offensive to men – and yet there are so few alternative models of masculinity on offer. In fact, there is an imaginative deficit within the mapped territory of masculinity. The stories that have been told about what men are and what they do are grand and wide and deep and deafening. They are unlike the flimsy, peripheral stories that have traditionally been told about women, who have been relegated to supporting characters in stories of male heroism – until very recently. Right now culture is finally making room for new role models for women and queer people. But straight men are still strait-jacketed by the stifling narratives of patriarchy.

Modern masculinity leaves so little room for stories that are not about conquest and violence, very little room at all for supple stories that involve uncertainty, gentleness, and all the undiscovered countries of the human heart. Modern masculinity is a cage, and men are locked inside it – and the rest of us are locked in with them. It will not be unlocked until it is considered less important to raise little boys to be men than it is to raise them to be human.

Hatred of masculinity and the prison it has become, is often confused with hating men. It's true that some people have been hurt enough in their lifetimes to lose hope in the entire gender, and that's a pity, but personally, it is out of respect for men that I consider it so important to talk about toxic masculinity, about rape culture and about patriarchy.

Modern masculinity is brittle and fragile. It reacts to any perceived threat by lashing out and shutting down. It is definitionally resistant not just to change, but even to the thought of change. I abhor these aspects of masculinity because I have seen too many men try with all their might to reject them, try bravely with no script, no safety rails, and no hope of a hero's reward, to believe that this narrow vision of masculinity is innate. I despair of it, sometimes, and despair is exhausting, and I won't settle for it. I still want to understand why men do what they do and how they can begin the work of change.

Because right now, too many men and boys seem to believe that change is impossible. A common fear among decent men struggling to know how to ethically exist in a male body in the modern age is that there is something inherently hateful and destructive in maleness itself, that there is some sort of original taint written into their genes, and that women as a whole might have correctly identified it. That's why the first and worst thing men say to women fighting for their own liberation is that they must 'hate men'. It assumes that asking men to change their behaviour is, and must be, the same as hating what they are on the deepest level.

But being a good guy isn't about who you are. It's about what you do. So many of the knee-jerk defences of men who have done violent things, celebrities and ordinary guys alike, start on the premise that they are 'not that sort of person'. In fact, everyone is that sort of person – everyone who grew up in patriarchy and learned that sex was both a terrible thing that women might one day suffer you to do to them and something that was vital to their identity as a man. That tension is a terrible thing to inhabit.

Somewhere around the frayed edge of my twenties, I realised I'd been wrong about men. I'd been putting the needs and feelings of men before my own, not because I'm an especially nice person, but because that was how I'd heard you stayed safe. I'd made a mistake about men. I'd thought, as so many of us had, that the reason the world was overrun by populist tyrants and far-right demagogues driving the clown car of culture towards climate collapse was that men were unhappy. White men in particular. Middle-class white men especially. I thought their comfort was more important than anyone else's consent. I was wrong.

One of the central delusions of modern masculinity is the notion that men are emotionally repressed. In fact, men and boys are emotionally illiterate – because a great proportion of them were raised to believe that emotional fluency is unmanly. How else could we have wound up in this toxic, twisted place where men so routinely mistake their own feelings for facts, where men who are in love or lust experience those desires as overwhelming imperatives that demand?

Men are not, in fact, less emotionally capable than women by nature. It's simply that women and girls are expected to learn to manage their own feelings – and to consider those of others – at a far earlier age. Decades of dissection and study of the human brain have found no gland for human empathy and emotional control that is missing in the males of the species. The issue is not that so many men are unable to cope with discomfort – it is that society as a whole is unable to cope with male discomfort, to the extent that it is considered unmanly to learn any of the basic emotional coping skills that carry a person through times of change and uncertainty. Where men's potential discomfort is a problem to be solved, women's pain is normalised, made invisible, and accepted – at least up to a certain degree – as our lot in nature and creation.

It is not anti-feminist to talk about men's emotions as if they matter. What is anti-feminist is to demand that men's feelings come first, to insist that men's experiences are taken more seriously, to bully or threaten women into placing men's comfort ahead of their own safety. It's not wrong to help men heal their hurts and grow and move on, but that healing and growth must not be prioritised over the safety and growth of a complete community.

But if we're really, honestly going to talk about men's feelings, it might hurt. It might mean poking at the soft and painful places beneath the carapace of masculine posturing. It might mean talking about the full spectrum of emotion, including vulnerability, disappointment, loneliness, embarrassment and fear – all of those unmanly feelings men and boys are bullied out of acknowledging.

Straight men are so often crushed by the contradictions of having to hate what they desire. We've already talked about the particular, predictable way in which broken men try to bury their own self-loathing in the bodies of women, flattening intimacy into an act of dominance – and it's impossible to do that to a person while also respecting them as an individual with their own equally precious life to live. The men I know who have done the most harm to women – and to me personally – are some of the most damaged individuals I've ever met. That is not an excuse. Not even close. Hurt people do not always and inevitably hurt others. We know this because so many male survivors of abuse and trauma find ways to break the cycle of abuse. They have been courageous enough to refuse to let their own trauma dictate the trajectory of their lives. They know that those willing to do that work can build better lives and better worlds.

Sexual revolution does not require men and boys to hate themselves. Shame and self-hate are not useful emotions. They don't make you a better person, or a better partner, or a better man. There are 7 billion human souls skulking around this planet and it is vanishingly unlikely that you or I are either the best or the worst of them. In fact, more often than not, hating yourself gets in the way of exactly the sort of rapid positive change the species needs right now. Everyone has met individuals so enamoured of their own self-loathing that it's impossible to talk to them about small, everyday, human mistakes. Individuals so invested in thinking that they are bad people that they are unable to become better ones.

But men as a political class are not too fragile to cope with the consequences of their actions. It is not a kindness to have low expectations of men, or to always be doing the emotional work for them. It is not a kindness to give in to the threat – so common in abusive relationships – that if we don't do what they want, they will do violence to themselves, or to us, or both. For a long time I thought that I was being loving to men by expecting less of them. I thought wrong. I was not being loving. I was not being kind. I was only being nice – and nice is not enough.

There's a savage self-loathing at the core of so many of our paradigms of masculinity. Most of the men I know who have hurt women feel deep shame, including about the women they've hurt. Sexual violence becomes a way of displacing that shame into someone else's body. That shame – the idea that men don't do bad things, that men *are* bad things – doesn't come from feminism. It comes from patriarchy. And fear of being 'found out' is the centre of that shame. It's not as if most men and boys don't know that there are problems with the way they sometimes behave. It's not as if most men and boys don't feel bad about it. The problem comes when you convince yourself that feeling bad is enough.

Meanwhile, women and girls are managing men's rehabilitation for them – and suffering in the process. Women and girls are doing the emotional labour of talking men through their difficult feelings about the violence they have done. Often these women and girls have suffered violence themselves – and yet when it happened to us there was no such support system. We were told, implicitly or explicitly, to keep quiet or face the consequences. Nobody was worried about the effect on our mental health of being shut out of communities or having our experience invalidated.

I've learned a lot, doing that. I've learned that there are men who truly, honestly don't know what they've done wrong, and don't know what to do now, and their pain, guilt and shame is visceral. But just because they are in pain does not mean that the process we're collectively going through is unjust. Justice is not synonymous with coddling men's discomfort.

In recent decades, as the idea of men's right to rule at home and in public life has become more and more rickety, new justifications have had to be found. If history can no longer be hammered around the shape of their shame, people search for other ways to explain away their own behaviour. One permission slip that patriarchy loves to give itself is the appeal to nature – specifically, to a particular idea of evolutionary biology that owes more to magical thinking than it does to scientific rigour. Male dominance is meant to be a manifestation of natural selection, and rape culture an evolutionary advantage. Men and boys are simply born violent and selfish – and if God didn't make them that way, nature did.

This approach to interpreting evolutionary science is known as 'sociobiology' or 'biological determinism'. It's a simple, seductive theory that has passed into folk wisdom. Right now the marketplace for ideas is in free fall, full of shady short-traders and rotten loans. Biological determinism is a convenient way of laundering shoddy ideas and sending them back to market.

In this hectic understanding of masculinity, men are simply animals, testosterone-driven beasts following laws of nature that play out in patterns remarkably similar to the laws of late capitalism: take what you want and screw the other guy. It's a simple story that hallucinates a world of heroism and hierarchy where every possible moral or ethical conundrum resolves itself into fight–fuck–kill.

Again, it's puzzling that more men aren't offended by the assumption that possession of a penis automatically cripples a person's ethical capacity. Perhaps it's because animals are allowed to be innocent. Animals are allowed to act on instinct. Allowing nature to take the fall for what culture did offers moral cowards an intellectual justification for abandoning personal responsibility. Young men in particular seem oddly eager to claim to be no better than animals when it suits them. Sociobiological arguments are recruited to explain away all sorts of gendered injustices, from inequality in the paid workplace (men have larger brains and are therefore more intelligent) to modern beauty standards (women are designed by nature to appeal to men sexually, which is why it's important for them to maintain an ideal waist-to-hip ratio). Scientists like Cordelia Fine have painstakingly explained why, 'contrary to the view that the brains of men and women are strikingly different, none of these differences were particularly substantial. Even for the very largest, the overlap between the sexes meant that about one in five women were more "male-like" than the average male.'[2]

The theory of evolution by means of natural selection is a rich, complex and beautiful hypothesis, but one thing it isn't and never has been is a moral argument of any kind. From the start, though, people have tried to squash it into the shape of one. Darwin himself got the chance to look at the emergence of the theory of eugenics – the argument that 'unfit human specimens' should be prevented from breeding – and turned away in disgust. And yet petty 'neo-masculinist' pop philosophers and YouTube televangelists routinely invoke Darwin's theories to legitimise bigotry – a misreading that insults both the man and the method.

It's not that there are no facts under the morass of evolutionary mysticism. It's not that there is no solid research, that there are no plausible theories in there; but these crisp slices of genuine scientific enquiry are battered in the heavy crumb of convenient fictions, deep-fried in received wisdom and smothered in the special sauce of popular prejudice so they're easier to swallow for those who already have their mouths full of comforting lies. That stuff isn't good for you. Eventually it settles in around your heart.

The notion that the natural inclination of the male human animal is towards dominance, violence and sadism is nothing but propaganda. Essentialism is invariably conservative, but the rallying cry of every weak apologist for misogyny – 'Not all men!' – deserves to be reversed. Not all men are shambling supplicants to their own biology. Not all men are incapable of change. When men do shitty things to women, they don't do it because that's the way men are, but because that's the way men feel, and men have been permitted very few ways to manage their emotions that are non-violent.

Within living memory it was women, not men, who were assumed to be unstoppably, uncontrollably sexual. In the nineteenth century it was the female sex drive that was supposed to be animalistic and in need of management. By contrast, modern culture imagines women as blank sexual canvases, erotic receptacles with no serious desires of their own. In fact, when women do feel desire, they are encouraged to treat it like every other hunger in their unruly bodies – as something dangerous, something that they need to stamp down on right away before it gets them into trouble.

As much as the natural fallacy excuses crimes against women, it utterly erases crimes against men and boys. If the behaviours commonly understood as masculine were really so natural, they would not have to be enforced with violence. If it were really so aberrant for little boys to be gentle, to be emotionally expressive, these behaviours would not be terrorised out of them. If little boys became men automatically, they wouldn't need anyone to tell them to man up. Biological determinism is an excuse – it lets us take a look at the wreck of modern masculinity, shrug our shoulders and say, well, we found it like this. It was broken when we got here.

The long-held presumption that violence – including sexual violence – is an inevitable extension of male sexuality and a fundamental aspect of male identity, is one of the most insidious lies currently holding the human species back from deeper healing. Social Darwinism repackaged man's inhumanity to man as a moral imperative. We tend to understand 'nature' according to the socioeconomic norms of our age, and right now the prevailing idea is that violence, sexual and racial injustice, and pitiless competition are not merely justified but somehow a biological duty.

Trying to explain human behaviour by looking at how animals behave is hardly more accurate than scrying for the future in the entrails of birds, as the ancient Romans did right before their cities were ransacked. But suppose, for a moment, that it was all true. Suppose that men really were designed by natural selection to be savage, sexually unhinged, aggressive, domineering and destructive, whereas women were designed to be passive, to nurture and to put up with men? Suppose all of that really was 'natural' – why would that make it a good idea? The universal assumption in all of these pleas to nature is that history and biology have come to a close – that adaptation and natural selection have already done their work, with modern man as the finished product.

This is a comforting idea for some. Progress is invariably condemned as unnatural by those who are confused by the present and afraid of the future, because the personal is not only political. It is also historical, economic and material.

In August 1941 the writer Dorothy Thompson wrote a taxonomy of Nazism for *Harper's Magazine*, suggesting a simple test to guess who, at any given social gathering, would turn fascist if tempted. 'Kind, good, happy, gentlemanly, secure people never go Nazi ... But the frustrated and humiliated intellectual, the rich and scared speculator, the spoiled son, the labor tyrant, the fellow who has achieved success by smelling out the wind of success – they would all go Nazi in a crisis.'[3] That sounds plausible. And there's plenty of evidence to suggest that misery and despair shovel a lot of people towards the nihilist cults of modern racism and sexism.

The trouble is that the stereotype doesn't tell the whole story. Plenty of anxious, heterosexual Caucasian gentlemen nursing ignoble but predictable anxiety about their status in the world have somehow managed not to drink the crypto-fascist Kool-Aid, refreshing though it surely looks to anyone lost in the desert of modern masculinity. We don't hear from those gentle, often desperate souls, but they're out there. I know, because I've met them. I know because, again, some of my best friends are depressed, anxious white men who rarely get laid and yet somehow manage to retain their grip on human decency. I've often heard them say, as the latest horrific massacre flashes across the rolling panic attack of the news, that in another life, that could have been them. But it wasn't them. Why not? A few months ago I was bored and wistful online, and I asked some of those men – friends and strangers – to tell me what exactly it was that stopped them going down that road. And they did.

It was my mother, one man wrote. She raised me to respect women. It was my father, said another. I saw how he treated my mother and sisters. I swore to be different. I escaped an oppressive Evangelist background, another man told me, and that led me to question everything. It was the love of Jesus, said another. My college girlfriend was patient with me. My wife had had enough. I have a daughter. I am a son. It was the girls in my online gaming group. It was my karate teacher. I got sober. I got dumped. I got better.

Every answer was different. The common thing was that they all *had* one. There was a moment, or a number of moments, where they decided to rewrite the story of their own lives. The difference between sexist and non-sexist men is not how depressed they are but how good their skills are for dealing with it. Despite the lack of a road map, despite their own terror, men and boys are still divesting from toxic masculinity, abandoning their sunk costs and going clear. And that is courage. That is resistance. Not the whole of it, but the start. Any fool can put on a white shirt and wave a tiki torch at strangers. It takes something more to stare down the smooth-talking, hate-dripping hard men promising to take away your pain and panic and say, 'Not today.' Cowardice is preferring a life of crabbed and paranoid violence because you're too scared to sit in a room and feel your own damn feelings. Actual rebellion is not marching behind whatever slick dog-whistling fascist happens to come down your street promising glory – but refusing to be spiritually crushed or co-opted. And maybe you don't feel better, but you at least carry on, and that is heroic.

The men I respect most are not perfect. They are human beings who have made mistakes. What sets them apart is that they have the backbone to change, to accept responsibility for their actions, to risk getting things wrong, to grow without expecting their personal growth to come at the expense of other people's suffering. There's a lot of room to get things wrong if you're willing to own it, pick yourself up and keep on stumbling forward. Even when you're afraid of messing up. Even when you'd rather stay calcified in your own safe little carapace for fear of being found out. That's what courage is.

Courage is knowing that emotional pain is not a competition. It's understanding that everybody's trauma is different, everybody's trauma matters, and feminism isn't to blame for the way men and boys suffer in this society. That masculinity doesn't need to be toxic, but toxic masculinity is killing the world. That we get through this together, or not at all.

So what does it mean to be a good man? The answer, the real answer, the one that more men need to be ready to hear, is that *it does not matter*. It does not matter, because the problem is not 'bad men'.

The real problem is an unjust social structure where men of every moral character have most of the power, meaning that the course of a woman's life is so often set by how many 'bad' men she encounters along the way. Most women I know who are partnered to 'good' men consider themselves lucky to have found a life partner who is not a controlling misogynist coward – but they still have to get lucky with their relatives, colleagues, teachers, doctors, employers and political representatives – or find a way to survive when the dice of male ethical dysphoria don't roll their way.

Men's moral choices still have a disproportionate impact on women's lives. If women and girls had an equal share of the power and resources in society, it would not have to matter as much as it does whether a man is 'good'. And that's the sticking point. This sexual revolution is not about making men better. This sexual revolution imagines a world where a woman's life does not depend on all of the men in it being 'good'.

13

TRUTH AND CONSEQUENCES

Abuse always has consequences. Up until now, the consequences of sexual abuse have mostly been shouldered by survivors. In fact, right back to the book of Genesis, women have been blamed for men's bad choices and punished for knowing too much – especially for knowing too much about men.

So how should culture respond to sexual and racial injustice, now that these things are so much harder to unsee? If men and women want to live differently, the consequences of abusing power are going to have to change. There must be consequences for sexual violence, for domestic violence, for misogyny and bigotry. The fact that generations of men have not faced the same consequences that are now being imposed might feel unfair. But naming violence makes violence visible. Generations ago, sexual violence was normalised in a way that we are only now coming to terms with. But generations ago, a lot of things were normal that we now abhor. Social change is painful. There is always a human cost – but it is never as high as the cost of opposing change.

For many centuries, abuses of power have been defined and dealt with by the powerful. Men have been allowed to decide what rape is and who deserves to be punished for it. In classical mythology, the shame and stigma of rape is borne by victims of rape. One of them, Cassandra, the daughter of the Trojan king Priam, is punished for refusing to have sex with the god Apollo by being cursed with useless foresight – to know the future but have nobody believe her. Most young women living in sexist societies know what it feels like to be disbelieved without having to be personally cursed by a minor deity. Nonetheless, Cassandra tries to warn her people that Troy is about be invaded. Nobody listens, and in the end, she is raped and murdered along with the rest of her family.

Then there's the legend of Lucretia, from ancient Rome. Lucretia, in the historian Livy's account, was a noblewoman who was raped and who killed herself to make sure nobody thought she had submitted willingly to abuse. The men of Rome then overthrew the monarchy to avenge her and established a republic. Over the subsequent centuries, Lucretia has been mythologised as a model of female chastity, her suicide held up as the noblest possible response to sexual violence. She has been romanticised by poets from Chaucer to Shakespeare; she has been painted, naked and in pain and in salivating detail, by Titian, Botticelli, Dürer and many others. But her own part of the story, as Sandra Joshel writes in 'The Body Female and the Body Politic', was over. 'Once Woman has played her role – to attract the villain whose actions set in motion other active males who construct the state, empire, and therefore history in the Roman sense – she must go … "How tragic!" sigh author and reader, finding pleasure in the pain of noble loss.'[1]

Times have changed, and male-dominated mass culture has graciously acknowledged the possibility that women who survive male violence might have other things to do in the story than die. The rape and murder of a lover or family member is still a standard way to give a male hero something to fight for, but occasionally women are allowed to complain about it, too – as long as they do it in men's language, and on men's terms. In fact, if you go by the endless movies made about revenge for sexual violence, what men as a whole seem to think the appropriate response to rape is one of two things: swooning followed by eventual lifelong commitment, or a guts-out killing spree.

Male violence is still ubiquitous in the stories men write about women but, curiously, this has not made men any more likely to acknowledge the existence of rape, much less stand against it.

There is a distasteful pattern in modern culture of grown men suddenly discovering the phenomenon of violence against women and responding by finding reasons to look at more of it. This usually involves some hand-waving about 'raising awareness', even though women and girls are already well aware, because they can't afford not to be. The question to male creators, whenever culture fetishises violence against women without challenging it, is simple: did you come to help, or did you just come to watch?

When I was a teenager in the early aughts, pop culture was one pouting parade of strong female characters written by men, who took bloody revenge on their oppressors while wearing skin-tight Lycra. Women who have been raped on film were damaged goods, and they took the only kind of revenge that patriarchy could safely imagine: they flipped out and started shooting things. The type of angry woman a man can handle is slightly underdressed, tragically self-defeating and, crucially, not pointing a finger at him.

The film my friends and I flocked to see when we were starting to be old enough to understand the power dynamics of sexuality without having a clue what to do with them was *Kill Bill*. The irony of a high-rolling rape-revenge fantasy being produced by serial rapist Harvey Weinstein is coruscating in retrospect. On the set of *Kill Bill*, lead actress Uma Thurman was bullied into doing a stunt scene that left her seriously injured. Asked a decade later how she felt about Harvey Weinstein being exposed as a predator, Thurman's red-carpet response to *Access Hollywood* was low, slow and chilling. Her face was a stiff mask of self-control as she told the reporter that 'I have learned that when I've spoken in anger, I usually regret the way I express myself. So, I've been waiting to feel less angry, and when I'm ready, I'll say what I have to say.'[2]

There was no sword and no shiny vinyl catsuit. There was only rage, real rage, the sort that cannot be stylised and resold, clear and calm and terrifying. This is what frightens powerful men far more than the vengeful heroine of limpid legend. Anger that does not scream and throw things but tells you instead how very, very disappointed it is. How it expected better. Anger that shows you the damage you did in a way you can't look away from. Anger that does not want you to die, but to live differently.

The question of what we do with abusers in our midst, abusers who some of us might love, has been tearing apart communities I have been close to for years. I have seen it happen again and again. Truths long hidden are spoken, and before long it is the people telling those truths – usually women – who are blamed, not for lying, but for causing harm – as if harm were not already being done, had not already been done, for years. I have watched the collective inability to deal with the fact that 'good' men might not always do good things fracture communities and friendships. I have been involved in restorative justice processes in activist circles. I know that the climate is, for once, less than merciful to men. I know that men are scared. I also know that this could not have happened any other way.

I don't want to live in a world where men don't change until you threaten to destroy everything they love. I wanted to believe that men would care enough about women to want to change of their own accord. I wanted to believe that male innocence and white innocence would not continue to be purchased at the price of everyone else's pain. But belief is not enough without evidence of action.

'Boys will be boys' is not an adequate moral response to fifteen centuries of cruelty. The sentiment, however, retains its hold on the popular imagination, and it's worth asking why. What does it mean for boys to be boys? And when is youth an excuse for cruelty?

This is a question I started asking myself seriously three years ago, when I spent time interviewing the young men following 'alt-right provocateur' Milo Yiannopoulos around America on his tour whipping up race hate on US campuses. I was struck not just by how young these men were, but by how young they seemed – how profoundly and dangerously immature in their alt-right Rumspringa, how fundamentally divorced they were from the concept of consequences. In the article, I called these young men 'lost boys', and on that basis it garnered more condemnation and threats from the political left than any piece of journalism I've ever done. In fact, the catastrophic immaturity of these young men was precisely what I found most chilling. Because they were young in a very particular way – young in a way that only boys, and usually only white boys, ever get to be.

That was when I truly realised in a new way how our experience and understanding of youth itself means something very different depending on who we are and where we come from. In many languages – and in archaic forms of English – when 'youth' is used as a noun, it only and always means a young man. Women rarely get to be 'youths' in the way that implies a state of unformed and rather adorable potential. Young women, and a great many young men of colour, are not understood to have potential – for different reasons. The 'potential' of young men of colour is not valued in the same way because so many cultures do not properly value the lives of people of colour, particularly not Black men. Grown women, meanwhile, are not understood to have 'potential' – by the time we reach puberty we are already supposed to be at the height of our social and cultural value.

'We value young women for what they are,' wrote Goethe, 'and young men for what they may become.'[3] Women in the public eye are not permitted the mistakes of youth that we routinely allow young men of a similar age. A twenty-one-year-old white boy is still halfway a child in the world's eyes and deserves tolerance and the benefit of the doubt; a twenty-one-year-old girl had better not make any mistakes, because she'll pay for every one of them down the decades.

Youth and ignorance are shabby excuses for cruelty. There's a young woman who I've known since we were both very small who has always, from infancy, struggled with her temper. She was rippling at the seams with pent-up energy and was also taller and stronger than many of her peers. She would boil over with frustration and lash out. Sometimes she would actually hit or shove, more often she would simply frighten other little girls in a way she hardly understood, because she was also a child. However, because she was a female child, she was expected to master her temper.

Hitting and shoving were not tolerated. Being young was no excuse; being in pain was no excuse. I watched my friend, over the course of years, struggle to manage and master her own propensity for violence. By her mid-teens she had done it. She's in her mid-twenties now, and still has a tendency to be stubborn, is quick to feel frustrated – that's just in her nature – and you can still, at moments of stress, see behind her eyes the tiny girl on the edge of a screaming, punching tantrum. But taking control of that part of her character has made her more patient, more considerate than most of my close friends. I admire restraint and gentleness in her far more than I do in those who have not had to struggle for it. I know how hard it was and I also know that she had no choice, and that there are times when a bit of rage in women can be a good thing. Society does not tolerate girls who are furious and physically rowdy. What if we also asked boys to be in complete control of their reactions by their mid-teens?

This is where our notion of what it truly means to be young is unbalanced in a way that the concept of privilege does not adequately explain. Every young person deserves a second chance: a chance to better themselves, to learn and grow and experiment, and that's something young women should be allowed to have, too. But no young person should be permitted to use their youth as an excuse for refusing to take responsibility for their actions or recognise the humanity of others.

Time works differently for girls. For women, being young – or at least appearing to be young – is an essential part of the social currency we're told is vital to respect and safety. We cannot expect to be valued once we start to become mature adults. We are valuable for the juicy ripeness of youth. Beyond our mid-twenties, we start to rot – in the language of pick-up artists and the alt-right, we 'hit the wall'.

The idea of the biological clock is a powerful one – and we apply it not just to fertility but to every field of a woman's life. It is as if, just as we start to get things figured out, we're told – that's it, you're done. The plain reason for this is because the world remains terrified of adult women, and of adulthood in women, even as it relies on them to do the bulk of the work that keeps society running – even as it refuses to allow women to ever, truly, be young.

Women are supposed to look young, but they are rarely allowed to actually *be* young, with all of the awkwardness and error and allowance that implies. This is not just unfair – it is an enormous waste of human talent. Everyone deserves time to develop, learn and make mistakes. If women get less time, we are running at a deficit. The persistent idea that women are entirely adult at the moment they hit puberty and cease to be of social or cultural importance the moment their fertility starts to tail off is bad for everyone.

The question is which causes more social harm: the extended grace period afforded to so many young men, or the truncated time women get to experiment and be truly young? The emotional stunting of men and the wastage of women's talent are both cultural wounds in their own right. Together they are a sociological disaster in the making, whereby those who are allowed time to mature are rarely required to do so, whereas those who are expected to shoulder adult responsibility way too young are not allowed time to develop the skills they might need to be an actual grown-up.

A broken value system is behind all this – a human metric whereby men and boys are valued as people, and women and girls, whatever their age, are valued as bodies. Women are assumed to be mature enough to consent to sexual activity as soon as they are physically post-pubescent – and this argument is still successfully used to acquit child rapists in courts of law, whereby simply looking sexually mature is frequently assumed to be, in and of itself, consent.

When maturity is discussed in the public sphere, it is couched in the language of traditional life milestones – things a person is supposed to do and, increasingly, to own. For men, in particular, adulthood is still supposed to consist of external commitments – to a wife, a family, a sensible full-time job, a house, a car. Part of what has been called the modern 'crisis in masculinity' relates to the sudden impossibility of acquiring any of these things – as every such crisis has done over centuries of capitalist accumulation. If you phrase manhood as something you can buy, what happens when most young men can't afford it?

For women and girls, by contrast, maturity is usually defined by their capacity to care for others. This means that the qualities deemed necessary to adulthood are strictly divided between the binary genders. It is still commonly assumed that 'girls mature faster than boys', but the truth is that girls are simply expected to grow up faster, to manage their own emotions and anticipate the needs of others in a way that men and boys are not asked to do until much later, if at all. This aspect of male privilege – the privilege to remain a perpetual adolescent who whines and lashes out when asked to consider other people's feelings – is corrosive to the character. The privilege to remain ignorant of the harm one is causing is more damaging still. This is, in part, because culture rarely expects from white men the maturity to be able to distinguish between wanting a thing and owning it, or the adult capacity to consider that one's desires must be balanced against the autonomy of others. That's a mood familiar to anyone who has tried to explain to a toddler, while gently prising their fingers off a stolen toy or treat, that just because they want a thing doesn't mean that the thing is theirs. That bawling, grasping impulse straight from the id is the sort of 'innocence' that deserves to be relegated to childhood – but it seems to have become increasingly forgivable in adult men in positions of power.

Our collective commitment to white male innocence costs our species much too much. Any society in which the amount of personal responsibility a person has to take for his emotions and behaviour is in inverse proportion to the amount of power and privilege he has – any society where poor girls have to grow up fast so they can take care of other people while rich men are allowed to be perpetual children, acting up and lashing out – will ultimately destroy itself.

Creating real social and professional consequences for abusers and predators is the only thing that will bring about the change we need. More often than not, when this has happened to men I have personally known – when they have been called to account for causing harm – they have not had careers to lose, because they were largely young and largely broke. Most of us are not working in glittering Hollywood studios or ancient government buildings, unless we're there to empty the bins. If you're on a zero-hours contract, your boss probably doesn't care how many bodies you have buried under your patio as long as you turn up on time to sweat for less than the living wage. Your friendship group, on the other hand, does care. Your family cares. Your reputation affects more than your ability to earn a wage – in fact, that's often the last thing to go. In workplaces and institutions there are at least processes to follow, even if they are rarely put into effect, even if it's easier to just shut down the victims. But the process for community justice, by its nature, is not formalised. Who decides when and whether it's right to let a person with a history of abuse back into a community?

Ostracism is brutal. It's a primal fear that predates and pre-empts any modern legal sanctions – so primal and so brutal that even talking about it can feel taboo, tempered with the childlike panic that by naming it we will invite it on ourselves. It is often employed by groups who, for whatever reason, have found the laws of their culture and community inadequate to the task of tackling bad behaviour. And it's not just fearful and uncomfortable for the person being ostracised – his friends, family, colleagues and followers are all implicated in the process, finding themselves torn between defending their friend and avoiding consequences themselves.

Ostracism is not a new solution. It has, in fact, been applied to the problem of abuse within communities and scenes for a long, long time – but within recent memory it was victims who were shunned. Don't talk to that girl – she's crazy. She's trouble. She's a wrecker. We all know how he gets at parties, and she's a slut anyway, if we all just ignore her, maybe she'll leave town.

Even if you know he's done something dreadful, it can be hard to watch someone you care about go through it. I know how hard it is because it has happened to me, too. I have been shunned by social groups, including when I lacked the sense to shut up about the first man who raped me, who was a popular, powerful older figure. I found myself disinvited from parties. Shut out of confidences. Talked about behind my back just loudly enough that I could hear exactly who thought I was a manipulative, unstable liar. I was nineteen and in college, so it wasn't as difficult as it would later become to move on and make new friends.

The point of punishment is to create consequences for antisocial behaviour, and the point of creating those consequences is to get people to behave better. I wish that the world at large had valued women enough to pay attention to their demands for change before they had to resort to ostracism and shunning. The anguish of so many men and boys in this awkward transition period is visceral. But it is the opposite of kindness to let things go, to forgive transgressions before they have been properly understood. Allowing people to escape the consequences of their actions is not kind, and it is not respectful. It's just nice – and too much damage has already been done by telling women and girls that they have to be nice to men, no matter the cost.

However we learn to live together in the future, if we do, we're going to have to build new social infrastructure as we go, figure out ways to actually process all of the pain and discomfort that we were previously obliged to bury alive. And yes, it's going to be messy. No, it's not going to be nice. But it will be kind, and it will be ethical, and it will, eventually, be worth it.

What I have said to the men I know and love, who are going through the sort of panicked personal reckoning where time telescopes down and it becomes impossible to imagine any sort of future – the first thing I want to say – is that you will survive this. I promise. We will survive it, together. I can't promise you'll be forgiven, but I'm willing to bet you'll get a second chance at intimacy and security in the future, as long as you work to deserve it now. My sympathy is slightly limited by the double standard at work here – the sort of social shunning and shaming women like me face for being a bit annoying is equivalent to what men face for being an actual sexual predator.

Because you know what's worse than being accused of rape? Being raped. You know what's worse than being worried that you can no longer flirt in the way you used to? Being unable to express desire in any way without fearing for your safety. Being told that your sexuality itself is an invitation to violence. Being told you have no agency at all, and having that repeatedly confirmed by men who treat you like so much walking meat.

You may feel as if you're at risk of losing everything, but that is not the case. The thing that is going to determine your character is not just what you did then, it's what you do now. This matters beyond any one individual or community. It matters for our societies on a much broader scale that you stay here in this place of discomfort. As we have seen earlier in this book, a great many young men are being courted by far-right, anti-democratic ideologies off the back of this collective mood. It makes clear emotional sense. When one group throws you out, you run to the group that will have you – I've done that before, and regretted it, though never with such high stakes. The new right laps up young and not-so-young men who feel wronged and misunderstood. They will fry your heart and eat it. Do not trust them.

I'm being blunt here not because I don't care, but because I do, and because I know what it's like. Really. I know something about how it feels to have the world at large think the worst of you, and to say so in no uncertain terms. I have been called out before. I have been flamed all over the internet and had people try to destroy my reputation. Sometimes I had things to answer for and sometimes I didn't, but it felt like having my self-esteem flayed alive every time. I have not recovered everything I have lost from the times I was mercilessly called out in public. But it is survivable, and sometimes, even in the heat of internet outrage, it is possible to stay in the room with people's rage and learn from it.

Part of what adulthood actually involves is learning, slowly and painfully, how to rectify past mistakes, make amends and move on. Many of us spend a lifetime learning how to do that within our intimate communities, and some of us never do. The dreadful truth, however, is that growing up in public as a political being is a wholly different experience now than it was in previous generations. We need to do it faster, smarter and with more flexibility than was required of our parents and grandparents.

To paraphrase Margaret Atwood, men are afraid that women will cancel them, and women are afraid that men will kill them.[4] This doesn't mean that the fear of being cancelled is insignificant, but feelings are not facts. For someone culturally influential, 'cancelling' may well be the worst thing they can possibly imagine happening, but that doesn't mean it is objectively the most dangerous tendency in modern politics.

Nobody can grow up, let alone do grown-up politics, without learning how to change their behaviour with good grace. Yes, fucking up is embarrassing and hurtful for everyone involved. It is also inevitable. It is part of learning how to be human in a volatile and fast-moving political culture. The plain fact is that if you want to be part of a cause that's bigger than yourself, you will, at some point, fuck up, unless you're among the rare subset of the human species who tumbled from the womb with perfect politics. So I do understand how it feels, and it's coming from a place of sympathy, as well as love, when I say that there are times when the only option is to sit with that discomfort, with that fear, and let it go.

Let it all go. Let go of your resentment at women's lack of patience, let go of your wounded pride, let go of your useless shame, and let go of the idea of being a 'good guy'. The world is not neatly divided into good and bad men. It never was, and we need to let go of the idea that it ever was, so that we can finally be better to one another, finally learn to deal with our shit like grown-ups in this strange new cityscape we're crawling through together, trying to find our way to the light. That's the only way we're going to move from a place of holding abusers to account into a future where abuse is less likely to happen.

To men who have hurt women and are unwilling to do the work of change, all I can say is – I'm sorry. I'm sorry that you hurt people. I'm sorry you weren't able to be better. I'm sorry that you have jeopardised all of the good work you've done in the world with your incapacity to treat the women you get involved with as human beings.

I'm sorry for the people you have hurt and for those who will be hurt anew by the revelations about your behaviour. I'm sorry that nothing I can say or do can save you from the consequences. For a long time I told myself that you did this because you were ill, and you are still ill. Everyone who cares about you was worried about you long before this happened. But the fact that you hate yourself is not an excuse for the harm you've done. Nor can you avoid being held accountable because you're unwell and in pain. Many of the people you have hurt were also unwell and in pain, and they're in more of it now because of how you treated them.

Private self-hatred is not a substitute for public justice. For men and boys struggling to resolve their sense of self with changing social expectations, it is important to remember one thing: beating yourself up does not help. Private self-hatred is not a substitute for public justice.

Most of the violent men I have known were deeply self-loathing. Most of them also believed that their own self-loathing was punishment enough – that their suffering was both explanation and excuse for the way they continued to behave towards women and people weaker than themselves. The most uncomfortable revelation is the fact that none of this, really, was that revelatory. A great many people knew. Maybe they didn't know all of it, but they knew enough to feel tainted by a complicity that hobbled their compassion.

It turns out that this isn't about individual monsters. It never was. This is about structural violence, about a culture that decided long ago that women's agency and dignity were worth sacrificing to protect the reputation of powerful men and the institutions that enabled their entitlement. Everyone, including the 'good guys', knew it was happening. We just didn't think it was all that wrong, or at least, not wrong enough to take action.

Except that now that really does seems to be changing. Now 'old dinosaurs' are wondering how to negotiate with the oncoming asteroid, while current or former 'stupid young men' are in a state of panic about their imminent introduction to the concept of 'consequences', leading to the question: what, precisely, is the age when men are expected to take responsibility for their behaviour?

The notion that women's agency and dignity might be more important than men's right to act like grabby children whenever they want may feel like uncharted territory, but some of us have lived here all along. Men and boys who don't know their way around yet are struggling to work out what they ought to do now. My friend's husband wants to know if he did the right thing in challenging a superior at work who said he was going to stop hiring 'hot women' because he'd only want to assault them. My photographer friend wants to know why he didn't listen properly to the rumours about predators in his industry, and if he can make up for that now. My environmental activist friend is worried that the stupid things he did as a teenager will invalidate the work he's doing today.

Nobody wants to be having these conversations, but they are necessary. Avoidance of these conversations has shaped our culture, because cultures are defined not only by the stories they tell, but also by the ones they don't. We have built entire lives, families and communities around the absence of this conversation. And yet here we are, having it anyway. So how do we handle what we know now about how women have been treated for so long?

This is a question in two parts. It's a question about how men should now relate to women in particular, and to their own sexuality in general. It is also a question about how we all cope with the consequences. How do we deal with suspecting what we suspect, with knowing what we know about our own past behaviour? The very first thing we must do is to continue to know it – to actively know it, rather than filing it away in the spam folder of our collective consciousness. We must stay here, in this difficult place. We must look at what we have done and have allowed to be done to others without flinching or making excuses.

Many of the men I have talked to about this have begun, of their own volition, to speak about 'no longer objectifying women'. To wonder whether they should just stop looking at pretty women at all, if the act of desiring another person is itself violent. It's sad that that confusion has arisen. It should, after all, be possible to desire someone without dehumanising them. But we have apparently created a world where it is incredibly difficult for a man to desire a woman and treat her as a human being at the same time.

Some men I speak to are worried, now, that 'having to ask' will mean more rejection. I would draw attention to the fact that even as women everywhere are confessing to crimes others have committed against them, describing lifetimes of humiliation and hurt, still the second or third thought on some men's minds is anxiety about whether this will affect their chances of getting laid.

Rejection feels awful. So awful that batteries of violence, shame and blame have been built to help men avoid it. If women's desire is absent from this conversation – if women are not thought of as desiring beings, if female desire is so terrifying we can barely speak of it without nervous laughter – then yes, we are going to remain confused about the difference between seduction and assault. That confusion is not human nature. Human nature is a lazy excuse for not doing the work of change here, and I'm sick of hearing it.

Men who believe they cannot change are already being shown up every day by the growing number of their fellow male humans who have changed, who are changing. We can rewrite the sexual script of humanity.

Unfortunately we are in one of those rare and curious moments where we have to do something unfair and hurtful in order to answer decades of pain and injustice. We didn't want to have to make an example of anyone. We tried to ask nicely for our humanity and dignity. We tried to put it gently, and our gentleness was mistaken for weakness, and nobody cared. Now that there are consequences, now that there is finally some sort of price to pay for treating women like interchangeable pieces of flesh and calling it romance, men are paying attention.

When women actively place their own needs first, even for a moment, polite society implodes in outrage. No, for once, we're not being gentle and forgiving. Yes, it's unfair that some men who have hurt women will be made examples of in their communities and workplaces while others who have done the same will face no consequences. It feels unfair that the cost of mistakes some men made in their youth may well be losing professional respect, job security, money and power. But it has been a lot less fair for a lot longer for all the people who were hurt and humiliated, disrespected and degraded, and who were expected to choose between shameful silence and blowing up their careers or communities by speaking out.

In 2016, Stanford student Brock Turner was given a nominal sentence of just six months after his father complained that Turner's life was being 'ruined' over 'twenty minutes of action'. The 'action' in question was a brutal rape that left Turner's victim bleeding, naked, behind a dumpster. In her statement to the court, the young woman told Turner and the world what the justice system lacks the means to articulate:

> You took away my worth, my privacy, my energy, my time, my intimacy, my confidence, my own voice, until today … The damage is done, no one can undo it. And now we both have a choice. We can let this destroy us, I can remain angry and hurt and you can be in denial, or we can face it head on, I accept the pain, you accept the punishment, and we move on.[5]

Feeling bad because you have harmed someone is not morally or ethically equivalent to feeling bad because you have been harmed but, as educator Nora Samaran notes:

There is a quality in guilt that paralyses. Worse, it leads those who feel it to lash out, like pythons or like some kind of wild animal guarding a nest of self-loathing. Do not look at the man behind the curtain, says the guilt, or I will attempt to destroy you just to stop you from getting near the core of my shame.[6]

A lot of men, right now, are wondering if forgiveness is possible. If amnesty is on the horizon. If you fish your crimes out of the past and lay them dripping in front of us, will women accept you, forgive you, let you back into the loving female place you've been told is the only respite you're allowed from the awfulness of the world?

The answer will eventually be yes. Well, *my* answer will eventually be yes. I can't speak for everyone, as I'm pathologically forgiving and have often been told by people who care about my well-being that my life would be better if I didn't let the men in it get away with quite so much because I expect no better. Still, my answer will always eventually be yes, yes, you are forgiven.

There will be time for apologies. We have the rest of our lives to do this differently. There will be time to reach out to those you may have wronged and say that you were a younger and different person, you are sorry, you didn't know, you tried not to know, you know now. There will be time to make it right, but it will take precisely that. It will take time.

And there will be time. Time for everyone to do better. Time to make a world where love and violence are not so easily confused. Time for a species of sexuality that isn't a game where women and girls are the prey to be hung bleeding on someone's bedroom wall.

And there must also be space for rage. Space for women and girls and queer people to be angry, to be unreasonable, even though our rage is more than reasonable. There has to be space for our pain and anger, because patriarchy made everything precious in our lives conditional on not making a fuss. Because we were forced to carry the weight of all the hurt in the world, and stifled if we dared to complain, and then praised for being strong and silent. We don't want to have to summon that strength any more – and we should not have to.

14

Abuses of Power

Sexual violence is essential to the logic of authoritarianism. To describe the violence at the centre of sexuality is to describe the cruelty clotting the arteries of our social systems. This means that describing rape culture is an act of political defiance. Most people who set out to bring their abusers to justice aren't looking for revolution. They just want to stop rapists getting away with it. Unfortunately we live in societies designed to let rapists and abusers get away with it, and a mortal challenge to one is inevitably a mortal challenge to the other.

It matters how powerful men treat women, not least because that's how they tend to treat everyone else. There are moments when the mask comes off. Moments when you can see the stitching come apart on the seamless story powerful men have told themselves about what justice means in the world and who deserves it. The naked, shameless demonstration of how little women's pain matters when weighed against the reputation of men has been a running theme of the past half-decade in the sleazy, high-stakes, reality-television disasterpiece of world politics.

In 2018, embattled patriarchy found its ultimate test case. The conservative judge Brett Kavanaugh, Donald Trump's pick for Supreme Court Justice, was accused of multiple counts of sexual assault by women who knew him as a young man. His chief accuser came forward to testify before the Senate, in an act of patriotism eerily akin to what Anita Hill went through in the 1990s, when she came forward to accuse Justice Clarence

Thomas of harassment and was publicly denounced as 'a little bit nutty and a little bit slutty'.[1]

Authority becomes abuse when it cannot be challenged without immense personal cost. Swallowing her tears, Dr Christine Blasey Ford described the high-school party in 1982 where, she said, a young Kavanaugh tried to rip off her clothes and shoved a hand over her mouth to stop her screams. She was subjected to a gruelling, hours-long interrogation in front of an audience of millions. Republicans on the Supreme Court selection committee made clear that, to them, whatever had happened, it was Kavanaugh who was the real victim. Critics said she was going too far, tutted that she should have shown more compassion for Kavanaugh and his children, asked why she chose to remain silent for so long – and why she had tried to stay anonymous. The answer of course, was fear – not for her good name, but for her life. Shortly after coming forward, Ford had to leave her home with her family because of death threats.[2] It's dangerous to get between a rich, powerful man and something he wants. Ford, like Anita Hill before her, will now always be the woman who accused a powerful judge of rape, and had her sanity and credibility publicly questioned, her sexual history vivisected, her life upset for ever. That she chose to come forward anyway was an act of courage and rebellion. It always is. To name someone as your abuser is a direct challenge to power; the more powerful the abuser, the more perilous the challenge. So who is the law supposed to protect? Is it supposed to protect women from violence, or men from consequences?

Ford told a Senate panel dominated by white, male Republican senators that she was 'terrified' but had come forward out of a sense of 'civic duty'. She remained calm, dignified and good-natured, repeating that she 'just wanted to be helpful', as she was questioned by a female outside prosecutor. Kavanaugh, by contrast, yelled, sneered and snarled on live television in front of an audience of millions in petulant rage that the world wasn't making this easy for him. He is now a Supreme Court Justice.

A display of rage from a man is strength; from a woman, a display of emotion is weakness and hysteria. Imagine if Hillary Clinton had hollered and hissed and shown her teeth at a Senate hearing. But the most fascinating aspect of the Kavanaugh hearings was how many of his defenders attempted to claim not that no assault had happened but that it didn't matter if it had.

This was the key to the whole thing. The Kavanaugh hearings forced American institutional patriarchy to come out and say how little it cares about women. As the hearings drew to a close, panicked men in public life and in the press queued up to make the case not simply just that Ford and the other accusers were lying about being assaulted, but to imply that *if they had been assaulted, it didn't really matter*. Boys will be boys, after all. If we condemn Kavanaugh on the basis of Ford's testimony, shouldn't we also condemn half the men in America? Our parents, our children, ourselves? To men like this, the outrage is not that women and children may have been hurt, but that men of good standing might be made uncomfortable.

This was hardly helpful to Kavanaugh, who has always insisted that he is innocent of assault. But for those unsure where their loyalties should lie, it was the argument with most impact. Kavanaugh clutched for it in an interview on Fox News, where he insisted that everyone 'makes mistakes in high school'. Well, of course we do. But how many of us got away with it? How many of us got the chance to move on and learn? The question is not whether teenagers – or, come to that, grown adults – do stupid, selfish things. The question is who has to pay for those 'mistakes' with their lives and their freedom, and who gets to stay 'innocent'.

Not everyone is innocent until proven guilty – not when male innocence comes at the cost of women's pain. As a circuit court judge, Kavanaugh tried to deny a seventeen-year-old pregnant immigrant girl the right to an abortion.[3] Clearly, the consequences of decisions you make when you are young and reckless are supposed to weigh heavier on girls than on boys.

In fact, the bodies of young women have long been considered collateral damage on the journey to manhood. From girlhood onwards, women are the ones who are supposed to carry the responsibility and suffer the consequences for men's teenage stumbles and errors of judgement, while boys are allowed to remain, in Kavanaugh's words, 'innocent'. Kavanaugh's own prepared statement admits that he was 'not perfect in high school'. Of course not. Young white men are people of whom perfection is not demanded.

This is only true for white boys, of course. Before a law that is supposed to be impartial, young men of colour learn not to expect leniency on account of their youth, their hormones, their misreading of a situation or, for that matter, their utter innocence of any crime whatsoever. This double standard has everything to do with punishing Black youth and nothing to do with protecting women.

In 1989, five Black teenage boys were arrested in New York for a crime they did not commit. The Central Park Five case, which ended with the wrongful imprisonment of five young men of colour for the rape of a white woman, gripped America.

Donald Trump, then a businessman in New York, paid a reported $85,000 to place a full-page advertisement in the city's newspapers calling for their execution. 'I want to hate these muggers and murderers,' wrote Trump in the advert, which ran before the boys had even been charged. 'They should be forced to suffer and, when they kill, they should be executed for their crimes.'[4]

'They must serve as examples so that others will think long and hard before committing a crime or an act of violence ... what has happened,' Trump wrote, 'is the complete breakdown of life as we knew it.'[5]

So whose suffering matters? Whose bodies deserve protection? Who gets to make mistakes, and what kind? Whose youth and foolishness are an excuse, and whose are a condemnation? And is one wealthy and powerful man's potential failure to attain even more wealth and power considered more of a loss to society than the life and dignity of young women?

'The legal system,' as Judith Lewis Herman observes, 'is designed to protect men from the superior power of the state, but not to protect women or children from the superior power of men. It therefore provides strong guarantees for the rights of the accused but essentially no guarantees for the rights of the victim.'[6]

When abusers cannot easily dismiss their own abuses, they reframe the issue, saying not simply that abuse does not occur, but that it doesn't matter. Because when has it mattered?

When has it mattered what men do to the women in their lives, or in their past, or in their way? What does one girl's suffering matter compared to a man's potential discomfort at being asked to change or apologise? He was young; he was just a boy, and anyway, she's only a girl. He has a bright future. Or he's grown and has a brilliant career. Or he's older and has an important legacy. He was just a boy. His story is what matters; she must find a way to live in its margins. This is how power operates in a rape culture. And this is why a culture of sexual violence and social exclusion of victims cannot be separated from the context of patriarchy.

Male violence at the highest levels of government has been tolerated for a very long time. Unfortunately for these men, women are no longer quite so willing to keep their mouths shut about it as they once were. This means that even voters who don't really care about male politicians assaulting women know that on some level they should care, which is why so many double down on frantic excuses. Nobody is more anxious to win the culture war than those who have already lost the moral argument.

The way these men choose to behave towards women is not incidental to the way they behave in office. It's not a side issue, and it's not a private matter. The way politicians treat women and children informs their attitude towards everything else. Men who bully, grope and harass because they feel entitled to do so will treat the electorate with the same violent contempt. Institutions that cover up and tacitly condone abuse will operate similarly. Sexual violence and abuse are central to our political culture, not least because they create something that men like Trump have always relied on: they create complicity, and complicity rallies the troops far faster than loyalty.

In a similar way, over the past decade, there has been an outcry against the sexual abuse of children within some of our oldest institutions of power – from the foster homes that were supposed to care for our most vulnerable young people to the boarding schools that were supposed to educate the most fortunate, all the way up to the top of the Catholic Church itself. Organisations that justified their very existence by their mission to offer guidance to the needy and direction to the lost.

For decades, the abuse of children by teachers and religious leaders was the stuff of popular comedies and folk wisdom; everyone had heard the one about the altar boy and the sacrificial wine – but the men who hurt these children were never made to answer for their shameful abuses. It was the children themselves who were expected to swallow the shame in silence, and when too many spoke up, the institutions closed ranks to move offenders on to a new posting – sacrifice the victims to protect power's image of itself.

The threat of sexual violence for men is associated with situations of absolute powerlessness – usually, and crucially, institutional powerlessness. Boarding schools. Prisons. Religious institutions. Decades before the Catholic Church was forced to acknowledge the endemic nature of child abuse by its clergy, the idea of the predatory priest was so common that it had been absorbed into popular narrative. The body politic should react against these ideas; instead, it reabsorbs the uncomfortable truth into its narrative.

This is how power works in patriarchy – right through to the top. The British boarding schools that educated some of my home country's most elite politicians have been revealed, in the past decade, to be hotbeds of sexual coercion and abuse. Ritual humiliation in childhood is still considered a necessary, forming part of the character of the modern citizen – and sexual and gender-based shaming has always been part of that obligatory informal curriculum. In mixed-gender schools in Britain, sexual abuse and harassment of girls has become so 'endemic' as to go unnoticed, according to activist Soma Sara, who collected thousands of accounts of victimisation in schools.[7] It is at schools and at colleges that boys learn how to become men by shaming women so as not to be shamed themselves. By performing violence so that violence might not be done to them in turn.

Those who are victims of abuse learn to normalise abuse, especially when they are very young, and especially when that abuse comes at the hands of those in positions of care and authority. When you cannot escape being hurt, it is dangerous to turn your rage on the people who have hurt you. Better to blame and shame the victims. That way you can stay safe.

This redirected shame calcifies into a culture of silence. Often it's women who are tasked with being the enforcers of that silence, to shame other women into shutting up, to protect the men they work for or rely on for their own status. They may not like doing it, but they may also have little choice. Women are the ones hired for the thankless roles that boil down to decades spent soothing male egos, and greasing the wheels of power by making all the difficult and dirty things go away. Women come in with the bucket to clear up the messes men make, including for other women, and if they refuse to do so, they can find themselves scrubbed away in turn.

Harvey Weinstein was surrounded by female assistants who ferried starlets to his hotel rooms or actively worked to make sure he could dine alone with whoever was on the menu that day. Women have chosen to support their husbands, their bosses, their fathers, time and time again, rather than supporting and believing one another, and often that decision has made absolute sense. It is often safer to enable the abusers than acknowledge the abuse. Social mechanisms are in place to keep women isolated from one another, competing with each other, pitted against each other for the attention and favours of men at work and outside it. For many, many years, there was simply no way for us to speak to one another honestly about what was happening, no spaces to tell a different story about power and desire.

This has been long been the implicit attitude of institutions across the political spectrum, from the Republican Party to the Nobel Prize Foundation. It is incorrect to suggest that these institutions have never had strategies in place to deal with sexual assault and abuse. It's merely that the strategies so far have been variations on the theme of 'just make sure nobody talks'. The strategy has been to tolerate a certain amount of abuse as normal, to protect abusers and sideline survivors.

The test for organisations and institutions in the years to come will not be whether or not abusers can be found amongst their ranks, but how they deal with them when they are. Getting rid of individual violent men, eventually, under extreme public pressure, will not do away with institutional misogyny – that will only happen when the consequences of not speaking out and protecting the vulnerable are greater than the consequences of complicity.

Most of us know, in our meek and yearning little hearts, that the men we've chosen to lead us – or had forced upon us – are swollen frat boys straight from the collective id. Most of us know that in a just world, Donald Trump would probably be in jail. But acknowledging that out loud would mean acknowledging an injustice so enormous we'd have to haul ourselves up and do something about it – and most of us have been exhausted for at least a decade. So it's easier to believe the perpetrator. It's easier to let him have what he wants.

Let's be honest with ourselves for a second, here. Let's admit that nobody votes for a Donald Trump or a Boris Johnson or a Jair Bolsonaro believing their candidate to be a sincere and morally upstanding specimen of humanity. All that is required from these spoiled thugs is all that has ever been required of them: the absolute bare minimum of plausible deniability, just enough of a flimsy fig leaf for browbeaten gatekeepers to feel OK about letting men like this off the hook, like they were always going to, whether the alleged offence is a hilarious, totally innocuous – definitely not racist – crack about Africans or raping someone in a changing room. It is uncomfortable to have to articulate what we have always known about these men. It is uncomfortable to acknowledge that when powerful men insist that their history of sexual violence is a 'private matter', what they mean is that it doesn't matter. That it shouldn't matter.

Here is what we are saying shouldn't matter. Here's how E. Jean Carroll describes her interaction with Trump in the 1990s:

> He seizes both my arms and pushes me up against the wall a second time, and, as I become aware of how large he is, he holds me against the wall with his shoulder and jams his hand under my coat dress and pulls down my tights ... he opens the overcoat, unzips his pants, and, forcing his fingers around my private area, thrusts his penis halfway – or completely, I'm not certain – inside me. It turns into a colossal struggle.[8]

That is a description of rape, and Carroll knows just what she is risking by making it part of the public record. Naming your abuser is an act of defiance, especially when your abuser's entire personal brand is about getting away with it. As Carroll herself noted:

> His admirers can't get enough of hearing that he's rich enough, lusty enough, and powerful enough to be sued by and to pay off every splashy porn star or Playboy Playmate who 'comes forward', so I can't imagine how ecstatic the poor saps will be to hear their favorite Walking Phallus got it on with an old lady in the world's most prestigious department store.[9]

I admire this woman. She's easily in my top twenty people ever to accuse the former president of the United States of violent sexual assault. But she doesn't talk like a good victim. A good victim is meant to be meek and ashamed. A better victim remembers that in a culture that values men's comfort over women's lives, being accused of rape and assault is worse than being assaulted or raped. The best victims of all are so silent that the men who hurt them can move on to ever-more-lucrative positions of political prominence – entirely undisturbed by conscience.

It's easier not to look. It's easier not to have to contemplate the emperor in his horrible nakedness. It's easier to cling desperately to the belief that the president is not a rapist than it is to acknowledge how many of our fellow citizens would rather elect a rapist than a woman. Perhaps the most provocative thing that the modern movements against sexism, racism and imperialism have done, the most shocking thing that has been responded to with most savagery by state forces, is simply to describe structural violence as it is. They have taken away the one thing the powerful and comfortable rely on to sleep at night: they have taken away the privilege of ignorance.

Abuses of power are scaffolded by an architecture of wilful ignorance. In *On the Origins of Totalitarianism*, Hannah Arendt tells us that one of the hallmarks of a tyrannical regime is the way it permits both oppressors and bystanders to preserve their own innocence – innocence in the original sense of the word, implying not purity but ignorance. It allows bystanders to dangle above the solid ground of moral responsibility on a parachute of suspended disbelief. It allows people not to know what they know.

Listen carefully the next time you hear a man warn his daughter, his sister or his friend not to walk alone down that street, not to accept that date, not to talk to strangers. Then watch that same man's face when you suggest that violence against women is an intolerable social calamity, that some women and girls have good reason to fear or even hate men. He's a decent person. He is not being dishonest. He has merely lived with hypocrisy so long that he has mistaken it for a moral programme. He has learned that male violence is at once everywhere and awful but somehow also natural and acceptable. The only permissible solution to male violence is more male violence. The only thing that can stop a bad man is a better man.

This has long been the logic of justice in a world where white men have the power to define all women's experience for them, where the majority of rapes go unreported and the majority of those that are reported go unpunished or even uninvestigated, while any woman bringing a charge of rape or assault can expect to suffer further for reporting the crimes committed against her.

One of the most damaging tendencies among people who like to think of themselves as fair-minded and reasonable is the assumption that the world works as it should. You can be a clever, kind, well-read person who recycles your rubbish and never throws away your small change, and still labour under the delusion that the society you live in is essentially just and reasonable – that incidents of violence and persecution and ignominy and corruption are rare.

This is known, in academic circles, as the 'just world theory'. The belief is more common among people who are right wing, but everyone is susceptible – including those to whom violence has been done. When you cannot stop someone hurting you, you find ways to persuade yourself that it doesn't really hurt, or that it shouldn't really hurt.

The notion that 'those to whom violence is done, go on to do violence' has passed into folk wisdom – but folk wisdom tends to favour the folk with most power. In fact, the vast majority of victims of abuse do not go on to abuse others. Abuse is not a taint, a shame that spreads on contact and cannot be controlled. And yet there remains a self-perpetuating superstition that speaking about abuse – like speaking about fairies, or vampires, or monsters from legend – invites it in.

Speaking about abuse is not without its dangers – as we have seen, one of the immediate consequences tends to be that perpetrators of abuse round on victims and attempt to threaten or shame them into silence. But before that, there is a cost to speaking about abuse even to yourself, or with safe, trusted loved ones. The cost of acknowledging abuse you have suffered is that you are obliged to process the pain and hurt, to summon the memories of traumas that happened when you could not protect yourself. In order to prevent hurt and injustice in the future, you have to face the hurt and injustice of the past. And that's harder to do than it is to write.

In 1948 the journalist Milton Mayer spent a year compiling a devastating account of the lives of former Nazi Party members in small-town Germany. To a man, none of them had known what was being done to the Jews. They'd heard rumours. They'd noticed their neighbours disappearing. But nobody knew for sure – nobody knew, and at the same time, everybody knew. They were able to choose ignorance because it was convenient not to connect the dots, and then, as Mayer recounts one former Nazi telling him:

> One day, too late, your principles, if you were ever sensible of them, all rush in upon you. The burden of self-deception has grown too heavy. Suddenly it all comes down, all at once. You see what you are, what you have done, or, more accurately, what you haven't done, for that was all that was required of most of us: that we do nothing.[10]

Doing nothing is always easier than taking a stand. Knowing nothing is always easier than choosing to see what's in front of you. Monsters grow in the dark matter of learned public ignorance, and the suspension of disbelief has long been compost for every type of predator, psychopath and petty demagogue. When the #MeToo movement broke, Hollywood didn't 'really' know what was going on, just like Silicon Valley didn't 'really' know, just like everyone in the Trump administration didn't 'really' know. Really knowing would have required everyone to act according to their consciences.

So nobody knew. And at the same time, everyone knew. Speaking out was too painful, and the risk was too great, so everyone looked away. The longer everyone looked away, the more awkward it would be to look again, because it was starting to look like the sort of nightmare public relations executives have when they fall asleep in front of the casting couch. It was more comfortable to look away, to discredit the abusers and disbelieve the evidence of your own senses, until nobody could look away any more. Until everyone was forced to know what they knew.

A culture of abuse and of complicity with abuse is part of how power operates. It's not just the woman hurt and humiliated at work, or the the line manager who violates her boundaries. It's her friend who stays silent for fear of losing her job, her colleague who can't see what she's making a fuss about, the CEO who decides that she's the one making trouble. It recruits entire industries in a psychodrama of secrecy and shame. *The cover-up is the point.*

And that pattern repeats at every stratum of society, because the relationship between state and citizen is structurally abusive. The exploitation of women and the subjugation of people of colour are the rotten core of the economic logic that sustains our societies and the culture that shapes our lives. That's a hard truth to hang on to. Most people don't want to know how much freer they might be. It is emotionally safer to let yourself be lied to. It's safer, when you have to watch petty despots bully and cheat their way to power, when you are forced to confront the real extent of rape and abuse being revealed all around you, to believe that somehow you chose this. That somehow you wanted it. Because the alternative is worse. The alternative, awful truth is that it doesn't matter what the vast majority of us choose, because none of the choices on offer are enough to protect us, or our families, or our communities from violence. Because the important choices were never ours to begin with. Because we are not living in an age of consent.

The same young men who grow up believing that they are entitled to exploit the bodies and trample the humanity of others go on to lead the institutions and write the laws that define our lives. The rest of us learn to look the other way, if we can bear it. It is always easier to sympathise with abusers than it is with victims of abuse. That's one strategy for surviving patriarchy. It's a strategy millions of us choose every day. All we have to do is nothing at all.

Endnote: Trauma Politics

Pain is not supposed to be part of anyone's political conversation. That's the rule, especially if people with political power have caused you pain. You don't talk about your trauma. You don't show the damage. You smile at abusers, including your own. You offer forgiveness to those who never even asked permission. You make things comfortable. No matter what outrages are inflicted on you and people like you, you suck it up and you move on.

In January 2021, armed white supremacists stormed the US Capitol. Representative Alexandra Ocasio-Cortez, a young congresswoman from New York, described her experience during the Capitol riots during an Instagram live broadcast. In footage that was seen by millions, she told the world how she had had to run from racists with guns, how she had been convinced she was about to die. She articulated the lasting horror of that moment and explained why it mattered. Conservatives, including those who had personally egged on the mob, exploded with outrage. The congresswoman was told, as survivors of abuse are always told, to *get over it already*. Sit down and shut up and stop making it awkward for the rest of us. Don't you have healing to do?

'These folks who tell us to move on, that it's not a big deal, that we should forget what's happened, or *even telling us to apologize* – these are the same tactics of abusers,'[1] Ocasio-Cortez said, drawing a deliberate link between the behaviour of her conservative opponents and the behaviour of sexual predators.

In the broadcast, Ocasio-Cortez shared that she is, like so many others, a survivor of sexual assault. Ocasio-Cortez directly compared the silencing tactics of sexual abusers to the behaviour of conservative apologists who, at this very moment, are frantically insisting everyone shut up about the four years of relentless civic vandalism and crypto-fascism culminating in an attempted white-supremacist coup.

Modern conservatism prides itself on being logical. It insists that all its arguments are based on undiluted fact. This claim to be evidence-based is made against all actual evidence, and it is made more urgent the more unhinged conservative figureheads become, the more hysterical their gun-clutching followers squeal to be the centre of attention at all times. The messier their divorce from reality gets, the louder they bellow that they are beings of pure reason. They're not swayed by emotion, not like weak and girlish liberals, wailing about made-up things like climate change and rape culture and racism.

According to conservative cultural dogma, it is progressives who are driven purely by emotion. 'Facts don't care about your feelings' is the inevitable retort when a woman of colour calmly explains what literally happened to her. What this means is that we don't care about your feelings, or the things that happened to you. Nor is it our responsibility to stop them happening again.

When we speak about trauma and violence, the English language deliberately smudges the distinction between suffering and delusion. For women, particularly women of colour, visible suffering is synonymous with delusion. If she speaks about harm that has been done to her, she is crazy by definition and can be safely ignored. Women's physical pain is routinely dismissed, including by medical professionals. In the US, Black women's pain is dismissed to the extent that they are routinely denied potentially life-saving treatment, which may explain why African American women are three times as likely to die in childbirth as their white neighbours.[2] Women of colour are expected to be 'strong' in a way that demands they never show the damage. The more pain a woman is socially expected to bear, the more she is praised for her strength.

Alexandra Ocasio-Cortez is one of a growing cohort of women refusing that sort of strength in the name of social justice. The notion that anyone might have a political priority more pressing than mollifying white male feelings is still shocking. Most of us, after all, have been raised to pay attention to the emotions of white men, to attempt to manage their moods, because not doing so might be dangerous. You can see how people who happen to be white and male might come away with the impression that their inner lives were more important than everyone else's. You can see how those people might eventually elevate their every pang of prejudice and sentiment to the status of unassailable fact.

This stubborn inability to tell the difference between facts and feelings is rotting our politics. In recent years autocrats around the world have exploited this tendency by simply presenting the public with a range of facts from which they can select whatever fits their mood. For a decade now, populist leaders have exploited that prejudice and been praised by swivel-eyed acolytes for 'telling it how it is'. When Trump warned Americans that their country was overrun with Mexican rapists, he was 'telling it how it is', just like when Jair Bolsonaro insists that only 'fairies' wear face masks in the middle of a pandemic.[3]

These men are not telling it how it is – they are telling it how it *feels*. In a culture held hostage to the psychic fragility of whiteness and the hysteria of straight masculinity, feelings apparently matter more than objective truth.

At a time of global crisis, our futures are in the sweaty hands of men who have built a mass movement around refusing to handle their emotions like adults. The further the new right drifts from the realm of reason, the more it loses control of its own emotions, the more it insists that its every tremor of feeling be treated as sacred fact.

This is not a new idea. More than three centuries ago, Mary Wollstonecraft wrote about the same cultural binary in *A Vindication of the Rights of Woman*. She warned about the dangers of confusing 'sentiment and reason' – feelings and facts. She explained that culture designates men as reasoning, thinking beings and women as creatures of emotion and sentiment, a strict binary that causes political problems at the highest level.

If men are unable to acknowledge their own emotions, they will start behaving as if their sentiments were simple fact, dressing their own subjective emotional responses up as objective truth. Wollstonecraft believed this was already happening in the revolutionary era of the late eighteenth century. What would she think now that politics has been overrun by a strain of toxic masculinity that has made emotional incontinence a moral good?

The idea that conservatives should exercise a shred of emotional self-control is now seen as censorship. But being asked to show basic regard for other human beings is not censorship, just as being made aware of harms you have done is not abuse. Censorship is what happens when you cannot speak about your own trauma without death threats.

Women are not specially endowed by nature with the capacity to tolerate trauma and endure violence without complaint, even though that capacity has become the definition of 'strength' in marginalised people.

Systems of violence require a final service from their victims. They require victims to protect abusers from awareness of their crimes. In order for systems of violence to continue, they must be normalised. In order for them to be made normal, they must be morally justified. And in order for them to be morally justified, victims must be coerced into silence, so that nobody has to actually face up to the human consequences of the harm that has been done in their name.

When people refuse to let atrocities stay buried at the crossroads of history, when they refuse to prioritise the comfort of abusers over everyone else's lives, that is an act of defiance. Ocasio-Cortez was not out of control. She simply refused to pretend that what had happened to her and so many others did not matter. She did the unforgivable. She refused to forgive.

And right now, refusing to forgive and forget is essential work. Because the idea, for example, that the attempted kidnap and murder of elected officials in the name of a defeated president is something anyone should just move on from, least of all those who were there, is repulsive, morally reprehensible and politically foolish. The world has spent far, far too long being held hostage to the emotions of powerful men.

There is a direct connection between the way people experience abuse within individual relationships and the way we all experience systemic oppression. This means that we can learn a great deal about how to think our way out of structural violence from those who have studied and survived intimate abuse and trauma. The patterns of abuse and repression are dynamically similar, from the way that shame is weaponised to deny victims their agency, to the extraordinary efforts of abusers to manipulate public perception, to the fight to normalise survivors' rights to dignity and safety.

The struggle of the human spirit against the intimate terrorism of interpersonal violence is a struggle against tyranny in microcosm, the struggle of consent against control. And the way we get free is the same. We get free by establishing basic safety, centring the experiences of the vulnerable and of survivors, by refusing to let those who abuse their power use that power to reshape reality or rewrite our collective history. The decades of work that have been done on the process of individual recovery from abuse and trauma must now be brought to bear on the long, difficult, essential process of recovery from collective injustice. Freedom is not just the unlocking of a cage door – it begins and ends with the belief that one does not belong in a cage.

When analysing collective political tendencies, the framework of trauma is essential. The nature of political power, of biopower – the power to 'make live or let die', as Foucault puts it – is always already exploitative. It is abusive by its very nature. Sometimes more, sometimes less, but always. What has changed recently is not simply the nature of the abuse but how little those in power care about disguising their own abuse. In fact, right now, the exercise of geopolitics is distinctly and nakedly abusive, in a way that all abusers get when they are losing control.

The question is not if power will change now that we have seen its true face, but how long those of us without it will stand by and watch authority become abuse at the highest level. These men told us who they were right from the start. What they don't get to do, however, is tell the rest of us who we are. We still have time to choose what sort of society we want to live in. We can choose to stop looking away.

We are led by men who have lost any earned authority they may have once had, and it is driving them mad. Our political leaders and elected officials are manifestly both unable to steer the world through the crisis they created and utterly uninterested in doing so. It is now impossible to kid ourselves that we are safe with these people with anything other than a superhuman effort at self-delusion.

For those of us who have realised and accepted that we are being abused and terrorised, it's often worse, because we don't yet know how to escape and we have lost the ability to believe that we can, except maybe individually. I have made a career speaking my version of truth to power, but my own truths still get stuck between my tongue and my teeth sometimes. For the longest time, I could not make them speakable at all. The fear of what would happen if I were to pronounce my pain out loud was so overwhelming that I shaped my life around the empty space of it. And like a lot of people, I've learned the hard way what happens when I make men uncomfortable. When I refused to make myself small and powerless so that others could feel large and in charge, there were consequences. Despite my many privileges, there were consequences – and something has gone horribly wrong when you have to rely on privilege to save you from the consequences of standing up for yourself.

It is painful, really and truly painful, for people to recognise and acknowledge that the structures they trusted and the people who are supposed to care for them are in fact violent and exploitative and pose an active threat to them and to their children. Most people don't leave abusive situations on the first try, especially not when escape is no guarantee of safety.

It is existentially horrifying to maintain awareness of crisis on this scale. Most people can't sustain that sort of awareness for long, so they rationalise, they make themselves feel safe, even though they know, rationally, that they are not.

The challenge is to allow people to sustain their awareness of crisis just enough to escape it – to maintain their awareness of crisis without triggering the response of collapse, despair and acceptance. That takes us back to those standard trauma responses: fight, flight, fawn or freeze. Most marginalised groups have been trained out of the fight response to trauma. When you are powerless and in constant danger of violence, 'fight' as a trauma response can get you brutalised or killed.

People's responses to trauma are predicated on their place in society. White men are more likely to respond to existential threat with violence and outwardly directed rage, because it is safer for them to do so. The relatively wealthy and secure are also more likely to fight on instinct. What the rest of us now have to wrestle with is our own sense that it is forbidden, even morally hazardous, to engage in any action which causes harm to the oppressor in any way. We have internalised the idea that it is wrong for us to fight. That is, in part, a learned response to sustained political trauma – it's what keeps the abuser in a position of power.

When systems of abuse are under attack, they defend themselves. Survivors of structural violence who speak out about injustice are routinely condemned as regressive acolytes of 'cancel culture' – reframing public conversation as if those who do violence to others are the real victims. Survivors are accused of 'playing the victim', as if a marginalised person speaking about their own suffering was always, by definition, in bad faith. We must hold firm against this sort of empty sophistry. To defy the shame and violence that wraps itself around the sclerotic heart of modern sexuality is not an attack on sex. To protest the rigid obligations of factory-issued female beauty is not to deny beauty in the world. To cry out when love is made conditional on accepting one's own subordination is not a betrayal of love. To disturb the sterile logic that flattens all possible pleasure and adventure into stale, violent transaction is to speak sex to power.

One of the finest acts of rebellion comes about when a person who has long learned that she must eventually be owned in some aspect by a man, that she owes her body and her desires to him, that she must be pretty and pleasant and good enough to be owned, suddenly refuses to be told what she should want and who she should please and chooses instead to please herself.

Every person on earth is entitled to own their own body and shape their own story. When a person who is not white or straight or male behaves as if she believes this of herself, she demands only her unclaimed share of what was already hers from her first breath and enriches both herself and society.

You don't have to believe it all at first. You don't have to wait until you're fully convinced that you are entitled to take up space in the world, that you don't owe your body to anyone or your allegiance to any orthodoxy that refuses you your full humanity. It's hard to believe these things all the time, especially when you've been taught not to. I know that in my life there are days when the weight of everything that has happened to me pins me to my bed, days when my whole life is superimposed by subtitles that translate everything I say into the old learned language of shame.

Consent is the opposite of authoritarianism and the inverse of shame. What is required is not a new set of rules about consent. What is required is a new ethics of consent, in public and private life, in our sexual and social interactions – everywhere that coercion and bullying are dressed up as choice and called freedom.

The ethics are simple. Every human being deserves agency over their own body and soul. No human being is less worthy of care, dignity and personal autonomy because of the body they were born with. Nobody is born with the right to use the body of another person for their own ends. Coercion and bullying are unacceptable, the pursuit of private gain by means of bullying and coercion is killing the world, and the price we have collectively been paying to protect the wealth of a few powerful men and the comfort of men everywhere is too high. A world beyond this culture of abuse and coercion requires all of us. Men and women, survivors and allies and everyone else. Everyone who is willing to try, to do the hard work that hope involves and to hold each other up along the way.

Resistance is an intimate art. It works from the inside out. It starts when you start to realise that wherever you are, whatever you have done, you deserve to live, you deserve to be part of a society that nurtures life and makes it worth living, and it's not too late to make one. That you can claim your part of a better, braver world when you know in your bones that you're worthy of it. That you are enough, for the future that is coming – ready or not.

NOTES

INTRODUCTION

1 Shulamith Firestone, *The Dialectic of Sex: The Case for Feminist Revolution* (London: Jonathan Cape, 1971), p. 126.

2 Paul Mason, *Clear Bright Future: A Radical Defence of the Human Being* (London: Allen Lane, 2019), p. 70.

3 Jessica Southgate and Lucy Russell, *Street Harassment – It's Not OK*, Plan International UK, 2018, plan-uk.org/file/plan-uk-street-harassment-reportpdf/download?token=CyKwYGSJ

4 '"Half of women" sexually harassed at work, says BBC survey', BBC News, 25 October 2017, bbc.co.uk/news/uk-41741615

5 *Violence Against Women: An EU-wide Survey*, FRA – European Union Agency for Fundamental Rights, 2014, fra.europa.eu/sites/default/files/fra-2014-vaw-survey-at-a-glance-oct14_en.pdf

6 Germaine Greer, *The Female Eunuch* (London: Paladin, 1970), p. 279.

7 More details about Gamergate here: en.wikipedia.org/wiki/Gamergate_controversy

8 Frank Browning, *The Fate of Gender: Nature, Nurture, and the Human Future* (New York: Bloomsbury USA, 2016), p. 34.

9 Ibid., p. 92.

10 Dan Cassino, 'Even the Thought of Earning Less than Their Wives Changes How Men Behave', *Harvard Business Review*, 19 April 2016, hbr.org/2016/04/even-the-thought-of-earning-less-than-their-wives-changes-how-men-behave

11 Amanda Marcotte, 'What's destroying democracy around the world? At least in part, misogyny and sexism', *Salon*, 10 September 2019, salon.com/2019/09/10/whats-destroying-democracy-around-the-world-at-least-in-part-misogyny-and-sexism/

12 Joshua Hawley, 'The Age of Pelagius', *Christianity Today*, 4 June 2019, christianitytoday.com/ct/2019/june-web-only/age-of-pelagius-joshua-hawley.html

13 Associated Press and Ashley Collman, 'Steve Bannon Says "Time's Up" Is "the Single Most Powerful Potential Political Movement in the World"', *Business Insider*, 15 September 2018, businessinsider.com/ap-steve-bannon-times-up-is-most-powerful-political-movement-2018-9?r=US

14 Isobel Thompson, 'Steve Bannon Is Obsessed with the Fall of the Patriarchy', *Vanity Fair*, 28 February 2018, vanityfair.com/news/2018/02/steve-bannon-is-obsessed-with-the-patriarchy

15 Leigh Goodmark, 'Stop Treating Domestic Violence Differently From Other Crimes', *New York Times*, 23 July 2019, nytimes.com/2019/07/23/opinion/domestic-violence-criminal-justice-reform-too.html

16 Elisabeth Mahase, 'Covid-19: EU states report 60% rise in emergency calls about domestic violence', *BMJ*, 11 May 2020, https://www.bmj.com/content/369/bmj.m1872

17 National Sexual Violence Resource Center, Statistics, nsvrc.org/statistics

18 'Why are rape prosecutions falling?', BBC News, 15 March 2021, bbc.co.uk/news/uk-48095118

19 'Number of rape charges at lowest level for 10 years', BBC News, 26 September 2018, bbc.co.uk/news/uk-45650463

20 Firestone, *The Dialectic of Sex*, pp. 10–11.

21 Caitlin Johnstone, 'Allowing #MeToo To Go Viral Is The Biggest Mistake The Establishment Ever Made', 10 November 2017, medium.com/@caityjohnstone/allowing-metoo-to-go-viral-is-the-biggest-mistake-the-establishment-ever-made-1c706d16783b

22 Wilhelm Reich, *The Mass Psychology of Fascism* (New York: Orgone Institute Press, 1946), p. 26.

23 Carole Pateman, *The Sexual Contract* (Cambridge: Polity Press, 1988).

24 Karah Frank, 'A Letter to My Abuser', theestablishment.co/a-letter-to-my-abuser-ff705dfec5cc/index.html, quoting George Orwell, *1984* (London: Penguin Books, 1974), pp. 204–5.

25 Judith Lewis Herman, *Trauma and Recovery: The Aftermath of Violence – From Domestic Abuse to Political Terror* (New York: Basic Books, 1992).

26 Audre Lorde, *Uses of the Erotic*, peacewithpurpose.org/ uploads/8/2/1/6/8216786/audre_lorde_cool-beans.pdf

1 WITHOUT OUR CONSENT

1 'Violence Against Women in the United States: Statistics', National Organization for Women 2021, now.org/resource/ violence-against-women-in-the-united-states-statistic/
2 'Statistics About Sexual Violence', National Sexual Violence Resource Center 2012, 2013, 2015, nsvrc.org/sites/default/files/ publications_nsvrc_factsheet_media-packet_statistics-about-sexual-violence_0.pdf
3 Zoe D. Peterson and Charlene L. Muehlenhard, 'A Match-and-Motivation Model of How Women Label Their Nonconsensual Sexual Experiences', *Psychology of Women Quarterly* 35(4), pp. 558–70, journals.sagepub.com/doi/pdf/10.1177/0361684311410210
4 Genevieve F. Waterhouse et al., 'Myths and legends: The reality of rape offences reported to a UK police force', *The European Journal of Psychology Applied to Legal Context*, 8, 1, January 2016, pp. 1–10, sciencedirect.com/science/article/pii/S1889186115000244
5 'Rape Case Judge Resigns Over "Good Family" Remark; State Orders Training', *New York Times*, 17 July 2019, nytimes. com/2019/07/17/nyregion/judge-james-troiano-resigning.html
6 'Irish outcry over teenager's underwear used in rape trial', BBC News, 14 November 2018, bbc.co.uk/news/world-europe-46207304
7 Conor Gallagher, 'Inside Court 12: the complete story of the Belfast rape trial', *Irish Times*, 28 March 2018, irishtimes.com/news/ crime-and-law/inside-court-12-the-complete-story-of-the-belfast-rape-trial-1.3443620
8 Peter Walker, 'Canadian judge who asked alleged rape victim why she didn't "just keep knees together" resigns', *Independent*, 10 March 2017, independent.co.uk/news/world/americas/judge-robin-camp-canada-ask-rape-victim-keep-knees-together-calgary-resigns-alexander-wager-a7621881.html
9 Nancy L. Paxton, *Writing Under the Raj: Gender, Race, Rape and the British colonial imagination, 1830–1947* (Rutgers University Press, 1999), pp. 9–12.

10 Cassidy L. Chiasson, University of Southern Mississippi, *Silenced Voices: Sexual Violence During and After World War II*, Honors Theses 340, aquila.usm.edu/cgi/viewcontent.cgi?referer=&httpsre dir=1&article=1336&context=honors_theses;Silenced

11 Lauren Duca, 'Donald Trump is Gaslighting America', *Teen Vogue*, 10 December 2016, teenvogue.com/story/donald-trump-is-gaslighting-america

12 Peter Pomerantsev, *Nothing is True and Everything is Possible: Adventures in Modern Russia* (Faber & Faber, 2017).

13 Alison Levitt and the Crown Prosecution Service Equality and Diversity Unit, 'Charging Perverting the Course of Justice and Wasting Police Time in Cases Involving Allegedly False Rape and Domestic Violence Allegations', March 2013, cps.gov.uk/sites/default/files/documents/legal_guidance/perverting-course-of-justice-march-2013.pdf

14 Helena Kennedy, *Misjustice: How British Law Is Failing Women* (London: Vintage, 2019).

15 Katie Heaney, 'Almost No One is Falsely Accused of Rape', *The Cut*, 5 Oct 2018, thecut.com/article/false-rape-accusations.html; André De Zutter, Robert Horselenberg and Peter Koppen, 'The Prevalence of False Allegations of Rape in the United States from 2006–2010', *Journal of Forensic Psychology*, 02, 2017.

16 'The Criminal Justice System: Statistics', RAINN, rainn.org/statistics/criminal-justice-system

2 THE HORIZON OF DESIRE

1 Catharine A. MacKinnon, *Feminism Unmodified: Discourses on Life and Law* (Cambridge, Mass.: Harvard University Press, 1987).

3 WE'RE ALL MAD HERE

1 Victims of Sexual Violence: Statistics, Rape, Abuse & Incest National Network (RAINN), rainn.org/statistics/victims-sexual-violence

2 'Harvey Weinstein speaks out: "I'm not doing OK"', ABC News, abcnews.go.com/GMA/video/harvey-weinstein-speaks-im-50432725

3   Katie Benner, 'Women in Tech Speak Frankly on Culture of Harassment', *New York Times*, 30 June 2017, nytimes.com/2017/06/30/technology/women-entrepreneurs-speak-out-sexual-harassment.html

4   Lundy Bancroft, *'Why Does He Do That'? Inside the Minds of Angry and Controlling Men* (New York: G. P. Putnam, 2002).

5   Jeffrey M. Masson, 'Freud and the Seduction Theory: A challenge to the foundations of psychoanalysis', *Atlantic*, February 1984, theatlantic.com/magazine/archive/1984/02/freud-and-the-seduction-theory/376313/

6   Sigmund Freud, 'The Etiology of Hysteria', quoted in Masson, 'Freud and the Seduction Theory', *Atlantic*, February 1984, theatlantic.com/magazine/archive/1984/02/freud-and-the-seduction-theory/376313/

7   Sigmund Freud, letter to Wilhelm Fliess, 4 May 1896, quoted in Jeffrey M. Masson, 'Freud and the Seduction Theory: A challenge to the foundations of psychoanalysis', *Atlantic*, February 1984, theatlantic.com/magazine/archive/1984/02/freud-and-the-seduction-theory/376313/

8   'One in eight of five to 19 year olds had a mental disorder in 2017 major new survey finds', *NHS Digital*, 22 November 2018, digital.nhs.uk/news-and-events/latest-news/one-in-eight-of-five-to-19-year-olds-had-a-mental-disorder-in-2017-major-new-survey-finds

9   Denis Campbell, 'Stress and social media fuel mental health crisis among girls', *Guardian*, 23 September 2017, theguardian.com/society/2017/sep/23/stress-anxiety-fuel-mental-health-crisis-girls-young-women

10 Patrick Butler and agency, 'Male suicide rate hits two-decade high in England and Wales', *Guardian*, 1 September 2020, theguardian.com/society/2020/sep/01/male-suicide-rate-england-wales-covid-19

4 BAD SEX

1   Alys Harte, 'A man tried to choke me during sex without warning', BBC Radio 5 Live Investigations Unit, bbc.co.uk/news/uk-50546184

2   Rhitu Chatterjee, '"Tip of the Iceberg" – 1 in 16 Women Reports First Sexual Encounter as Rape', *NPR*, 19 Sept 2019, npr.org/sections/health-shots/2019/09/16/761201571/tip-of-the-iceberg-1-in-16-women-report-first-sexual-experience-as-rape

3   Christopher Ingraham, 'The share of Americans not having sex has reached a record high', *Washington Post*, 29 March 2019, washingtonpost.com/business/2019/03/29/share-americans-not-having-sex-has-reached-record-high/

4   'No sex please, we're millennials', *The Economist*, 4 May 2019, economist.com/united-states/2019/05/02/no-sex-please-were- millennials

5   Tribune collectif, 'Nous défendons une liberté d'importuner, indispensable à la liberté sexuelle', *Le Monde*, 9 January 2018, lemonde.fr/idees/article/2018/01/09/nous-defendons-une-liberte-d-importuner-indispensable-a-la-liberte-sexuelle_5239134_3232.html; nytimes.com/2018/01/09/movies/catherine-deneuve-and-others-denounce-the-metoo-movement.html

6   Andrew Sullivan, 'It's time to resist the excesses of ♯MeToo', Intelligencer, *New York magazine*, 12 January 2018, nymag.com/intelligencer/2018/01/andrew-sullivan-time-to-resist-excesses-of-metoo.html

7   R. D. Clark and E. Hatfield, 'Gender differences in receptivity to sexual offers', *Journal of Psychology & Human Sexuality*, 2(1), 1989, pp. 39–55, doi.org/10.1300/J056v02n01_04

8   'Would You Go to Bed With Me?', BBC Radio 4, 2 November 2018, bbc.co.uk/programmes/m0000z50

9   Clark and Hatfield, 'Gender differences in receptivity to sexual offers', doi.org/10.1300/J056v02n01_04

10 Miss Cellania, 'The Historical Horror of Childbirth', *Mental Floss*, mentalfloss.com/article/50513/historical-horror-childbirth

11 Colin Barras, 'The real reasons why childbirth is so painful and dangerous', *BBC Earth*, 22 December 2016, bbc.com/earth/story/20161221-the-real-reasons-why-childbirth-is-so-painful-and-dangerous

12 'Maternal Mortality – key facts', *World Health Organization*, 19 September 2019, who.int/news-room/fact-sheets/detail/maternal-mortality

13 Nina Martin, 'U.S. Has The Worst Rate Of Maternal Deaths In The Developed World', NPR, 12 May 2017, npr.org/2017/05/12/528098789/u-s-has-the-worst-rate-of-maternal-deaths-in-the-developed-world?t=1604872591938

14 Hannah Summers, 'Black women in the UK four times more likely to die in pregnancy or childbirth', *Guardian*, 15 January

2021, theguardian.com/global-development/2021/jan/15/black-women-in-the-uk-four-times-more-likely-to-die-in-pregnancy-or-childbirth

15 Katie Zezima, Deanna Paul, Steven Rich, Julie Tate and Jennifer Jenkins, 'Domestic slayings: Brutal and foreseeable', *Washington Post*, 9 December 2018, washingtonpost.com/graphics/2018/investigations/domestic-violence-murders/

16 Khalida Sarwari, 'Domestic Violence Homicides Appear to Be on the Rise. Are Guns the Reason?', *News@northeastern*, 8 April 2019, news.northeastern.edu/2019/04/08/domestic-violence-homicides-appear-be-on-the-rise-a-northeastern-university-study-suggests-that-guns-are-the-reason/

17 Emily Nagoski, *Come as You Are: The Surprising New Science that Will Transform Your Sex Life* (London: Simon & Schuster, 2015), pp. 10–11.

18 Brian Alexander, 'Sorry, guys: Up to 80 percent of women admit faking it', NBC News, 30 June 2010, nbcnews.com/id/wbna38006774

19 Angelique Chrisafis, interview with Virginie Despentes, 'What is going on in men's heads when women's pleasure has become a problem?', *Guardian*, 31 August 2018, theguardian.com/books/2018/aug/31/virginie-despentes-interview-baise-moi-vernon-subutex

20 Neil Strauss, *The Game: Penetrating the Secret Society of Pickup Artists* (Regan: HarperTorch, 2006).

21 Thomas Hobbes, 'The Deregulation of the Sexual Marketplace', *Return of Kings*, 29 November 2014, returnofkings.com/48312/the-deregulation-of-the-sexual-marketplace

22 bell hooks, *The Will to Change: Men, Masculinity and Love* (New York: Atria Books, 2004).

23 Akeia A. F. Benard, 'Colonizing Black Female Bodies Within Patriarchal Capitalism: Feminist and Human Rights Perspectives', *Sexualisation, Media, & Society*, Oct–Dec 2016, 1–11, p. 3, journals.sagepub.com/doi/pdf/10.1177/2374623816680622

5 BEAUTIFUL TROUBLE

1 Sarah Berry, 'This trait makes men more attractive to women', *Sydney Morning Herald*, 7 June 2016, smh.com.au/lifestyle/

this-trait-makes-men-more-attractive-to-women-20160607-gpd5to.html

2 Karl Marx, *Economic and Philosophical Manuscripts of 1844*, XXII, marxists.org/archive/marx/works/1844/manuscripts/labour.htm

3 Body image report – executive summary, Mental Health Foundation, 13 May 2019, mentalhealth.org.uk/publications/body-image-report/exec-summary

4 Naomi Wolf, *The Beauty Myth* (New York: William Morrow, 1991), pp. 13–14.

5 National Association of Anorexia Nervosa and Associated Disorders (ANAD), Eating Disorder Statistics, anad.org/get-informed/about-eating-disorders/eating-disorders-statistics/

6 Kelsey Miller, 'Study: Most Girls Start Dieting by Age 8', *Refinery 29*, 26 January 2015, refinery29.com/en-us/2015/01/81288/children-dieting-body-image

7 '"Too fat to be a princess?" Young girls worry about body image, study shows', *Science Daily*, 26 November 2009, sciencedaily.com/releases/2009/11/091124103615.htm

8 Sarah Marsh, 'Eating disorders: NHS reports surge in hospital admissions', *Guardian*, 2 February 2018, theguardian.com/society/2018/feb/12/eating-disorders-nhs-reports-surge-in-hospital-admissions

9 Wolf, *The Beauty Myth*, p. 187.

10 Sarah Marsh, 'Eating disorders: NHS reports surge in hospital admissions', *Guardian*, 2 February 2018, theguardian.com/society/2018/feb/12/eating-disorders-nhs-reports-surge-in-hospital-admissions

11 beateatingdisorders.org.uk/media-centre/eating-disorder-statistics

12 Candida Crewe, *Eating Myself* (London: Bloomsbury, 2006).

13 Wolf, *The Beauty Myth*, p. 187.

14 Timothy A. Judge and Daniel M. Cable, 'When It Comes to Pay, Do the Thin Win? The Effect of Weight on Pay for Men and Women', *Journal of Applied Psychology*, 20 August 2010, timothy-judge.com/Judge%20and%20Cable%20%28JAP%202010%29.pdf

15 Ruth Umoh, 'Study finds you're less likely to get hired if you're overweight. Here's how to avoid this bias', CNBC, 3 November 2017, cnbc.com/2017/11/03/study-finds-youre-less-likely-to-get-hired-if-youre-overweight.html

16   Jess Zimmerman, 'Hunger Makes Me', *Hazlitt*, 7 July 2016, hazlitt. net/feature/hunger-makes-me

6 LABOURS OF LOVE

1   bell hooks, *All About Love* (New York: William Morrow, 1999), p. 137.
2   Moira Weigel, *Labor of Love: the Invention of Dating* (FSG, 2017), p. 5.
3   Dalia Gebrial, 'Decolonising Desire: The Politics of Love', blog, *Verso*, 13 February 2017, versobooks.com/ blogs/3094-decolonising-desire-the-politics-of-love
4   Linda R. Hirshman and Jane E. Larson, *Hard Bargains: The Politics of Sex* (New York: Oxford University Press, 1998), p. 258.
5   Miguel de Cervantes Saavedra, *Don Quixote*, translated from the Spanish by J. M. Cohen (London: Penguin, 1975), p. 108.
6   Kate Manne, *Down Girl: The Logic of Misogyny* (London: Penguin, 2019), p. 15.
7   Ibid.
8   Various, including Linda J. Waite and Maggie Gallagher, *The Case for Marriage: Why Married People Are Happier, Healthier, and Better Off Financially* (New York: Doubleday, 2000).
9   Rebecca Traister, *All the Single Ladies: Unmarried Women and the Rise of an Independent Nation* (New York: Simon & Schuster, 2016).

7 BODIES OF WORK

1   Maryam Jameel and Joe Yerardi, 'Workplace discrimination is illegal. But our data shows it's still a huge problem', *Vox*, 28 February 2019, vox.com/policy-and-politics/2019/2/28/18241973/ workplace-discrimination-cpi-investigation-eeoc
2   M. Lynn, *Determinants and Consequences of Female Attractiveness and Sexiness: Realistic Tests with Restaurant Waitresses*, 2009, semanticscholar.org/paper/Determinants-and-Consequences-of-Female-and-Tests-Lynn/2a084f30461d15d974293e30129e42584 1269fbb?p2df

3 *The Glass Floor: Sexual Harassment in the Restaurant Industry*, The Restaurant Opportunities Centers United Forward Together, 7 October 2014, chapters.rocunited.org/wp-content/ uploads/2014/10/REPORT_The-Glass-Floor-Sexual-Harassment-in-the-Restaurant-Industry2.pdf

4 Ai-Jen Poo, 'Female Domestic and Agricultural Workers Confront an Epidemic of Sexual Harassment', American Civil Liberties Union (ACLU), 4 May 2018, aclu.org/blog/ womens-rights/womens-rights-workplace/female-domestic-and-agricultural-workers-confront

5 Julia Wolfe et al., 'Domestic workers' chartbook', Economic Policy Institute, 14 May 2020, epi.org/publication/domestic-workers-chartbook-a-comprehensive-look-at-the-demographics-wages-benefits-and-poverty-rates-of-the-professionals-who-care-for-our-family-members-and-clean-our-homes/

6 Ibid.

7 *Cultivating Fear: The Vulnerability of Immigrant Farmworkers in the US to Sexual Violence and Sexual Harassment*, Human Rights Watch, 2012, hrw.org/sites/default/files/reports/us0512ForUpload_1.pdf

8 Madison Marriage, 'Men Only: Inside the charity fundraiser where hostesses are put on show', *Financial Times*, 23 January 2018, ft.com/content/075d679e-0033-11e8-9650-9c0ad2d7c5b5

9 Margarita Noriega, '13 sexist vintage airline ads from the '60s: "Someone may get a wife"', *Vox*, 7 August 2015, vox. com/2015/8/7/9113743/vintage-sexist-airline-ads

10 For more on age, appearance and weight requirements see: en.wikipedia.org/wiki/Flight_attendant#History

11 Maya Oppenheim, 'Women being plagued with debt due to gender pay gap, skyrocketing childcare costs and sexism, campaigners say', *Independent*, 13 December 2019, independent.co.uk/news/ uk/home-news/women-debt-stress-mental-health-credit-payday-loan-pay-gay-a9235621.html

12 Sarah Davidge and Lizzie Magnusson, 'The Domestic Abuse Report 2019: The Economics of Abuse', Women's Aid Federation of England Report, p. 3, womensaid.org.uk/wp-content/uploads/ 2019/03/Economics-of-Abuse-Report-Summary-2019.pdf

13 Arlie Russell Hochschild, *The Managed Heart* (Berkeley, CA: California University Press, 1983).

14 Rachel Moran, *Paid For: My Journey Through Prostitution* (Dublin: Gill Books, 2013).

15 Emma Goldman, 'The Traffic in Women', in *Anarchism and Other Essays* (New York & London: Mother Earth Publishing Association, 1911), pp. 183–200.

8 THE HOME FRONT

1 Jess Zimmerman, '"Where's My Cut?": On Unpaid Emotional Labor', *The Toast*, 13 July 2015, the-toast.net/2015/07/13/emotional-labor/

2 'Time to Care: Unpaid and underpaid care work and the global inequality crisis', *Oxfam*, 19 January 2020; Gus Wezerek and Kristen R. Ghodsee, 'Women's Unpaid Labor is Worth $10,900,000,000,000', *New York Times*, 5 March 2020, nytimes.com/interactive/2020/03/04/opinion/women-unpaid-labor.html

3 D. Del Boca et al., 'Women's and men's work, housework and childcare, before and during COVID-19', *Review of Household Economics* 18, 2020, 1001–17, doi.org/10.1007/s11150-020-09502-1

4 Ester Bloom, 'The Decline of Domestic Help', *Atlantic*, 23 September 2015, theatlantic.com/business/archive/2015/09/decline-domestic-help-maid/406798/

5 Arlie Russell Hochschild, with Anne Machung, *The Second Shift* (London: Penguin Books, 1989, revised edition 2012), p. 32.

6 Dawn Foster, *Lean Out* (London: Watkins Publishing, 2016), p. 148.

7 Hannah Arendt, *The Human Condition* (1958; University of Chicago Press, 1998).

8 Nancy Fraser, 'Contradictions of Capital and Care', *New Left Review*, July–August 2016, newleftreview.org/issues/II100/articles/nancy-fraser-contradictions-of-capital-and-care

9 Patrick Butler, 'Welfare spending for UK's poorest shrinks by £37bn', *Guardian*, 23 September 2018, theguardian.com/politics/2018/sep/23/welfare-spending-uk-poorest-austerity-frank-field

10 Heather Stewart, 'Women bearing 86% of austerity burden, Commons figures reveal', *Guardian*, 9 Mar 2017, theguardian.com/world/2017/mar/09/women-bearing-86-of-austerity-burden-labour-research-reveals

11 Brigid Schulte, 'The U.S. Ranks Last in Every Measure When It Comes to Family Policy, in 10 Charts', *Washington Post*, 5 April 2019, washingtonpost.com/blogs/she-the-people/wp/2014/06/23/global-view-how-u-s-policies-to-help-working-families-rank-in-the-world/

12 Aliya Hamid Rao, 'Even Breadwinning Wives Don't Get Equality at Home', *Atlantic*, 12 May 2019, theatlantic.com/family/archive/2019/05/breadwinning-wives-gender-inequality/589237/

13 Selma James, *Sex, Race and Class* (Falling Wall Press, 1973), la.utexas.edu/users/hcleaver/sexraceclass.html.

14 Claire Cain Miller, 'The Costs of Motherhood Are Rising and Catching Women Off Guard', *New York Times*, 17 August 2018, nytimes.com/2018/08/17/upshot/motherhood-rising-costs-surprise.html

15 Melinda Cooper, *Family Values: Between Neoliberalism and the New Social Conservatism* (New York: Zone Books, 2017).

16 'American Time Use Survey – 2019 Results', *American Department of Labor*, 25 June 2020, bls.gov/news.release/pdf/atus.pdf

17 Sophie Lewis, *Full Surrogacy Now: Feminism against the Family* (London: Verso, 2019), p. 22.

18 George Lakoff, *Moral Politics: What Conservatives Know that Liberals Don't* (Chicago: University of Chicago Press, 1996), p. 5.

19 Ibid.

20 Ibid., p. 8.

21 Lidia Yuknavitch, *The Chronology of Water: A Memoir* (Portland, Oregon: Hawthorne Books, 2016), p. 447.

9 THE MEANS OF REPRODUCTION

1 'Coping with a difficult birth experience and where to get help', The Birth Trauma Association (BTA), birthtraumaassociation.org.uk/PDFs/text_only_english.pdf

2 Janis M. Miller et al., 'Evaluating Maternal Recovery from Labor and Delivery: Bone and Levator Ani Injuries', *Research Gynecology*, vol. 213, no. 2, 5 May 2015, ajog.org/action/showPdf?pii=S0002-9378%2815%2900450-0

3 'Saving Lives, Improving Mothers' Care 2018: Lay Summary', Nuffield Department of Population Health, npeu.ox.ac.uk/ assets/downloads/mbrrace-uk/reports/MBRRACE-UK%20 Maternal%20Report%202018%20-%20Lay%20Summary%20 v1.0.pdf

4 *National Mortality Profile of Active Duty Personnel in the U.S. Armed Forces: 1980–1993*, cdc.gov/niosh/docs/96-103/ pdfs/96-103.pdf; Sarah Griffiths, 'The effect of childbirth no one talks about', BBC Future, 24 April 2019, bbc.com/future/ article/20190424-the-hidden-trauma-of-childbirth

5 Maria Caspani, 'Support for abortion rights grows as some U.S. states curb access: Reuters/Ipsos poll', Reuters, 26 May 2019, reuters.com/article/us-usa-abortion-poll-idUSKCN1SW0CD

6 Judith Jarvis Thomson, 'A Defense of Abortion', *Philosophy & Public Affairs*, 1 (1), Fall 1971. Reprinted in *Intervention and Reflection: Basic Issues in Medical Ethics*, 5th edn, ed. Ronald Munson (Belmont: Wadsworth 1996), pp. 69–80, spot.colorado. edu/~heathwoo/Phil160,Fall02/thomson.htm

7 Tony Tinderholt, interviewed by Lyanne A. Guarecuco in 'Lawmaker: Criminalizing Abortion Would Force Women to be "More Personally Responsible"', *Texas Observer*, 23 January 2017, texasobserver.org/texas-lawmaker-no-abortion-access-would-force-women-to-be-more-personally-responsible-with-sex/

8 Mark Joseph Stern, 'Georgia Just Criminalized Abortion. Women Who Terminate Their Pregnancies Would Receive Life in Prison', *Slate*, 7 May 2019, slate.com/news-and-politics/2019/05/hb-481-georgia-law-criminalizes-abortion-subjects-women-to-life-in-prison.html

9 Zoila Acevedo, 'Abortion in Early America', *Women & Health*, summer 1979, 4 (2), pp. 159–67, pubmed.ncbi.nlm.nih.gov/ 10297561/

10 Ibid.

11 Andrew Hochman, 'Race suicide', *Eugenics Archives*, 29 April 2014, eugenicsarchive.ca/discover/tree/535eedb87095aa0000000250

12 'Republican congressman: civilization threatened by "somebody else's babies"', *Guardian*, 13 March 2017, theguardian.com/ us-news/2017/mar/12/steve-king-iowa-congressman-geert-wilders-immigration

13 Adeel Hassan and Alan Blinder, 'Alabama Executes a Murderer a Day After Banning Abortions', *New York Times*, 16 May 2019, nytimes.com/2019/05/16/us/michael-samra-execution.html

14 Priscilla Alvarez, 'Parents of 628 migrant children separated at border still have not been found, court filing says', CNN Politics, 3 December 2020, edition.cnn.com/2020/12/02/politics/family-separation-us-border-children/index.html

15 'Preventing Unsafe Abortion', *World Health Organization*, 25 September 2020, who.int/news-room/fact-sheets/detail/preventing-unsafe-abortion; Lale Say et al., 'Global causes of maternal death: a WHO systematic analysis', *Lancet*, 2 (6), 5 May 2014, doi.org/10.1016/S2214-109X(14)70227-X

16 Emma Kasprzak, 'Why are black mothers at more risk of dying?', BBC News, 12 April 2019, bbc.co.uk/news/uk-england-47115305; Nina Martin, 'Black Mothers Keep Dying After Giving Birth. Shalon Irving's Story Explains Why', NPR, 7 December 2017, npr.org/2017/12/07/568948782/black-mothers-keep-dying-aftergiving-birth-shalon-irvings-story-explains-why?t=1618400035616

17 Professor Tressie McMillan Cottom, *Thick and Other Essays* (New York: The New Press, 2018).

10 WHITE LIES

1 Harriet Sherwood, 'Polish Magazine's "Islamic Rape of Europe" Cover Sparks Outrage', *Guardian*, 18 February 2016, theguardian.com/world/2016/feb/18/polish-magazines-islamic-of-europe-cover-sparks-outrage.

2 Irene Zempi, 'Veiled Muslim women's responses to experiences of gendered Islamophobia in the UK', *International Review of Victimology*, 2020, 26 (1), pp. 96–111.

3 'Germany shocked by Cologne New Year gang assaults on women', BBC News, 6 January 2016, bbc.co.uk/news/world-europe-35231046

4 'Charleston shooting: Dylann Roof named as suspect', BBC News, 19 June 2015, bbc.co.uk/news/world-us-canada-33189325

5 Sojourner Truth, 'Ain't I a Woman', speech at the Ohio Women's Rights Convention in Aron, Ohio, 29 May 1851, thehermitage. com/wp-content/uploads/2016/02/Sojourner-Truth_Aint-I-a-Woman_1851.pdf

6 Victoria Richards, 'Woman holds sign at feminist rally saying "there is no rape culture in the West"', *Independent*, 11 June 2015, independent.co.uk/news/world/americas/woman-holds-sign-feminist-rally-saying-there-no-rape-culture-west-10310370.html

7 'An examination of the 2016 electorate, based on validated voters', *Pew Research*, pewresearch.org/politics/2018/08/09/an-examination-of-the-2016-electorate-based-on-validated-voters/

8 Andrea Dworkin, *Right-Wing Women* (New York: Perigee Books, 1983), p. 15.

9 Saim Saeed, '950 attacks on Muslims recorded in Germany last year', *Politico*, 3 March 2018, politico.eu/article/germany-islam-950-attacks-on-muslims-recorded-in-germany-last-year

10 Angela Davis, 'Rape, Racism and the Capitalist Setting', *The Black Scholar*, 12, 6, 1981, pp. 39–45, JSTOR, www.jstor.org/stable/41066856, p. 39; Angela Davis, *Women, Race and Class* (London: Penguin, 2019), p. 155.

11 Reni Eddo-Lodge, *Why I'm No Longer Talking to White People About Race* (London: Bloomsbury, 2017), p. 72.

11 ANGRY YOUNG MEN

1 'You Will Not Replace Us', Hate Slogans/Slang Terms, Anti-Defamation League, adl.org/education/references/hate-symbols/you-will-not-replace-us

2 'Guns and Violence Against Women: America's Uniquely Lethal Intimate Partner Violence Problem', 17 October 2019, Everytown Research & Policy, 23 October 2020, everytownresearch.org/report/guns-and-violence-against-women-americas-uniquely-lethal-intimate-partner-violence-problem/

3 'Ten Years of Mass Shootings in the United States', Everytown For Gun Safety, maps.everytownresearch.org/massshootingsreports/mass-shootings-in-america-2009-2019/

4 'When Women Are the Enemy...', adl.org/resources/reports/when-women-are-the-enemy-the-intersection-of-misogyny-and-white-supremacy

5   George Hawley, 'The Demography of the Alt-Right', *Institute for Family Studies*, ifstudies.org/blog/the-demography-of-the-alt-right

6   Ibid.

7   Hussein Kesvani, 'When YouTube Red-Pills the Love of Your Life', *MEL Magazine*, 16 January 2019, melmagazine.com/en-us/story/youtube-red-pill-men-right-wing-hate-radicalization

8   Quoted in Bob Garfield, *American Manifesto: Saving Democracy from Villains, Vandals, and Ourselves* (Berkeley, California: Counterpoint, 2020).

9   Robin Hanson, 'Two Types of Envy', *Overcoming Bias*, 26 April 2018, overcomingbias.com/2018/04/two-types-of-envy.html

12 NO MORE HEROES

1   G. Willow Wilson, *Ms Marvel*, Book 1, *No Normal* (New York: Marvel, 2014).

2   Cordelia Fine, *Testosterone Rex: Myths of Sex, Science and Society* (New York: W.W. Norton, 2017), p. 91.

3   Dorothy Thompson, 'Who Goes Nazi?', *Harper's Magazine*, August 1941, harpers.org/archive/1941/08/who-goes-nazi/

13 TRUTH AND CONSEQUENCES

1   Sandra Joshel, 'The Body Female and the Body Politic' in Amy Richlin, ed., *Pornography and Representation in Greece and Rome* (Oxford: OUP, 1992), pp. 112–30, faculty.washington.edu/alain/Lat422Livy/Joshel.pdf

2   'Uma Thurman vents anger at Weinstein', BBC News, 24 November 2017, bbc.co.uk/news/entertainment-arts-42106916

3   Johann Wolfgang von Goethe, *Wilhelm Meister's Apprenticeship*, translated from the German by Thomas Carlyle (New York: A. L. Burt, 1839; Project Gutenberg, 2011), gutenberg.org/files/36483/36483-h/36483-h.htm

4   Margaret Atwood, 1982 lecture, 'Writing the Male Character'. See extract here: wist.info/atwood-margaret/25926/

5   Andrew Buncombe, 'Stanford rape case: Read the impact statement of Brock Turner's victim', *Independent*, 2 September 2016,

independent.co.uk/news/people/stanford-rape-case-read-impact-statement-brock-turner-s-victim-a7222371.html

6 Nora Samaran, 'Own, Apologize, Repair: Coming Back to Integrity', 10 February 2016, norasamaran.com/2016/02/10/variations-on-not-all-men/

14 ABUSES OF POWER

1 Ruth Marcus, 'Opinion: Have we learned nothing since Anita Hill?', *Washington Post*, 22 Sept 2018, washingtonpost.com/opinions/have-we-learned-nothing-since-anita-hill/2018/09/21/bdc649a4-bddb-11e8-8792-78719177250f_story.html

2 Tim Mak, 'Kavanaugh Accuser Christine Blasey Ford Continues Receiving Threats, Lawyers Say', NPR, 8 November 2018, npr.org/2018/11/08/665407589/kavanaugh-accuser-christine-blasey-ford-continues-receiving-threats-lawyers-say

3 Kira Lerner, 'Brett Kavanaugh falsely claims 17-year-old immigrant didn't meet requirements for an abortion', *Think Progress*, 5 September 2018, archive.thinkprogress.org/brett-kavanaugh-falsely-claims-17-year-old-immigrant-didnt-meet-requirements-for-an-abortion-25b9c759d63c/

4 Jan Ransom, 'Trump Will Not Apologize for Calling for Death Penalty Over Central Park Five', *New York Times*, 18 June 2019, nytimes.com/2019/06/18/nyregion/central-park-five-trump.html

5 Donald Trump, 'Bring Back The Death Penalty. Bring Back Our Police!' *New York Daily News*, 1 May 1989, Section B, p. 6, apps.frontline.org/clinton-trump-keys-to-their-characters/pdf/trump-newspaper.pdf

6 Judith Lewis Herman, *Trauma and Recovery: The Aftermath of Violence: From Domestic Abuse to Political Terror.* (Basic Books, 2015), p. 72.

7 'School abuse: "Rape culture" warning as 8,000 report incidents', BBC News, 29 March 2021, bbc.co.uk/news/uk-56558487

8 Jean E. Carroll, 'Donald Trump assaulted me in a Bergdorf Goodman dressing room 23 years ago. But he's not alone on the list of awful men in my life,' *The Cut*, 21 June 2019, thecut.com/2019/06/donald-trump-assault-e-jean-carroll-other-hideous-men.html

9   Ibid.

10 Milton Mayer, *They Thought They Were Free: The Germans 1933–45* (Chicago: Chicago University Press, 1966), p. 171.

ENDNOTE: TRAUMA POLITICS

1   E. J. Dickson, 'Alexandria Ocasio-Cortez Said Something Genuine, So Of Course Men Reacted Poorly', *Rolling Stone*, 2 February 2021, rollingstone.com/culture/culture-features/alexandria-ocasio-cortez-sexual-assault-instagram-live-1122515/

2   Nina Martin, 'Black Mothers Keep Dying After Giving Birth. Shalon Irving's Story Explains Why', NPR, 7 December 2017, npr.org/2017/12/07/568948782/black-mothers-keep-dying-after-giving-birth-shalon-irvings-story-explains-why?t=1618400035616

3   Tom Phillips, 'Brazil: Bolsonaro reportedly uses homophobic slur to mock masks', *Guardian*, 8 July 2020, theguardian.com/world/2020/jul/08/bolsonaro-masks-slur-brazil-coronavirus

BIBLIOGRAPHY

BOOKS

Bancroft, Lundy, *'Why Does He Do That?' Inside the Minds of Angry and Controlling Men* (New York: G. P. Putnam, 2002)

Browning, Frank, *The Fate of Gender: Nature, Nurture, and the Human Future* (New York: Bloomsbury USA, 2016)

Cervantes Saavedra, Miguel de, *Don Quixote*, translated from the Spanish by J. M. Cohen (London: Penguin, 1975)

Crewe, Candida, *Eating Myself* (London: Bloomsbury, 2006)

Davis, Angela, *Women, Race and Class* (London: Penguin, 2019)

Dworkin, Andrea, *Right-Wing Women* (New York: Perigee Books, 1983)

Eddo-Lodge, Reni, *Why I'm No Longer Talking to White People About Race* (London: Bloomsbury, 2017)

Firestone, Shulamith, *The Dialectic of Sex: The Case for Feminist Revolution* (London: Jonathan Cape, 1971)

Foster, Dawn, *Lean Out* (London: Watkins Publishing, 2016)

Greer, Germaine, *The Female Eunuch* (London: Paladin, 1970)

Herman, Judith Lewis, *Trauma and Recovery: The Aftermath of Violence – From Domestic Abuse to Political Terror* (New York: Basic Books, 1992)

Hirshman, Linda R. and Jane E. Larson, *Hard Bargains: The Politics of Sex* (New York: Oxford University Press, 1998)

Hochschild, Arlie Russell, *The Managed Heart* (Berkeley, CA: California University Press, 1983)

—, with Anne Machung, *The Second Shift* (London: Penguin Books, 1989; revised edition 2012)

hooks, bell, *All About Love* (New York: William Morrow, 1999)

—, *The Will to Change: Men, Masculinity and Love* (New York: Atria Books, 2004)

Kennedy, Helena, *Misjustice: How British Law Is Failing Women* (London: Vintage, 2019)

Lakoff, George, *Moral Politics: What Conservatives Know that Liberals Don't* (Chicago: University of Chicago Press, 1996)

MacKinnon, Catharine A., *Feminism Unmodified: Discourse on Life and Law* (Cambridge, Mass.: Harvard University Press, 1987)

Manne, Kate, *Down Girl: The Logic of Misogyny* (London: Penguin, 2019)

Mason, Paul, *Clear Bright Future: A Radical Defence of the Human Being* (London: Allen Lane, 2019)

Mayer, Milton, *They Thought They Were Free: The Germans 1933–45* (Chicago: Chicago University Press, 1966)

Nagoski, Emily, *Come as You Are: The Surprising New Science that Will Transform Your Sex Life* (London: Simon & Schuster, 2015)

Orwell, George, *1984* (London: Penguin Books, 1974)

Reich, Wilhelm, *The Mass Psychology of Fascism* (New York: Orgone Institute Press, 1946)

Rich, Adrienne, 'Diving into the Wreck', from *Diving into the Wreck: Poems 1971–1972* (New York: W. W. Norton, 1973)

Sandberg, Sheryl, *Lean In: Women, Work and the Will to Lead* (New York: Penguin Random House, 2013)

Strauss, Neil, *The Game: Penetrating the Secret Society of Pickup Artists* (Regan: HarperTorch, 2006)

Waite, Linda J. and Maggie Gallagher, *The Case for Marriage: Why Married People Are Happier, Healthier, and Better Off Financially* (New York: Doubleday, 2000)

Wolff, Naomi, *The Beauty Myth* (New York: William Morrow, 1991)

Yuknavitch, Lidia, *The Chronology of Water: A Memoir* (Portland, Oregon: Hawthorne Books, 2016)

ARTICLES

Associated Press and Ashley Collman, 'Steve Bannon Says "Time's Up" Is "the Single Most Powerful Potential Political Movement in the World"', *Business Insider*, 15 September 2018, www.businessinsider.com/ap-steve-bannon-times-up-is-most-powerful-political-movement-2018-9?r=US

Benner, Katie, 'Women in Tech Speak Frankly on Culture of Harassment', *New York Times*, 30 June 2017, nytimes.com/2017/06/30/technology/women-entrepreneurs-speak-out-sexual-harassment.html

Bloom, Ester, 'The Decline of Domestic Help', *Atlantic*, 23 September 2015, theatlantic.com/business/archive/2015/09/decline-domestic-help-maid/406798/

Butler, Patrick, 'Welfare spending for UK's poorest shrinks by £37bn', *Guardian*, 23 September 2018, theguardian.com/politics/2018/sep/23/welfare-spending-uk-poorest-austerity-frank-field

Carroll, Jean E., 'Donald Trump assaulted me in a Bergdorf Goodman dressing room 23 years ago. But he's not alone on the list of awful men in my life', *The Cut*, 21 June 2019, thecut.com/2019/06/donald-trump-assault-e-jean-carroll-other-hideous-men.html

Chrisafis, Angelique, interview with Virginie Despentes, 'What is going on in men's heads when women's pleasure has become a problem?', *Guardian*, 31 August 2018, theguardian.com/books/2018/aug/31/virginie-despentes-interview-baise-moi-vernon-subutex

Clark, R. D. and E. Hatfield, 'Gender differences in receptivity to sexual offers', *Journal of Psychology & Human Sexuality*, 2 (1), 1989, pp. 39–55, sciencefriday.com/wp-content/uploads/2016/04/gender-differences-in-receptivity-to-sexual-offers.pdf

Davis, Angela, 'Rape, Racism and the Capitalist Setting', *The Black Scholar*, 12, 6, 1981.

Frank, Karah, 'A Letter to My Abuser', *The Establishment*, 20 October 2016, theestablishment.co/a-letter-to-my-abuser-ff705dfec5cc/index.html

Fraser, Nancy, 'Contradictions of Capital and Care', *New Left Review*, July–August 2016, newleftreview.org/issues/II100/articles/nancy-fraser-contradictions-of-capital-and-care

Gebrial, Dalia, 'Decolonising Desire: The Politics of Love', blog, *Verso*, 13 February 2017, versobooks.com/blogs/3094-decolonising-desire-the-politics-of-love

Hanson, Robin, 'Two Types of Envy', *Overcoming Bias*, 26 April 2018, overcomingbias.com/2018/04/two-types-of-envy.html

Harte, Alys, 'A man tried to choke me during sex without warning', BBC Radio 5 Live Investigations Unit, bbc.co.uk/news/uk-50546184

Ingraham, Christopher, 'The share of Americans not having sex has reached a record high', *Washington Post*, 29 March 2019, washingtonpost.com/business/2019/03/29/share-americans-not-having-sex-has-reached-record-high/

James, Selma, 'Sex, Race and Class', la.utexas.edu/users/hcleaver/sexraceclass.html

Judge, Timothy A. and Daniel M. Cable, 'When It Comes to Pay, Do the Thin Win? The Effect of Weight on Pay for Men and Women', *Journal of Applied Psychology*, 20 August 2010, timothy-judge.com/Judge%20and%20Cable%20%28JAP%202010%29.pdf

Kesvani, Hussein, 'When YouTube Red-Pills the Love of Your Life', *MEL Magazine*, 16 January 2019, melmagazine.com/en-us/story/youtube-red-pill-men-right-wing-hate-radicalization

Lewis, Sophie, *Full Surrogacy Now: Feminism against the Family* (London: Verso, 2019)

Lorde, Audre, *Uses of the Erotic*, peacewithpurpose.org/uploads/8/2/1/6/8216786/audre_lorde_cool-beans.pdf

Mak, Tim, 'Kavanaugh Accuser Christine Blasey Ford Continues Receiving Threats, Lawyers Say', *NPR*, 8 November 2018, npr.org/2018/11/08/665407589/kavanaugh-accuser-christine-blasey-ford-continues-receiving-threats-lawyers-say

Marcotte, Amanda, 'What's destroying democracy around the world? At least in part, misogyny and sexism', *Salon*, 10 September 2019, salon.com/2019/09/10/whats-destroying-democracy-around-the-world-at-least-in-part-misogyny-and-sexism/

Marsh, Sarah, 'Eating disorders: NHS reports surge in hospital admissions, *Guardian*, 2 February 2018, theguardian.com/society/2018/feb/12/eating-disorders-nhs-reports-surge-in-hospital-admissions

Marx, Karl, *Economic and Political Manuscripts of 1844*, XXII, marxists.org/archive/marx/works/1844/manuscripts/labour.htm

Masson, Jeffrey M., 'Freud and the Seduction Theory: A challenge to the foundations of psychoanalysis', *Atlantic*, February 1984, theatlantic.com/magazine/archive/1984/02/freud-and-the-seduction-theory/376313/

Miller, Claire Cain, 'The Costs of Motherhood Are Rising and Catching Women Off Guard', *New York Times*, 17 Aug 2018, nytimes.com/2018/08/17/upshot/motherhood-rising-costs-surprise.html

Miller, Janies M. et al., 'Evaluating Maternal Recovery from Labor and Delivery: Bone and Levator Ani Injuries', *Research*

Gynecology, 213, 2, 5 May 2015, ajog.org/action/showPdf?pi i=S0002-9378%2815%2900450-0

Morrow, Lance, 'Opinion: A Spectral Witness Materializes', *Wall Street Journal*, 17 September 2018, wsj.com/articles/a-spectral-witness-materializes-1537225498

Ransom, Jan, 'Trump Will Not Apologize for Calling for Death Penalty Over Central Park Five', *New York Times*, 18 June 2019, nytimes. com/2019/06/18/nyregion/central-park-five-trump.html

Relman, Eliza, 'The 26 Women Who Have Accused Trump of Sexual Misconduct', *Business Insider*, 17 September 2020, businessinsider. com/women-accused-trump-sexual-misconduct-list-2017-12

Richards, Victoria, 'Woman holds sign at feminist rally saying "there is no rape culture in the West"', *Independent*, 11 June 2015, independent. co.uk/news/world/americas/woman-holds-sign-feminist-rally-saying-there-no-rape-culture-west-10310370.html

Sarwari, Khalida, 'Domestic Violence Homicides Appear to Be on the Rise. Are Guns the Reason?', *News@northeastern*, April 8, 2019, news.northeastern.edu/2019/04/08/domestic-violence-homicides-appear-be-on-the-rise-a-northeastern-university-study-suggests-that-guns-are-the-reason/

Schulte, Brigid, 'The U.S. Ranks Last in Every Measure When It Comes to Family Policy, in 10 Charts', *Washington Post*, 5 April 2019, washingtonpost.com/blogs/she-the-people/wp/2014/06/23/global-view-how-u-s-policies-to-help-working-families-rank-in-the-world/

Sherwood, Harriet, 'Polish Magazine's "Islamic Rape of Europe" Cover Sparks Outrage', *Guardian*, 18 February 2016, theguardian. com/world/2016/feb/18/polish-magazines-islamic-of-europe-cover-sparks-outrage

Stewart, Heather, 'Women bearing 86% of austerity burden, Commons figures reveal', *Guardian*, 9 Mar 2017, theguardian. com/world/2017/mar/09/women-bearing-86-of-austerity-burden-labour-research-reveals

Thompson, Dorothy et al., 'Who Goes Nazi?', *Harper's Magazine*, August 1941, harpers.org/archive/1941/08/who-goes-nazi/

Thompson, Isobel, 'Steve Bannon Is Obsessed with the Fall of the Patriarchy', *Vanity Fair*, 28 February 2018, vanityfair.com/ news/2018/02/steve-bannon-is-obsessed-with-the-patriarchy

Thomson, Judith Jarvis, 'A Defense of Abortion', *Philosophy & Public Affairs*, 1 (1), Fall 1971. Reprinted in *Intervention and*

Reflection: Basic Issues in Medical Ethics, 5th edn, ed. Ronald Munson (Belmont: Wadsworth 1996), pp. 69–80, spot.colorado. edu/~heathwoo/Phil160,Fall02/thomson.htm

Traister, Rebecca, 'Single Women Are the Most Potent Political Force in America', *The Cut*, 21 February 2016, thecut.com/2016/02/ political-power-single-women-c-v-r.html

Truth, Sojourner, 'Ain't I a Woman', speech at the Ohio Women's Rights Convention in Aron, Ohio, 29 May 1851, thehermitage. com/wp-content/uploads/2016/02/Sojourner-Truth_Aint-I-a-Woman_1851.pdf

WHO, 'Preventing Unsafe Abortion', World Health Organization, 25 September 2020, who.int/news-room/fact-sheets/detail/ preventing-unsafe-abortion

Zezima, Katie Deanna Paul, Steven Rich, Julie Tate and Jennifer Jenkins, 'Domestic slayings: Brutal and foreseeable', *Washington Post*, 9 December 2018, washingtonpost.com/graphics/2018/investigations/ domestic-violence-murders/

Zimmerman, Jess, 'Hunger Makes Me', *Hazlitt*, 7 July 2016, hazlitt.net/ feature/hunger-makes-me

ACKNOWLEDGEMENTS

Thanks must go, first of all, to my agent Veronique Baxter, and to the whole team at Bloomsbury – Alexa von Hirschberg, Jasmine Horsey, Callie Garnett, Sara Helen Binney and Kate Quarry. Bill Swainson, who I have been lucky enough to work with for a decade, took on the job of shaping and editing this book, and I am as grateful to him as ever.

Over the years I've also been privileged to have editing help and feedback from Michelle Weber, Lucie Elven, Meredith Peskin, Meredith Yayanos, Charlie Hallam, Lauryn Ipsum, Katrina Duncan and Samuel Braslow. Eva Galperin helped in ways only she knows, and is a hero in ways the world knows.

Just as importantly, this book came out of many long nights of conversation with dear friends and comrades – especially Christina Austin, Neil Gaiman, Margaret Killjoy, Jason Porath, Natti Vogel, Madhuri Shekar, Irvine Welsh, Frankie Boyle, Paul Clarkson, Michael Clarkson, Elizabeth Sutcliffe, Mara Wilson, Pam Shaffer, Emma Felber, Sasha Garwood, Alex Davison and Quinn Norton. Many others offered me their trust on condition of anonymity, and I won't name them here, but they know who they are.

I'm grateful to all the writers I've never met whose words and work have formed and challenged my thinking for so many years, including Shulamith Firestone, Ellen Willis, bell hooks, Angela Davis, Barbara Ehrenreich, Andrea Dworkin, Leslie Feinberg and Silvia Federici. I'm just as grateful to the feminist trailblazers of today whose work exists in conversation with mine, including Lidia Yuknavitch, Sophie Lewis, Kate Manne, Rebecca Traister, Anita Sarkeesian, Clementine Ford, Rebecca Solnit, Ijeoma Oluo, Jude Doyle, Reni Eddo-Lodge, Adrienne Maree Brown and Kitty Stryker.

Thanks go to Jane Penny, Eleanor Penny, Georgia Barnett and Mike Penny, for their encouragement and their patience when I had to run away and work over various Christmases. Thanks for his lifelong support to Raymond Barnett, whose memory is a blessing.

When I wasn't sure I could finish this book, Catherine Howdle and Cat Harris offered me their guest room in Brussels, and took care of me with soup and silliness. Redfern Barrett and Darren Cadwaller did the same in Berlin in the summer of 2018, when this book was just beginning.

Thank you to my 2020 quarantine writing group for creating a space where we could crank out words while the world was ending: Katherine Bergeron, Wayne Myers, Ted Mills, Paul Jeremiah Hayes, James Zapfletts, Joanne Williams, Adam Fleischmann, Adam Glinglin, Jacob Wellman, Elly Hayden, Mehran Baluch, Sarah Trick and everyone else who's joined.

Above all, thanks are due to my supporters on Patreon, who stuck by me through the years and encouraged me to take the time I needed to make this book what it had to be. *Sexual Revolution* would not exist without them.

Finally, to David Boarder Giles, who makes it possible to work as if we lived in the early days of a better nation.

INDEX

A NOTE ON THE AUTHOR

Laurie Penny is an author, journalist and screenwriter from London. They are a culture writer for Wired magazine and their celebrated columns and essays have appeared in the *Guardian*, the *New Statesman*, the *New York Times*, the *Baffler*, *Longreads*, *Time* magazine and many more. They are a graduate of the Nieman Foundation Fellows' programme at Harvard University and the Clarion West Writer's Workshop. *Sexual Revolution* is their 9th book.

A NOTE ON THE TYPE

The text of this book is set in Linotype Sabon, a typeface named after the type founder, Jacques Sabon. It was designed by Jan Tschichold and jointly developed by Linotype, Monotype and Stempel in response to a need for a typeface to be available in identical form for mechanical hot metal composition and hand composition using foundry type.

Tschichold based his design for Sabon roman on a font engraved by Garamond, and Sabon italic on a font by Granjon. It was first used in 1966 and has proved an enduring modern classic.